# OUT OF THE SHADOW: ARTISTS OF THE WARHOL CIRCLE THEN AND NOW

**DEBRA MILLER**

**UNIVERSITY GALLERY**
**UNIVERSITY OF DELAWARE**

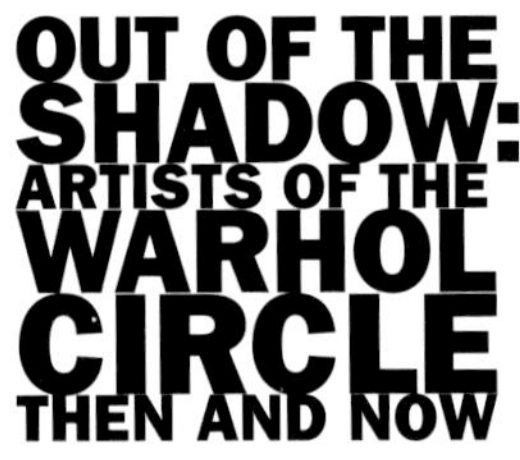

# OUT OF THE SHADOW: ARTISTS OF THE WARHOL CIRCLE THEN AND NOW

by
## DEBRA MILLER

with contributions by
Deborah Beris, Susanne Pepperman, and Ricki Sablove

essays by
Callie Angell, Ira Cohen, Robert Heide, Gerard Malanga,
Sur Rodney (Sur), George and Maria Warhola

and art by
Christopher Makos, Gerard Malanga, Allen Midgette,
Billy Name, Ultra Violet, and James Warhola

7 September - 30 October, 1996

## UNIVERSITY GALLERY
## UNIVERSITY OF DELAWARE



All dimensions are in inches except where noted.

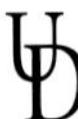

# CONTENTS

## ACKNOWLEDGMENTS

The University Gallery is pleased to have this opportunity to present "Out of the Shadow: Artists of the Warhol Circle, Then and Now." We appreciate the generous support received from numerous sources that made this exhibition and catalogue possible. These include the Delaware Division of the Arts, a state agency devoted to promoting the visual arts in the state; and at the University of Delaware, the Cultural Activities and Public Events Committee of the Faculty Senate, Visiting Minorities Scholars Fund, Visiting Women's Scholars Award Program, the Master of Arts in Liberal Studies Program, and the Departments of Art and Art History.

A special debt is owed to guest curator Debra Miller, who tirelessly toiled to bring this project to fruition.

Belena S. Chapp
Director
University Gallery

I am indebted to the following individuals and institutions for their invaluable assistance and generous support in the preparation of this catalogue and exhibition: Deborah and Antony Beris; Sally Cohen Donatello; Suzy and John Hoffmann; Alexandra Linett; Maria J. Keane; Barbara Macklem; Gavin Brown; Suzan Cooper; Jedi Weinberg; Howard Shakespeare; Ray Costello; Gerald Lyons; William and Mary Miller; Just Bob Morrison; Joe Moskal; Tom Moskal; Andrea Raphael and Alan Walker; the AIDS Information Network of Philadelphia; the director and staff of the University Gallery (Belena S. Chapp, Janet Broske, and Jimmie Lee Myers); Meg Williamson and Cynthia Smith of the University of Delaware Publications Office; Lenis Northmore and Jennifer Hintlian of the Slide Library; the Department of Art and Department of Art History, and the Masters of Arts in Liberal Studies Program. Finally, I would like to express my gratitude to my students, who contributed catalogue entries (Deborah Beris, Susanne Pepperman, and Ricki Sablove); to the guest essayists (Callie Angell, Ira Cohen, Robert Heide, Gerard Malanga, Sur Rodney (Sur), and George and Maria Warhola); to the artists (Christopher Makos, Gerard Malanga, Allen Midgette, Billy Name, Ultra Violet, and James Warhola); and, especially, to Andy Warhol, for recognizing their talents and creativity and for bringing them into the public eye.

Debra Miller
Guest Curator

## FOREWORD

The University of Delaware seems an unlikely place for the reunion of a number of prominent artists whose names are inextricably tied to the historical and cultural phenomenon known as Andy Warhol. This exhibition, which endeavors to forge their past lives (spent both in and out of his shadow) to their present preoccupations as artists, owes its existence to the persistent, even driven, efforts of Debra Miller. She conceived the idea in concert with the curriculum she developed on Warhol's legacy for the Master of Arts in Liberal Studies Program, with which she was affiliated.

Her research on Billy Name, and her intimate association with the other artists who collaborated closely with Warhol, enabled Dr. Miller to create a riveting, authentic experience teaching this subject in the classroom. Over the last two years, all of the artists included in this exhibition have given generously of their time to our students, providing an "eyewitness" view of perhaps the most pivotal period in contemporary art history. Their visits to campus have given us an unparalleled entrée into the turbulent, frenetic, sometimes hedonistic, and ultimately, all-consuming environment of the Sixties in which they were involved—one that gave birth to a surge of creative activity that continues to influence popular culture today. Thirty years later these artists may work in the seclusion of singular pursuits, but their productivity is no less intense.

They not only survived the Sixties: They have endured.

Belena S. Chapp
May 29, 1996

## DEDICATION

For my students and, as always, for Andy.

*Debra Miller* (signature)

Debra Miller

# INTRODUCTION
## OUT OF THE SHADOW: ARTISTS OF THE WARHOL CIRCLE, THEN AND NOW

by Debra Miller

22 February 1997 marks the tenth anniversary of Andy Warhol's untimely death. In the intervening decade, Warhol has received much overdue attention in the scholarly literature and has continued to fascinate the mass media, with the auctioning of his movable estate (Sotheby's New York, 23 April-3 May 1988),[1] the opening of the Andy Warhol Museum in Pittsburgh (13 May 1994),[2] the operations of the Andy Warhol Foundation for the Visual Arts, Inc. (headquartered in New York), and the exhibition and restoration of his films (a joint undertaking by the Museum of Modern Art and the Whitney Museum of American Art in New York).[3]

Among the most celebrated aspects of Warhol as an artist was his reliance upon collaboration.[4] Andy constantly surrounded himself with creative people in the visual, literary, and performing arts who provided him with ideas, assisted him with the execution of his works, appeared in his movies, and immeasurably contributed to the fame and mystique of the Factory (as his studio, housed in a former hat factory on East 47th Street in Manhattan, was known.)[5] As a result of the very public activities of the Pop artist and his Superstars (Warhol's featured company of artists and performers), his atelier became one of the most renowned in history, and its denizens, with their colorful monickers and extravagant personalities, became household names, as well as Pop celebrity icons.[6]

Paradoxically, both the popular press and scholars continue to lament those of the Warhol circle who died tragically young—frequently of the excesses in which they indulged in the Sixties[7]—yet largely fail to recognize Warhol's survivors and their significant accomplishments.[8] This is especially surprising in light of the fact that several of these Warholian "celebrities" have remained dedicated and serious artists for more than thirty years. They represent an important, but hitherto overlooked, aspect of Andy's legacy and the continuing tradition of Pop art.

This multimedia exhibition examines the artistic and cultural achievements of six living artists who first gained prominence through their association with Andy Warhol, and who continue to practice their arts to the present day. The group comprises several generations of Warhol's associates. It begins with those who played an integral role in founding the famous silver Factory in the early 1960s (Gerard Malanga and Billy Name) and those who were attracted to Andy and his studio in its early years (Ultra Violet and Allen Midgette); extends to one who entered Warhol's circle after his move to Union Square in 1968, and then to the final location on 33rd Street (Christopher Makos); and concludes with Andy's own nephew (James Warhola), who carries on the artistic tradition within the Warhola family. Each artist is represented by a mini-retrospective of ten works, surveying the varied media and phases of his or her career. It marks the first time all six of these artists have shown their works together, or have been professionally reunited since their revolutionary collaborations with Warhol.

The show is entitled "Out of the Shadow: Artists of the Warhol Circle, Then and Now," after Andy Warhol's silkscreened self-portrait of 1981, depicting himself as the mysterious legend of early radio.[9] It refers to the six exhibiting artists' beginnings with the Master of Pop, by whom they have long been overshadowed. But it also indicates that the time has now come for Gerard Malanga, Billy Name, Ultra Violet, Allen Midgette, Christopher Makos, and James Warhola to move into the spotlight, as mature artists in their own right. This in no way denigrates the seminal impact Warhol exercised upon them, or the significant influence they had on him. To the contrary, their works display countless interconnections with Andy's, and with each other's, that bespeak a common breeding ground, shared interests, and a mutual vision. These include themes of human sexuality (homosexual, heterosexual, and transvested), spirituality (Christian subjects and Zen philosophy) and death and disaster (guns and car accidents); a fascination with famous people and Native Americans, with physical beauty and international travel, and with conceptual art and its progenitors (especially Marcel Duchamp, Man Ray, and John Cage); the union of word and picture (in the art of illustration, in inscriptions on artworks, in concrete poetry, and in poetic/photographic memoirs); and the appropriation and replication of images (through photography, photo-silkscreening, and photocopying).

Perhaps the most important aspect of the symbiotic relationship between Warhol and his circle is their common embracing of experimentation. When Andy began his career as a filmmaker in 1963, he had no previous training in the medium. Nevertheless, he forged ahead, and with the help of those more experienced, went on to produce a groundbreaking body of cinematic work.[10] Warhol later expanded from his initial painting, printmaking, and filmmaking into photography, the production of music (with the Velvet Underground), publishing (with *Interview* magazine), theater (with *Pork*), writing (with more than a half-dozen texts to his credit), television (including *Andy Warhol's Fifteen Minutes* for MTV), videos (among them, "Hello Again" for the rock group The Cars), acting (including an appearance on *The Love Boat*), and modeling (for both Zoli and Ford).[11] His followers, too, have become proficient in a wide variety of media through hands-on practice, with little or no professional instruction beyond their primary areas of expertise. Gerard Malanga, for example, began his public life as a poet, but then took on the role of Warhol's silkscreening assistant, and soon became one of his first male Superstars, as well as a dancer with the Factory's traveling multimedia production, the Exploding Plastic Inevitable. Subsequently, Malanga also turned to filmmaking and photography, at which he has become eminently masterful. And so it is with Billy Name, who began as a theatrical lighting designer, but further increased his talents to include set construction, appearing in underground films, still photography, concrete poetry, and conceptual sculpture. Ultra Violet effortlessly shifts from performing, to writing, to painting and printmaking; Allen Midgette from acting, to fashion design, to fine art;

James Warhola from oil painting to watercolor, from science-fiction and fantasy to children's book illustration; and Christopher Makos from photography, to photo-silkscreening, to writing, to hosting his own TV show, and now, to moving into cyberspace with his own site on the World Wide Web.

This catalogue is organized as a series of six short monographs on the individual artists, arranged in the chronological order of their association with Warhol, and tracing each of their lives and careers through a selection of ten representative works. Following these entries, the unique talents and imaginations of Warhol and the artists of his circle are eloquently addressed in a series of essays by the friends, family members, and colleagues who have known them and their *oeuvres*, and who have understood their artistic sensibilities. The personal reminiscences of Gerard Malanga, Robert Heide, Ira Cohen, Sur Rodney (Sur), and George and Maria Warhola give an intimate glimpse into the artists' psyches and into the socio-cultural milieus in which they worked and evolved. Callie Angell's sensitive consideration of the Warhol films underlines the profound import of collaboration in his studio, and the wealth of contributions his followers have made. And their impact extends far beyond the parameters of the art world. These influential artists, performers, and writers broke down social barriers, allowing the ethnic working class to mingle with wealthy debutantes, and giving sexual minorities and the creatively disenfranchised a forum for self-expression. As a result of the activities of Warhol and his atelier, being different was no longer deemed unacceptable in our culture; it became desirable.

# GERARD MALANGA (b. 1943)

Gerard Malanga's simultaneous careers as poet, photographer, filmmaker, curator, and archivist have brought him a large international following. His childhood, spent growing up in New York, was followed by education at the University of Cincinnati and Wagner College in Staten Island, where he studied poetry and underground filmmaking with the legendary Willard Maas and his wife, Marie Menken. He went to work for Andy Warhol in 1963 as silkscreening assistant and soon became a major influence on the art and films created in Warhol's Factory; his contributions cannot be overestimated. He starred in numerous Warhol productions (including the epic *The Chelsea Girls* and *Vinyl*) and introduced many of Warhol's most noteworthy collaborators into the Factory (among them, Paul Morrissey, the Velvet Underground, Nico, and International Velvet). Together Warhol and Malanga founded *Interview* magazine in 1969. After a decade of travels during the 1970s, Malanga returned to New York. In 1985 he was appointed first photo archivist to New York City's Department of Parks and Recreation; in 1988 he joined the Society of American Archivists. In a career spanning over a quarter century, Malanga has authored more than twenty-five books in limited or extended formats, as well as numerous articles. His photographs and films have been exhibited worldwide. Presently, Gerard Malanga lives in the Berkshires in western Massachusetts and is a Fellow at Simon's Rock of Bard College.

## 1. THE YOUNG MOD

In 1962, Andy Warhol began work on his series of silkscreens focusing on the themes of death and disaster. His imagery was appropriated from the chilling examples of contemporary photo-journalism that he collected: scenes of criminals, suicides, executions, accidents, illnesses, funerals, natural catastrophes, and socio-political unrest.[1] The original press photographs, stockpiled at the Factory, also inspired Warhol's collaborators to create their own versions of the inescapable subject matter that seemed to permeate the media in the 1960s.

Billy Name, residing at the Factory, mechanically reproduced many of Warhol's morbid source photographs in 1964, on Andy's newly arrived Thermo-Fax machine (see cat. #12). Gerard selected a group of Billy's sepia-toned copies, and also made some Thermo-Faxes himself, on which he then typed or wrote original poems at the bottom of each page, in the space below the picture. These mixed-media works, completed in 1964-65, are extremely rare; fewer than twenty-five were made, and the present location of the majority of them is unknown.[2]

*The Young Mod* is dedicated to Jean Shrimpton, epitome of the British "Mod" style as London's most celebrated, top model of the early 1960s (prior to Twiggy, in the second half of the decade).[3] The composition combines two seemingly incongruous elements: the graphic depiction of a gruesome car crash, with bodies strewn amidst the wreckage; and a descriptive verse that conjures visions of youth and beauty, of wealth, fashion, and leisure.[4] The pleasurable lightness of the poem, with its references to "sun and sea" and to "clean white" "weightless" fabric, is a welcome contrast to the oppressive darkness of the ponderous pictorial image. But then Malanga startles us with his closing lines, which disturbingly interweave the themes of unexpected death by automobile with the good life of the model setting off on a quick vacation getaway. The theme was a timely one. In 1960, there were approximately 61,700,000 cars registered in the United States, and the U.S. Department of Commerce reported 38,137 deaths involving motor vehicles.[5] Following in the long artistic tradition of the *memento mori* or *vanitas* subject, the poet reminds us of the transiency of life on earth and the omnipresence of human mortality.

Malanga later published "The Young Mod" as the final poem in his book of verse entitled *Chic Death*, which also reproduced five of Warhol's "Death and Disasters" paintings.[6] The Thermo-Faxed image exhibited here was not included with the poem.

THE YOUNG MOD

for Jean Shrimpton.

The model, vigorous, attractive, modern, is for
touring the tennis courts and terraces
in a two-piece ensemble of weightless
naked wool.  The dress a clean white sleeveless
sweep of shape, with its own double
breasted jacket; it will never show
signs of travel fatigue.  The port shelters
a sleek assemblage of yachts.  But she
is leaving the race with the clock to others
and forgetting the crowds and confusion.
The naked wool bolero-back skimmer
is just the sort of almost-nothing weight
she'll need for sun and sea.  A man lies
dead along the wreckage of his auto.
Another is still pinned behind the steering wheel.

-Gerard Malanga.

1. Gerard Malanga
*The Young Mod* 1964
Thermo-Fax and typed poem
14 x 8 1/2

## 2. VINYL

Although Malanga began his association with Warhol in June 1963 as Andy's paid silkscreening assistant, his intense good looks and aggressive sexuality made him a prime candidate for Superstardom. Before long he became a featured player in Warhol's films. His appearances include segments in *Kiss* (1963), *Couch* (1964), and *13 Most Beautiful Boys* (1964-65), and the central roles in *Vinyl* (1965), *Camp* (1965), *Bufferin* (1966), and reel #8 of *The Chelsea Girls*, "The Gerard Malanga Story" (1966).

Malanga was not unaccustomed to performing in public. Even prior to his affiliation with Warhol, he was known in artistic circles as one of the up-and-coming young poets of his generation, already having given noteworthy readings of his original material for both academic and avant-garde venues.[7] It was, in fact, through the poets Charles Henri Ford and, indirectly, Willard Maas (Gerard's creative writing professor at Wagner College in Staten Island) that Malanga first made Warhol's acquaintance.[8] Later, in 1966, Warhol would immortalize Malanga reading wittily censored excerpts from his secret diaries and poems in the single-reel film *Bufferin*. In it, a tolerant but focused Malanga, despite the repeated, chiding interruptions of Rona Page, intones his writings with a good-natured determination and commanding presence.

The first film by Warhol to feature Malanga as its main protagonist was *Vinyl*, shot in March 1965 and based on Anthony Burgess's novel *A Clockwork Orange*. Warhol bought the rights to the story, playwright and scenarist Ronald Tavel wrote the script, and Gerard Malanga originated on film the role of the amoral delinquent Victor.[9] Prior to filming, Warhol distracted the cast from studying their lines, with the apparent intent that they should read them aloud from cue cards, for the first time, with the camera rolling. The resultant performance by Malanga (a trained poet who was adept at reading to an audience) is a directorial tour-de-force of underground filmmaking. Malanga's blatantly difficult and halting delivery of the unfamiliar script, augmented by his Bronx accent and street-toughened attitude, purposefully evokes the essence of his remorseless working-class character. The antihero's cinematic scenes of torture and frenetic dancing, furthermore, foretell of Malanga's future participation in Warhol's multimedia production the Exploding Plastic Inevitable, for which he performed his infamous sado-masochistic "whip dance" to the live music of the Velvet Underground (see cat. #3).

## 3. EXPLODING PLASTIC INEVITABLE

One of the countless contributions Gerard Malanga made to the Factory was his introduction of Andy Warhol and assistant Paul Morrissey to the Velvet Underground.[10] In mid-December 1965, at the invitation of his friend Barbara Rubin—an experimental filmmaker who had trained with Jonas Mekas and appeared in Warhol's film *50 Fantastics and 50 Personalities* (1964-66)—Malanga attended a performance of the hitherto unknown band at the Cafe Bizarre in Greenwich Village. Following

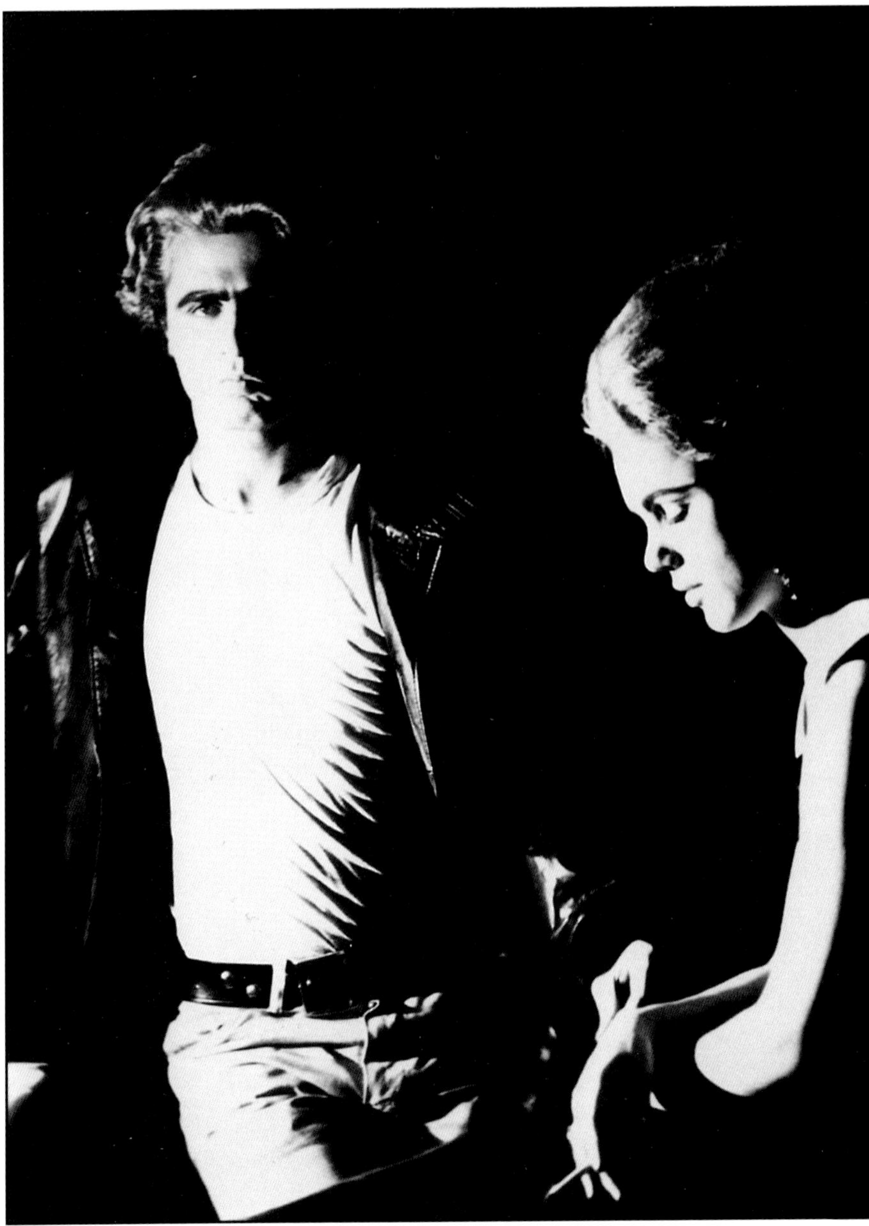

2. Gerard Malanga and Edie
   Sedgwick in Andy Warhol's
   *Vinyl* 1965
   13 1/2 x 9 1/4
   Photograph by Billy Name

Rubin's suggestion, Gerard brought his whip so that he could dance to the group's sado-masochistic repertoire. This was not Malanga's first foray into the medium. When he was a teenager, he had danced regularly to "Top 40" hits on disc jockey Alan Freed's *Big Beat* television show, and Rubin had witnessed his virtuosity as a go-go dancer on film in Warhol's *Vinyl* (see cat. #2). That evening at the Bizarre, two members of the Velvet Underground, Lou Reed and John Cale, expressed their appreciation of Gerard's dancing during their performance and invited him to come back and dance again.

At the time, Warhol and Morrissey had been approached by Broadway producer Michael Myerberg to promote a new discotheque he planned to open in Queens. Consequently, they were in search of a rock group to produce and to manage. Malanga, serving as talent scout, brought them to see the Velvets perform at the Cafe Bizarre on the night following his own visit.[11] Impressed with their explosive, abrasive, revolutionary style, Andy invited them to the Factory, became their impresario, added the European chanteuse Nico to the group,[12] and

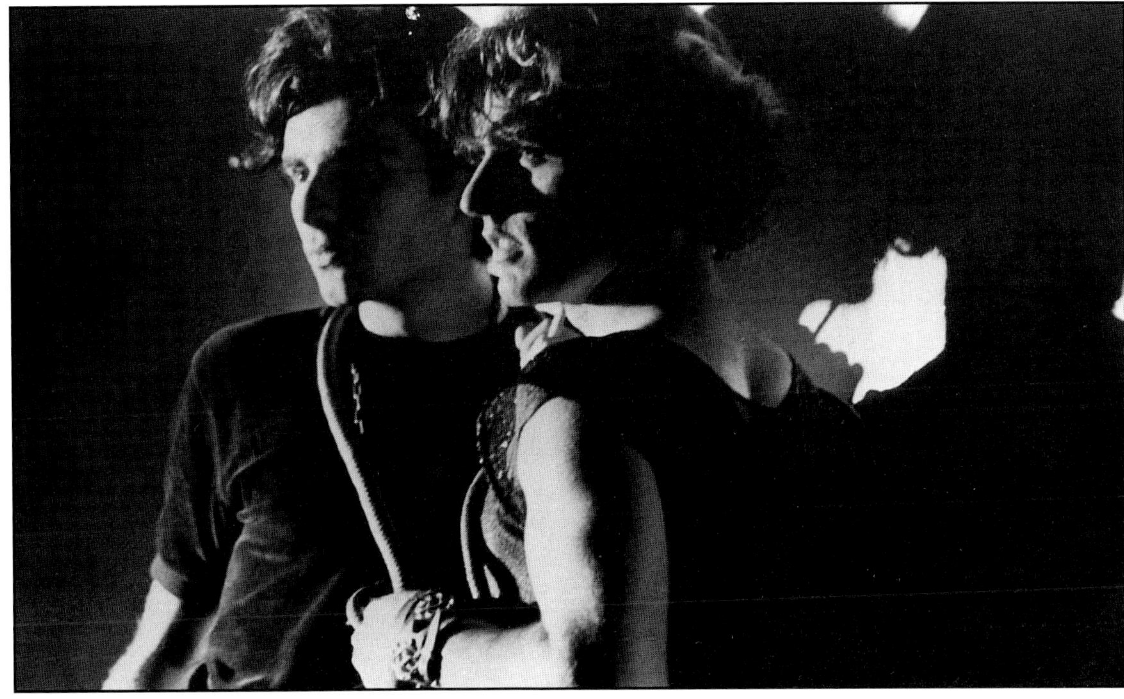

3. Gerard Malanga and
Ronnie Cutrone as Dancers
in the Exploding Plastic
Inevitable  1966
6 1/4 x 9 1/2
Photograph courtesy of
Suzan Cooper Archives

designed a multimedia show around them, of which
Malanga and his interpretive "whip dance" became an
integral part.[13] First called "Andy Warhol, Up-Tight," then
"Andy Warhol's Underground New York," and finally the
"Exploding Plastic Inevitable," the psychedelic audio-
visual presentation incorporated light and slide shows and
Factory films projected on and around the live musicians
and dancers (see cat. #15). The latter comprised a
constantly changing cast of Factory regulars (including
Ingrid Superstar, Edie Sedgwick, Mary Woronov, Eric
Emerson, and Ronnie Cutrone) who joined Malanga on
stage.

In a typical performance, Gerard, clad in black leather
and brandishing his whip, jerked and gyrated wildly to
the Velvets' music. At times during his dance he would
hold a pair of long flashlights that bobbed and beamed at
random into the audience; at other times he would
entangle himself in phosphorescent green lengths of Day-
Glo plastic, or strike a pose of crucifixion, or feign
shooting up heroin. Malanga danced and toured with the
Exploding Plastic Inevitable until his departure from New
York for Italy in August 1967. By that time, the year-and-
a-half-long professional relationship between the Velvet
Underground and Warhol had come to an end, but not
before having changed the course of rock-and-roll
history. With fellow writer Victor Bockris, Malanga, from
his inside perspective, later chronicled their story in the
co-authored book, *Up-Tight*.[14]

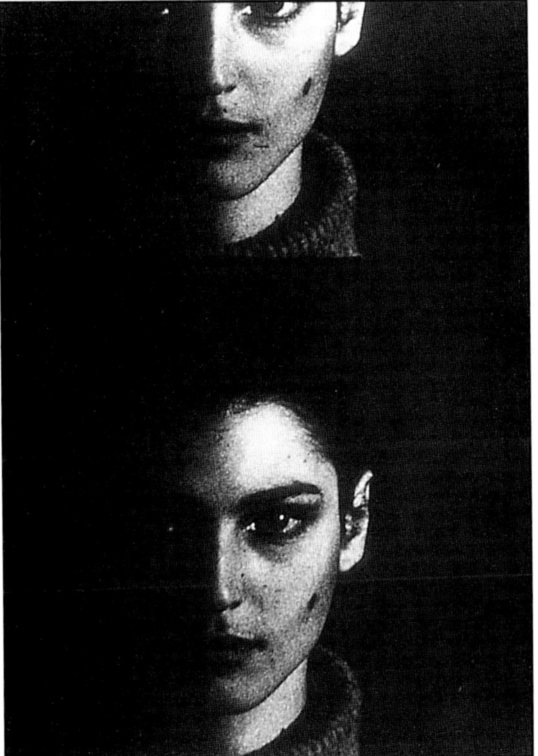

4. Gerard Malanga
(and Andy Warhol)
*Still from Benedetta
Barzini's Screen Test*  1966
Gelatin silver print
20 x 16

## 4. STILL FROM BENEDETTA BARZINI'S SCREEN TEST

From 1964 to 1966, all visitors to the Factory who were
rich, famous, beautiful, talented, interesting, or who
otherwise exhibited a certain star quality, were invited by
Warhol to sit for a screen test. The largely standardized
cinematic portraits were captured on 100-foot rolls of
black-and-white film, approximately three minutes in
length, by Andy's silent Bolex camera, which had been
mounted on a tripod and stationed before a plain
backdrop in the studio. Warhol, Malanga, and Billy Name
took turns behind the camera, adjusting the lights, placing
the sitters, and giving them instructions to remain as still
as possible and to stare directly into the lens, preferably
without blinking. The screen tests thus captured not only
the physical appearances of the subjects, but also their
psychological responses to taking direction, and their
emotional reactions to the unwavering scrutiny of the
camera that was trained on them. Consequently, Malanga
characterized the films as "studies in subtle sadism…
[t]he results [of which] were often brutal."[15]

In 1967, Malanga and Warhol collaborated on *Screen Tests/A Diary*, a book of selected stills from the films with poems devoted to the sitters.[16] The authors selected 54 subjects from the approximately 500 screen tests shot at the Factory. Inclusion in the book was based upon four main criteria: the consistent compositional format of a tightly framed close-up head shot; the subjects' consent to signing a release form; the socio-cultural significance of the person in the portrait; and Malanga's inspiration to poetize the individual depicted. The film negatives generated for the book remained in the possession of Malanga, who produced from them a portfolio of large-scale photographic prints, each measuring 20 x 16 inches. Among them is the portrait of Benedetta Barzini, the globe-trotting Italian-born model to whom *Screen Tests/A Diary* was dedicated.

Benedetta was the strong-willed daughter of prominent journalist and writer Luigi Barzini, author of the best-selling book *The Italians*. On 7 February 1966, Malanga was introduced to the twenty-two-year-old model by art dealer Leo Castelli at a party at Robert Rauschenberg's loft in New York. He felt an immediate attraction to her, which resulted in a brief romantic involvement spanning from early October to 7 November of that year.[17] Of more lasting value than the couple's short-lived romance was the creative spark Barzini ignited in Gerard. He subsequently published four volumes of poetry devoted to his muse,[18] and his cinematic treatment of Benedetta and her father, titled *In Search of the Miraculous* (1967), was the Official American Entry for that year's 10th International Film Festival in Bergamo, Italy.

In the screen test/portrait, Barzini's dark angular features, large eyes, heavy brows, and the trademark mole on her cheek are accentuated by the strong raking light that eerily illuminates the right half of her face. The rest of Benedetta's visage is obscured in deep shadow, evoking a sinister tone that hints of an unstable childhood, early estrangement from her family, three periods of commitment in a mental institution, and a ten-year bout with anorexia and amenorrhea.[19] The image is both haunting and penetrating.

## 5. PORTRAIT OF CHARLES OLSON

In 1954, at the age of twelve, Gerard received a Kodak Brownie camera as a gift from his parents. With it, on 12 May 1955, he documented the final day of service on the Manhattan section of the Third Avenue elevated train, which ran to and from his neighborhood in the Bronx. This historic occasion from childhood marked the beginnings of Malanga's recurrent interest in photography as a means of recording ephemera—the places, people, and events that, without his pictures, would exist only as memories in his mind's eye. He cites Henri Cartier-Bresson on this compelling stimulus:

> We photographers deal in things which are continually vanishing, and when they have vanished, there is no contrivance on earth which can make them come back again. We cannot develop and print a memory.[20]

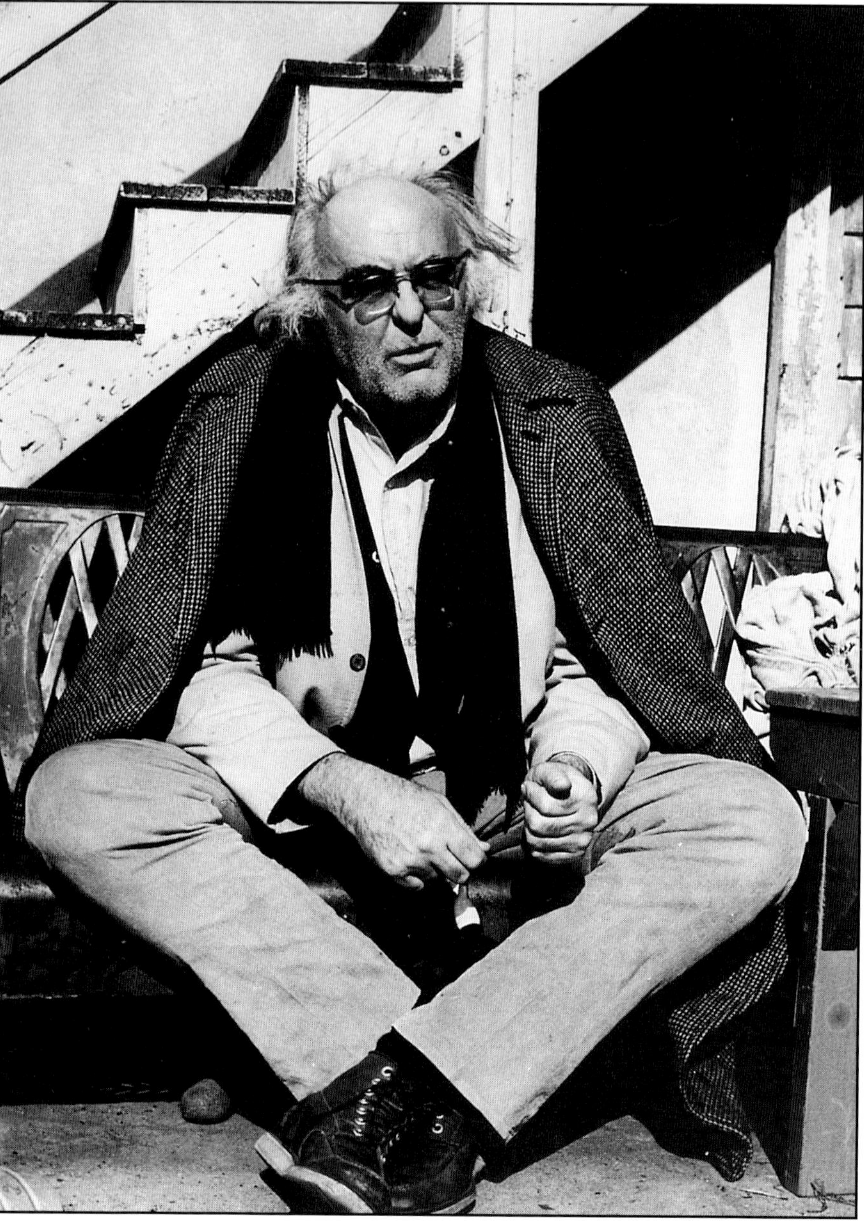

5. Gerard Malanga
*Portrait of Charles Olson*
1969
Gelatin silver print
17 x 14

As an adult, Malanga would go on to become a photo-historian for our culture,[21] capturing for posterity many of the noteworthy artists, musicians, writers, and celebrities of his era: people like William Burroughs, John Cage, Allen Ginsberg, Abbie Hoffman, Mick Jagger, Lou Reed, and others too numerous to mention. Gerard, as friend and colleague to his renowned sitters, had entrée into their private world—a world that others could come to know only through the media.

A watershed in the evolution of Malanga's career as "photographer of the famous" occurred on 16 April 1969, with the portrait he made of Charles Olson (1910-70). Gerard visited the eccentric, influential poet at his apartment at 28 Fort Square in Gloucester, Massachusetts, to interview him for *The Paris Review*'s "Writers at Work" series.[22] During the visit, Malanga shot the portrait that was destined to become the most familiar image of the failing Olson, who died of cancer on the following January 10. Gerard also filmed some brief footage of his host, which he later inserted into his cinematic scrapbook *cum* travelogue *April Diary* (1970), a visual record of his trip from Manhattan to the

Berkshire Mountains in western Massachusetts, and the people he encountered *en route*.

Olson, by all accounts, was a man of great primal energy and imposing stature (6'7" tall), known for his brilliant intellect, radical individualism, inspired spontaneity, and rambling harangues.[23] After being "uneducated" at Wesleyan, Yale, and Harvard universities, Olson held a number of professional positions. Most notable among them, for the future of the avant-garde and the conceptual breeding of the artists of the Warhol circle, was his five-year tenure in North Carolina as rector at Black Mountain College (1951-56), the experimental educational community that had such a seminal impact on the American arts and counter culture of the second half of the twentieth century.[24]

That day in Gloucester, Gerard diligently pursued his prepared questions and completed the interview with amazing grace and professionalism, but the published conversation reveals Olson to be a difficult subject—at times uncooperative, pompous, and downright crotchety. The same raucous verve evinced by Olson in the interview is betrayed in Malanga's photographic portrait, which captures the spirit of the man with extraordinary visual acuity and frank realism. The viewer is confronted with an Olson who is unshaven, whose hair is uncombed, who squints at the sunlight and scowls at the camera. With portraits like these, Malanga truly has created "souvenirs [sic] of vision"[25] and experience.

Gerard accompanied fellow poet Robert Creeley to visit Olson in New York Hospital shortly before his death.

6. Gerard Malanga
*Candy Darling* 1971
Gelatin silver print
64 1/2 x 44 1/2

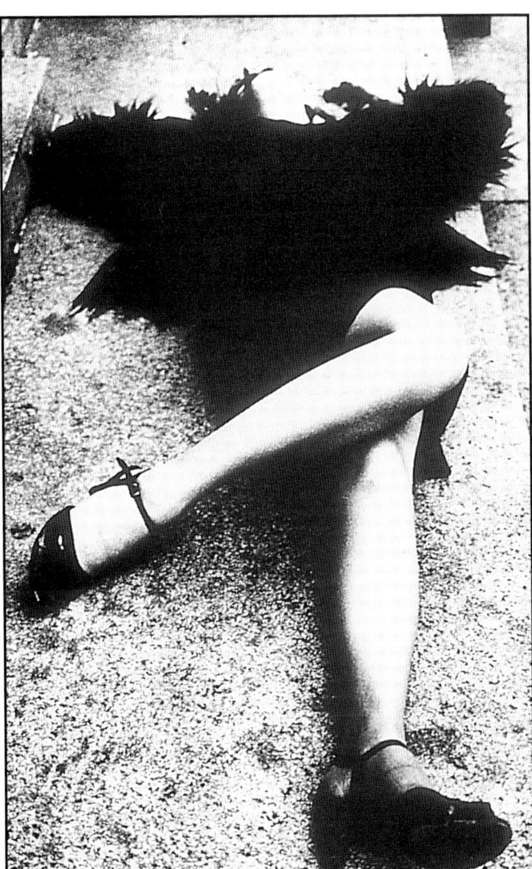

According to Creeley, Olson had been "delighted" with *The Paris Review* interview and "beamed" when Gerard entered his room.[26] Olson did not die without leaving an assessment of his younger disciple:

> Malanga's a POET to contend with among the poets of his generation because of his total commitment to POETRY. He makes no compromises. And for this reason he is unique. There is no one else quite like him and I like that in a person. He's got VISION. I wish this gentleman warrior well.[27]

## 6. CANDY DARLING

"This was the summer I met Candy Darling."[28]

So Andy Warhol described with forceful impact and unadulterated respect the momentous occasion of 1967. It is the only isolated sentence in *POPism*, a single-line remembrance visually and conceptually set off by double spaces above and below. Elsewhere in his autobiographical account of the Sixties, Warhol celebrated Candy as "the most striking drag queen I'd ever seen. On a good day, you couldn't believe she was a man."[29]

Candy Darling began her life as Jimmy Slattery in Massapequa, Long Island. Since childhood, she nourished herself on the mystique of Hollywood, avidly watching the "Million Dollar Movie" on television, poring over *Photoplay* and *Modern Screen* magazines, and idolizing the great female stars like Kim Novak, Lana Turner, Joan Bennett, and Yvonne DeCarlo.[30] At the same time, the starstruck youth began experimenting with his mother's clothes and make-up, and acting out scenes from his favorite films.

Andy fortuitously encountered "Hope Slattery" (as Candy was calling herself then) with fellow drag queen Jackie Curtis on the streets of Greenwich Village one hot August afternoon. In the course of the next year, Candy made a brief, scene-stealing appearance in the Warhol production of *Flesh* (1968; written and directed by Paul Morrissey), following a run in co-star Curtis's off-Broadway parody *Glamour, Glory, and Gold.* In 1971, the year in which Gerard Malanga photographed Candy Darling lying face-up on a sidewalk in New York,[31] she was starring with Curtis and Holly Woodlawn in *Women in Revolt*, a feature-length satire on feminism by the filmmaking team of Warhol and Morrissey.[32]

The radically foreshortened perspective of Malanga's photograph emphasizes the long, elegant line of Candy's milky white legs, which dominate the composition. He reduces her head to a few dramatic smudges of eye make-up and lipstick, two tenebrous nostrils, and some delicate wisps of platinum hair framing an alabaster neck and jawline. The fairness of Candy's flesh provides a marked tonal contrast to the dark dress and 1940s-style, open-toed shoes she wears, reminiscent of old Hollywood and the stars she emulated. The jagged silhouette of her monkey fur jacket is splayed out like the wings of a fragile dead bird or an exquisite fallen angel, recalling the words of Candy's own self-description:

> …I know I have a look of refinement
> and nobility which is sometimes thought of
> as being angelic and athereal [sic].[33]

The histrionic pose of Candy, collapsed on the sidewalk, poignantly gives substance to another passage from her private journal:

> I have always been the goddess above it
> all untouchable… I was born to be a
> queen and every time I come down from my
> thrown [sic] I am humiliated for it and
> suffer many indignities.[34]

Renowned playwright Tennessee Williams featured the actress in his off-Broadway production *Small Craft Warnings* in 1972, the same year in which Lou Reed immortalized her in his rock-and-roll classic "Walk on the Wild Side."[35] But Candy never did realize her dreams of Hollywood stardom, nor did she ever fully complete her physical transition to womanhood. In 1974, still in her twenties, Candy Darling died of pneumonia and cancer, possibly brought on by the female hormones she was taking. As Andy noted in his bitter-sweet postscript, she did have "the movie star's funeral she'd always wanted, uptown at Frank Campbell's."[36]

## 7. OBVIOUSLY A DANCER

The expansion of Malanga's career from poetry into photography is not surprising, in light of the visual imagery that characterizes his writing and the literal descriptiveness of his photographic style. Surely his professional association with Warhol and the Factory also reinforced his appreciation for the visual arts and gave him constant exposure to its photographic processes (i.e., still photography, filmmaking, and photo-silkscreening). As Gerard himself noted, "[v]irtually all of Andy Warhol's work includes aspects of photography whether directly applied or appropriated."[37]

Since the time of his earliest published volumes in the 1960s, Malanga would incorporate a few plates or a pictorial cover to illustrate the focus of his poems. These included photographs of Benedetta Barzini by Stephen Shore, Richard Avedon, and Billy Name;[38] examples of Warhol's "Death and Disasters" paintings for *Chic Death* (Cambridge, MA: Pym-Randall, 1971); and stills from the Warhol films for *Screen Tests/A Diary* (New York: Kulchur Press, 1967). By the mid-1980s, he began to combine his own photographs and poetry. *This Will Kill That* (Santa Barbara: Black Sparrow Press, 1983) featured architectural portraits by Malanga of the buildings inhabited by the women who inspired his accompanying verses. In *Autobiography of a Sex Thief* (New York: Lustrum Press, 1984) he presented, for the first time in print, the erotic photographs he shot as visual evidence of what he verbally documented in his poems. And *Three Diamonds* (Santa Barbara: Black Sparrow Press, 1991) represents a culmination of that evolving synthesis of Malanga's love poetry with erotic photography.

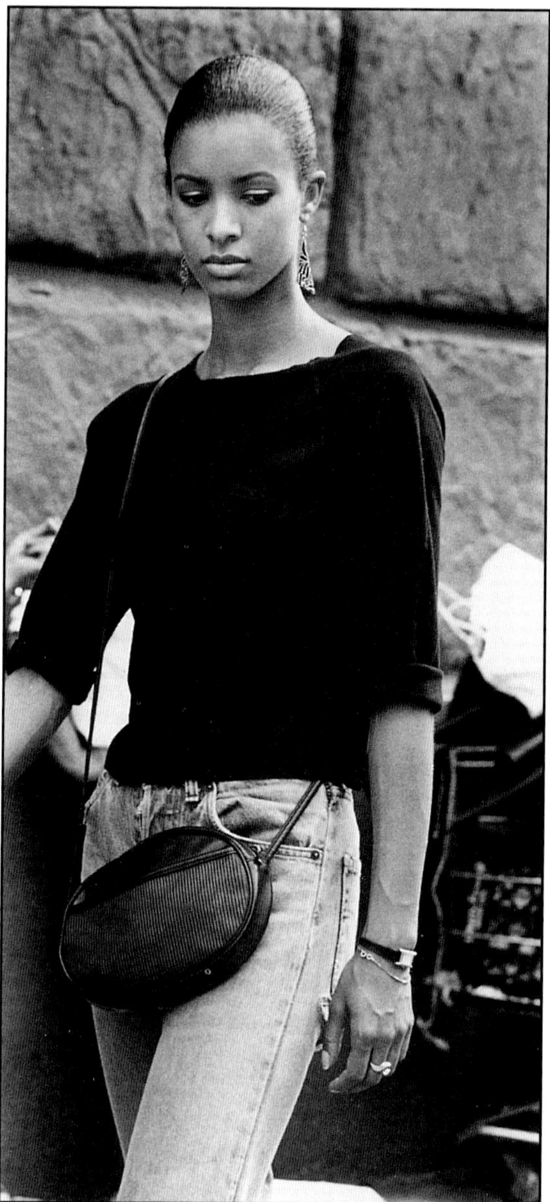

7. Gerard Malanga
*Obviously a Dancer* 1982
Gelatin silver print
22 1/2 x 10 1/4

*Obviously a Dancer* is one of the images included in *Three Diamonds*; it serves as an iconic counterpart to the poem "Extended Sonnet," which extols the "immediate image of heightened awareness/of individual identity, of loveliness."[39] Taken as a whole, the photographs in *Three Diamonds* promote an urban aesthetic. They document women from a wide variety of ethnic backgrounds, seen on crowded beaches and city streets, in casual clothes or *en deshabillé*. In essence, they represent the experiences of a New Yorker—of a poet and photographer moved by his daily observations to create works of verbal and visual art.

According to Malanga:

> Observations that lead up to and are poems
> have never been a voluntary decision and yet
> the way in which I focus in on what I see is
> very much a specific act of participation.[40]

As was the case with many of the subjects in this book, the unwitting "model" was unknown to Malanga. He spotted her on several occasions in his neighborhood in Manhattan, became familiar with her movements, and acted on his plan to capture her beauty on film—a plan that necessarily anticipated the fleeting moment and the urgency of wasting no time. On the day he sighted her approach from Astor Place, near Cooper Union, he set up his camera, pre-focused, and shot his picture at the very instant she passed by.[41] Malanga then framed his candid composition in a narrow, vertical format that psychologically elongates and attenuates the woman's already tall, thin, and graceful body. Finally, he assumed the tone of an archivist/poet when he catalogued her, in verse, to complete his covert act of documentation: "obviously a dancer. She is the origin of motion."[42]

## 8. SHULAMITE

Malanga's photographic work comprises two main categories. Along with his portraiture, he has produced, since 1970, a body of erotic photographs focusing on the sexual allure of the female. These, in turn, can be sub-divided into two groups: candid shots of unaware strangers, friends, and passersby who caught his eye and fired his imagination (see cat. #7); and pictures of first-time models who are spontaneous and unrehearsed, yet who have been directed during their photo sessions to use Malanga's studio props, costumes, and accessories, and who, consequently, are fully cognizant of playing to the camera.[43] This corpus of nudes, semi-nudes, and clothed figures is extremely personal; it reveals as much about the artist's taste as it does about his subjects' forms. Clearly, his aesthetic is that of the *demi-vierge*. In general, his models tend to be very young,[44] thin, small-breasted, and firm; they wear little or no make-up, and represent for him "purity without innocence."[45]

8. Gerard Malanga
*shulamite* 1987
Gelatin silver print
20 x 16

With but a few exceptions, Gerard does not shoot full-length nudes or fully nude figures. Rather, he prefers to frame close-up details of his models (see cat. #9), or to depict his models either partially nude or in the act of undressing. He explains:

> It is in the "revealing," in the undressing, not in the nude, that the gesture becomes sexually arousing, because one becomes subliminally involved in a sexual, intimate experience.[46]

Thus, in the tradition of Warhol, the artist embraces an art of voyeurism, but recognizes that it is "a subjective word. It expresses what would be considered degenerate and… carries with it negative connotations."[47] Therefore, he prefers the less familiar term *scopophilia*—the "love of looking"—to define his artistic desire to capture these transitory, private actions on film.

Gerard observes further that "voyeurism in photographs does not exist apart from that which informs it (exhibitionism)."[48] That interplay surely is in evidence here. The pubescent model looks directly into the camera and makes unabashed eye contact with the viewer; her gaze is at once condescending and smoldering. She is adorned with tastefully understated accents of expensive jewelry, perfectly manicured and polished nails, and the well-trimmed hair that suggest a background of refinement and privilege. Perhaps then it is best not to draw a rigid distinction between Malanga's nudes and his portraits. Although the girl's identity is unknown to us, the photograph speaks volumes about her character. It is, in essence, a visual biography: the story of a well-bred "good girl" anxious to be naughty in her desire for womanhood. The wanton attitude and stunning seductiveness elicited by his camera inspired Gerard to entitle the photograph *shulamite*, after the cherished bride of the Old Testament's poetic Song of Solomon—an ancient collection of rapturous Israelite love poems that sings the praises of a maiden renowned for her beauty in boldly erotic terms.[49]

## 9. MARBLE OF FLESH

With this traditional study of the female nude,[50] Malanga moves beyond his self-professed voyeuristic themes of eroticism and physical desire (see cat. #8) to the pictorial realms of abstraction and ideal beauty. Here the photographer takes a formal approach to the classic simplicity of the unadorned body and focuses on the essence of pure form.[51] In so doing, he recalls the values of ancient Greek statuary, and simultaneously, pays homage to the marbles of antiquity with a trick of textural reversal. Whereas the sculpture of Praxiteles has been renowned for its sensuous evocation of flesh,[52] Gerard's photograph imparts a marmoreal firmness to his flesh-and-blood subject.

To depersonalize the composition, Malanga excludes his anonymous model's head and hands, framing her figure from mid-back to mid-thigh in a three-quarter posterior view. He further removes her from our individual, quotidian world by placing her before a neutral backdrop that offers no distractions from the significant elements of shape, tone, and contour. Gerard's skillful use of side lighting—a combination of natural and incandescent illumination with reflectors set up in his studio[53]—enhances the figure's plasticity, brought out by the subtle gradations in shading that impart a fully rounded effect to the buttocks. The body's rhythmic sequence of curves and hollows gently animates the balanced stasis of its pose. By employing a limited depth of field, Malanga creates a mood of evanescence, as the softened, hazy contours of the left side of the figure dissolve into the surrounding atmosphere. In contrast, the hard edges of the silhouetted right leg and buttock come into sharp focus and the surface texture and details of their skin are revealed. Thus, without being pornographic or even overtly sexual, Gerard retains the totality of a fleeting sensuous impression and expresses the refined thrill of witnessing the beauty of natural form.

## 10. BRAID-SNITCHING

This is a rare example in Malanga's *oeuvre* of a preconceived, staged photograph. Its concept dates back to the Victorian era and the Freudian tradition known as "braid-snitching." A.A. Brill, the Hungarian-born American colleague and translator of Freud, described it as an antiquated form of "sadistic perversion":

> In the old days there were the "braid-snitchers," who cut off one or both braids from women, but I have not seen this type since the ladies gave up wearing long hair.[54]

Upon reading this passage in his personal copy of Brill's *Lectures*, Gerard made the following annotation to himself in the lower margin of the page: "photo of a pair of sheers about to cut off a braid."[55]

There is, in Malanga's photographic visualization of Brill's words, an underlying psychological tension between the [unseen boy's] aggressive act of cutting and the unknowing girl's victimization—a sadistic metaphor for rape that evokes the latent sexual repression of the Victorian period. Gerard published this image twice: first, in 1984, as the cover for his collection of poems and photographs entitled *Autobiography of a Sex Thief* (New York: Lustrum Press); and then as the frontispiece for *Good Girls* (Tokyo: Kawade-Shoboshinsha Co., Ltd., 1994), his first book of erotic photographs *sans* poetry.

This sexually charged composition can be appreciated on two levels: it is naturalistic as well as symbolic. As a highly successful study in textural differentiation, it invites both a visual and a tactile response. The viewer senses the hard metal blades of the scissors against the silky plait of blond hair, the delicate honeycomb of cotton lace, and the shiny satin ribbon. The photographer's sharp focus renders visible each individual strand of hair, but does not lose sight of the hypnotic flow of its gentle interweaving and curvilinear plays. Here Malanga has perfectly balanced exacting detail with the overall unity of a pleasing design. But then our revelry in the sensuousness of the hair is cut short by our awareness of the scissors and the implicit damage they will do. The composition's close-up, cut-off format serves to thrust the viewer into the situation and to heighten our sense of intimacy with the pictorial image. We are left feeling uneasy, and perhaps a bit guilty, at our inability to prevent the impending loss of beauty, youth, and innocence represented by the schoolgirl's braid.

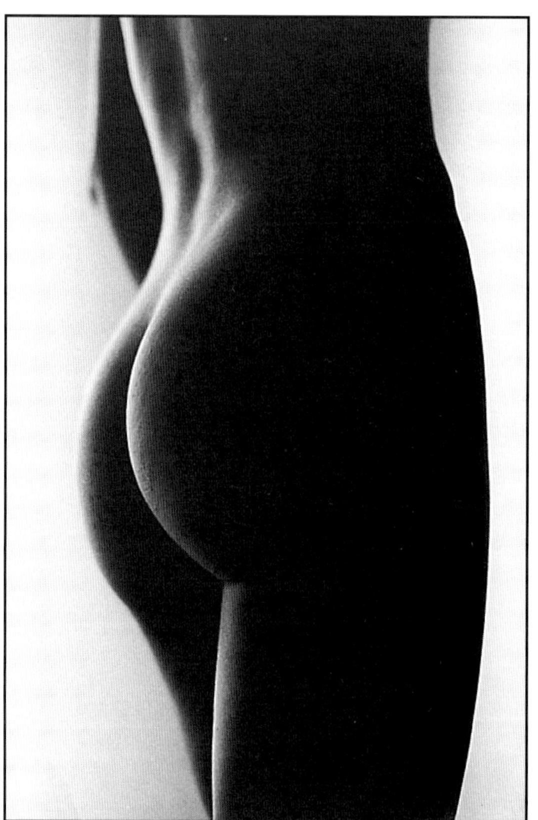

9. Gerard Malanga
*Marble of Flesh* 1987
Gelatin silver print
20 x 16

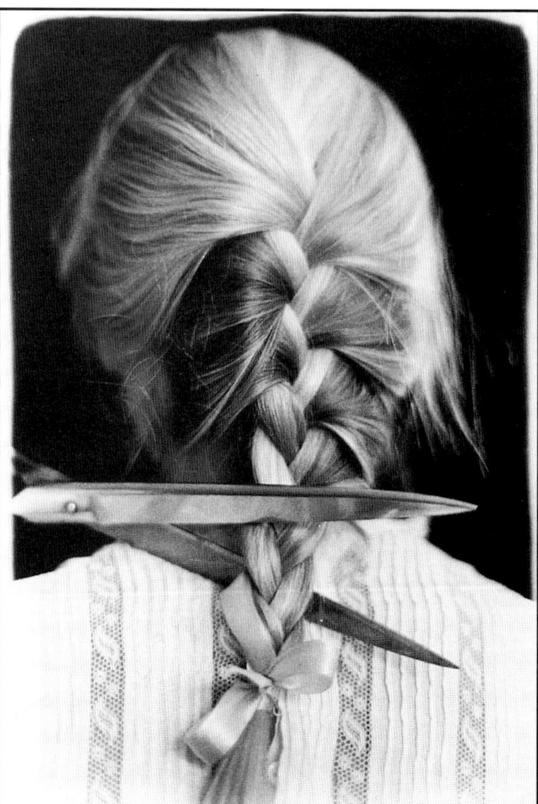

10. Gerard Malanga
*Braid-Snitching* 1981
Gelatin silver print
20 x 16

# BILLY NAME (b. 1940)

Billy Name was born William Linich in Poughkeepsie, New York in 1940. Although he is best known as Andy Warhol's Factory Fotographer, his formative years as an artist were spent in the underground theater. Upon moving to Manhattan in 1960, he became active in lighting design at such seminal avant-garde venues as the New York Poets Theater, the Living Theater, and Judson Memorial Church, and attended the Spoleto Festival of Two Worlds as assistant to lighting designer Nick Cernovich. In 1963, Billy Name met Andy Warhol; his creative input into Warhol's art and celebrity is inestimable. From 1964 to 1970, he served as *major domo*, in-house photographer, lighting and set designer, book designer and editor, and Superstar to Warhol, appearing in such films as *Haircut*, *Lupe*, and *Couch*. He was responsible for the famous silvering of the Factory's interior, and for documenting life in Warhol's circle during this most creative period. In the 1970s, Billy Name moved to San Francisco and developed his concrete poetry canon. He returned to New York state in 1977, where he remains active today as a photographer, concrete poet, and conceptual sculptor. His works have appeared in virtually all publications devoted to Andy Warhol, and have been exhibited in the United States, Europe, Asia, and Africa. The first monograph on his photography (Debra Miller, *Billy Name: Stills from the Warhol Films,* Munich and New York: Prestel Verlag) was published in 1994. In 1995, he was named Resident Photographer of the Gershwin Hotel, New York. His photographs are handled by the Gavin Brown Gallery in Manhattan.

"hair-cutting salons" at his apartment on East 5th Street, the interior of which he had completely covered with silver paint and aluminum foil. Ray Johnson brought Warhol to one of these parties. As a result, Andy was inspired to have Billy decorate his new studio on East 47th Street, the Factory, in the same glittering style as the apartment, and to feature Billy in a series of his films, clipping the hair of his co-stars.

The first three of these films were shot, to the best of Billy's recollection, in November or December 1963.[2] One, showing fellow lighting designer Johnny Dodd having his hair cut by Billy, was premiered by the Film-Makers' Cooperative at the Gramercy Art Theater on 10 January 1964;[3] another, filmed in a kitchen, was not documented and is not yet restored; a third included dancer Freddy Herko and choreographer James Waring in its cast,[4] observing Billy cutting the hair of art historian John Daley. Billy then reprised his early role twice, in 1965, when Andy videotaped him (using equipment loaned by the Norelco Company) cutting Edie Sedgwick's hair on a fire escape, and filmed him giving her a trim in the second reel of *Lupe* (Warhol's treatment of the death of Hollywood's "Mexican spitfire," Lupe Velez).

In addition to starring in *Haircut*, Billy Name was also responsible for its lighting. Here his background in theatrical illumination is clearly evident. The dramatic spotlighting he employed in the film creates the intense tonal contrasts that soon would come to characterize his photographic style, as well (cf. cat. #16). Abstract plays of brilliant highlights and tenebrous darkness, solid and void, lines and planes take on an aesthetic life apart from the figures themselves. Seen in this atmosphere, Billy's simple, everyday action of cutting hair evokes a highly charged, homoerotic mood, reminiscent of the Baroque art of Caravaggio.[5] Billy's silent, focused, near-mystical concentration recalls the words of Andy Warhol:

> I picked up a lot from Billy, actually—just studying him. He didn't say much, and when he did, it was either very practical and mundane or very enigmatic—like if he was ordering from the Bickford's coffee shop downstairs, he'd be completely lucid, but if you asked him what he thought of something, he'd quietly say things like, "You cannot be yes without also being no."[6]



1. Billy Name and John Daley in Warhol's *Haircut* 1963
4 1/2 x 6 3/8
©1994 The Andy Warhol Foundation for the Visual Arts, Inc. All rights reserved. Photograph courtesy of The Andy Warhol Film Project, The Whitney Museum of American Art. Used with permission.

## 11. HAIRCUT

In 1963, when Billy Linich (later Billy Name) was first introduced to Andy Warhol by their mutual friend, the proto-Pop artist Ray Johnson, he was living on the Lower East Side of Manhattan, working as a waiter at Serendipity—a restaurant frequented by Warhol—and doing theatrical lighting design for several avant-garde venues downtown.[1] Along with his other talents, Billy was quite adept at cutting hair, a skill he had learned from his grandfather, a barber in his native Poughkeepsie, New York. Because many of his friends at the time were struggling artists and performers who could not afford to have their hair professionally trimmed, Billy would hold

## 12. FLOATING HANDGUN

The replication of images played a major role at Warhol's Factory. Through the use of a broad range of artistic techniques (e.g., serigraphy and photography) and mechanical devices (such as the Thermo-Fax), Warhol and his collaborators were able to produce unlimited serial repetitions of their favorite compositions and subjects. Andy's proclivity for such mass-production is well documented. Among the most frequently quoted of

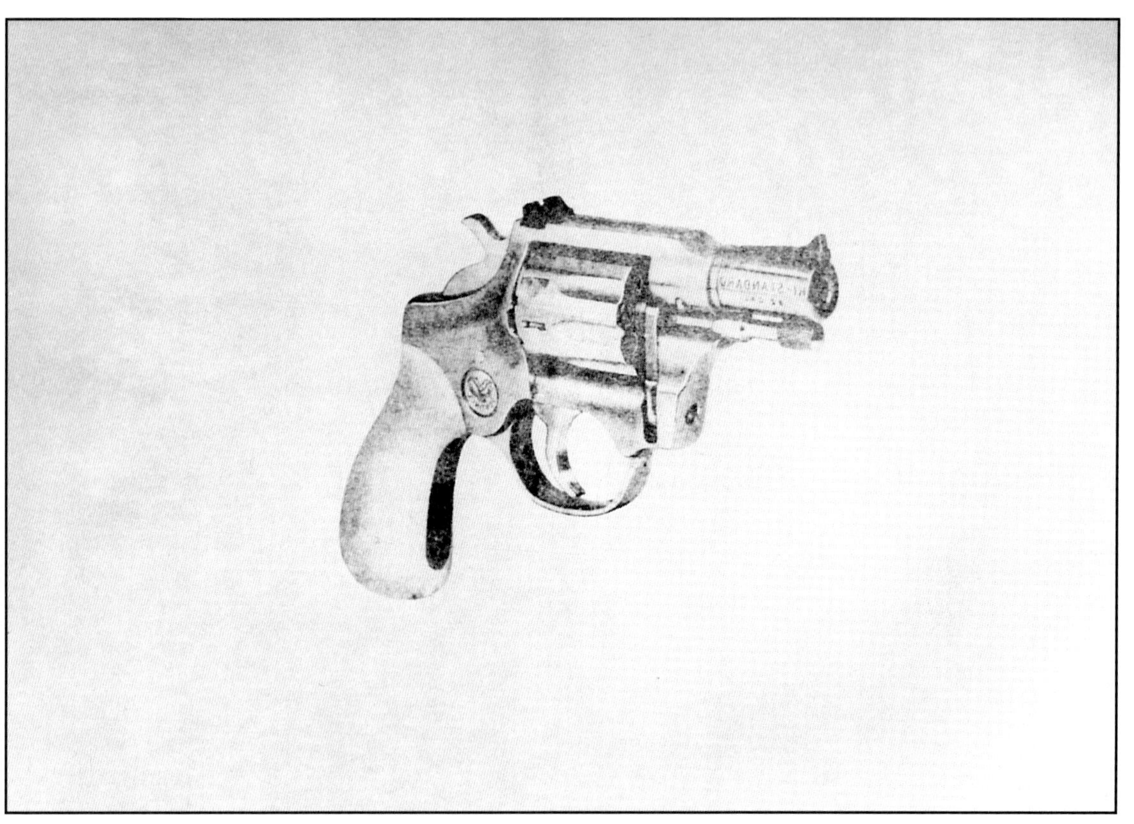



his philosophical proclamations on art and life are his assertions that "Whatever I do, and do machine-like, is because it is what I want to do;" "I like things to be exactly the same over and over again;" and "When you see a gruesome picture over and over again, it doesn't really have any effect."[7]

Andy recalled:

> We had one of those early copying machines at the Factory, a Verifax—sprayed silver, naturally—and Billy used to fool around copying photographs and negatives on that.[8]

The Thermo-Fax machine, a forerunner of the Xerox copier, arrived at the Factory in 1964.[9] It employed chemically-coated heat-sensitive paper (rather than the light-sensitive photocopying process of Xerox) to register by reflex a duplicate of an original, two-dimensional image exposed to infrared radiation. The dark areas of the source image absorb the infrared rays, which are then converted to heat, locally affecting the coating of the copying paper in contact with the original.

Historically, the process of mechanical mass-production was conceived by the American inventor, Eli Whitney. Between 1800 and 1802, Whitney developed the method to produce massive quantities of guns rapidly for the United States government.[10] Thus, Billy's *Floating Handgun* inadvertently represents the perfect subject for mass-production by Thermo-Faxing; it depicts the ultimate mass-produced killing machine, selected during the period in Warhol's *oeuvre* (1962ff.) when he was focusing on gruesome themes of violent death and unexpected disaster (cf. cat. #1).[11] The strength and significance of this Thermo-Faxed image was not lost on Andy. According to Billy, "Andy said that guns seemed to him to be Manhattan icons. He said he thought of doing a

series of paintings."[12] In 1981, Warhol finally produced his own monumentalized, close-up version of the same subject in Billy's Thermo-Fax—a .22 caliber Hi-Standard Sentinel turned in three-quarter view (*Gun*, acrylic and silkscreen ink on canvas, 70 x 90").[13] Billy notes:

> A lot of [my] work is parallel to what Andy did because we both had the same resources. We both had the same file of movie photographs, newspaper criminology photographs— some of which he selected for his images and some of which I selected for my images.[14]

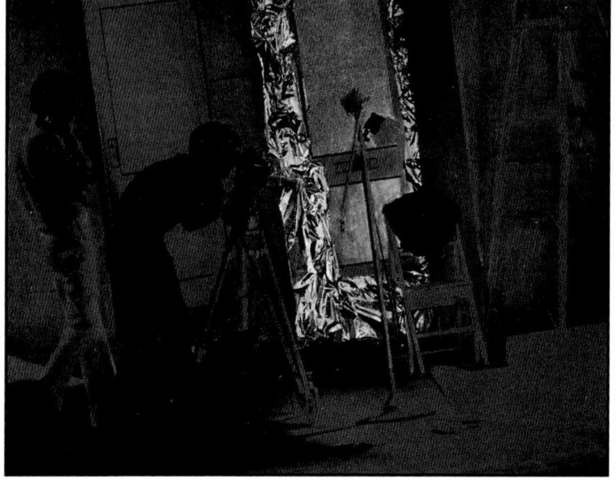



But the two works differ in format, as well as scale. Billy shows the gun in reverse, with its lettering seen in mirror image, whereas Andy creates a double impression through his characteristic off-register printing. In so doing, each artist implies the presence of a fallible human hand that controls the machine. Statistics further underscore the dangerous combination of the human hand with the gun. In 1960, guns were involved in most of the 10,000 murders committed in the United States. Ten

16

years later, the rate rose 50 per cent, to 15,000. By the early 1980s, when Andy issued his silkscreen, over 20,000 murders by handgun per year occurred in America.[15] And the violence continues to escalate. In the 1990s, the National Education Association estimates 100,000 students carry guns to school every day in the U.S., and one out of every four teenage deaths is due to gunshot wounds.[16]

## 13. ANDY WARHOL FILMING AT THE FACTORY

Andy Warhol, reminiscing about 1964, explained how Billy Name came to be the pre-eminent photographer at the Factory:

> I'd gotten myself a 35-mm camera and for a few weeks there I was taking photographs, but it was too complicated for me. I got impatient with the f-stops, the shutter speeds, the light readings, so I dropped it. But Billy started using the camera…[17]

Although Billy had no formal training in photography, his transition from designing lighting for stage and film (see cat. #11) to capturing images in black and white through the action of light in a camera, and then in a darkroom, was a logical evolution. He carefully studied the equipment manuals and taught himself the mechanics of shooting, developing, and printing. But Andy noted in Billy the inherent artistry that cannot be learned by simply following instructions:

> …his "Factory Fotos" caught the exact mood of everything that was happening—

embalmed-in-action… Billy had the magic timing that could get it all at the right split second.[18]

*Andy Warhol Filming at the Factory* evinces the significance of Billy's pictures as both documentary photography and fine art. As a visual document, it gives us a glimpse of the behind-the-scenes activities, the denizens, and the interior of Warhol's legendary studio on East 47th Street. Andy is caught behind his silent 16mm Bolex movie camera, intent on the act of shooting; a quartz halogen lamp, or "sun-gun," is directed towards his subject. Behind him walks Stephen Shore, the aspiring young photographer and filmmaker who, like Billy Name, would produce a significant collection of Factory Fotos in the 1960s.[19] The sheets of aluminum foil with which Billy decorated the Factory are in evidence at the center of the composition. But then the playful artist takes license with the realistic depiction of the interior that he himself silvered,[20] by hand-coloring his black-and-white photograph with electric-hued felt-tip markers. The shades of hot pink, neon orange, and chartreuse evoke the mood of the psychedelic Sixties, as does Billy's trademark isotropic angle of vision, achieved by tilting his camera off-axis before shooting. Typically, during this early phase of his career, Billy printed full-frame images on organic fiber paper, which he then ferrotyped by hand to create a glossy surface finish.

## 14. MARIO MONTEZ

Among the many aspects of life in Warhol's circle to be documented by Billy Name's Factory Fotos was the prolific filmmaking activity with which Andy occupied himself from 1963 to 1968.[21] The stills Billy shot of

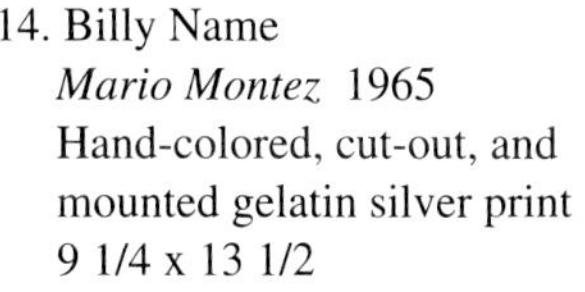

14. Billy Name
   *Mario Montez*  1965
   Hand-colored, cut-out, and
   mounted gelatin silver print
   9 1/4 x 13 1/2

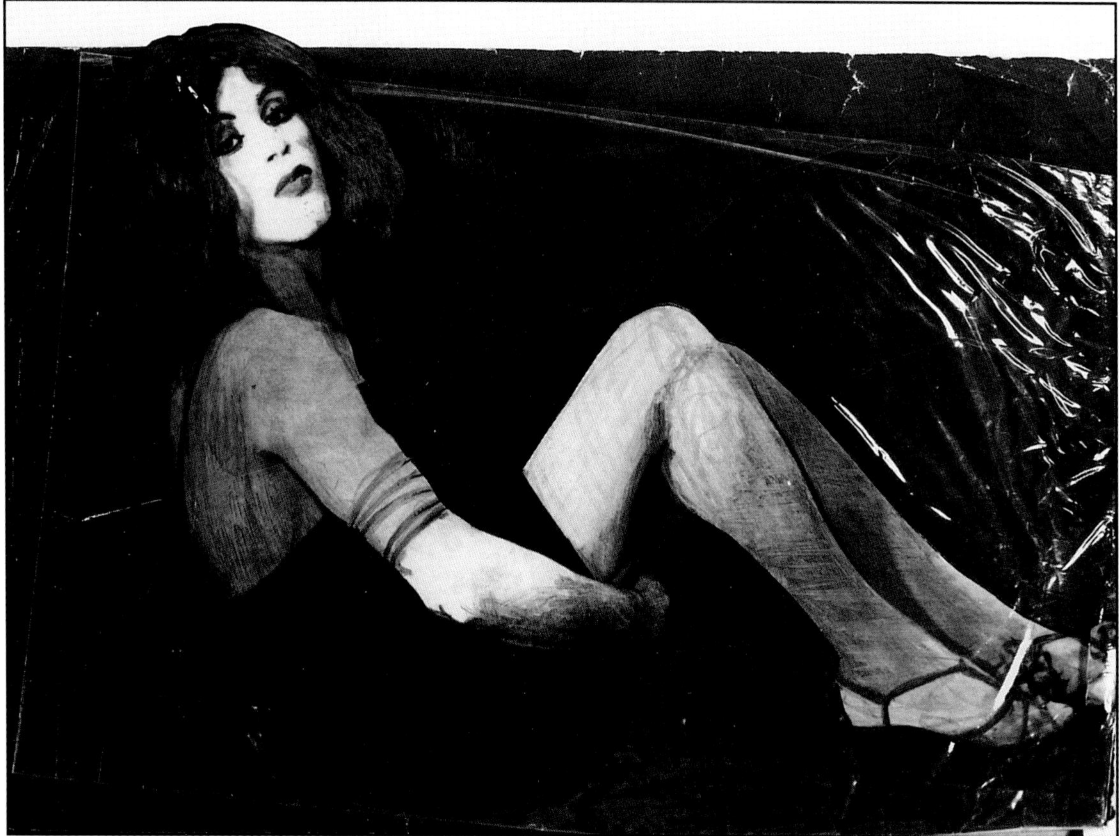

Warhol and his Superstars in action were circulated to the media, both as promotions for the individual films and as publicity for the Factory in general.

In December 1964, Warhol invited the poet and writer Ronald Tavel—a Brooklyn native to whom he had been introduced by Gerard Malanga—to create a series of scenarios for his Factory films. One of the earliest of these collaborations was *Screen Test #2*, shot in January 1965. In it, an aspiring 'actress,' played by drag queen Mario Montez, is given a try-out before the camera, while being directed and harassed from off-screen by Tavel.[22] As was frequently the case, in the afternoon, prior to Warhol's filming, Billy Name did a lighting check and photo session with the star.

The Puerto Rican-born Mario Montez was a well-known player in the new American cinema.[23] Before his association with Warhol, he had appeared as a female Spanish dancer in Jack Smith's *Flaming Creatures* (1962), and later in Smith's *Normal Love* and *The Borrowed Tambourine*. By that time, the actor had already assumed his pseudonymous persona, modeled after the exotic Hollywood screen idol, Maria Montez—a custom that would become extremely popular with Warhol's subsequent Superstars.

While posing for Billy Name's stills, Montez's sense of high camp and avant-garde theatricality exploded. In the several rolls of both black-and-white and color film that Billy shot, Mario postured and played to the camera, primping and preening in an auburn wig, black mini-jumpsuit, white stockings, and strappy high heels. The photographer selected one particularly glamorous frame of his model coyly seated on the floor of the Factory, which he enlarged, cut out, hand-colored, and mounted in cellophane against a glossy green background,[24] thus transforming his gelatin silver print from photograph to art object. Billy's aesthetic manipulation of his image is similar to Warhol's cropping of source photos for silkscreening (e.g., Gene Kornman's famous publicity still for the film *Niagara*, which Andy used as the basis for his own versions of *Marilyn*),[25] in that it imparts a greater focus and immediacy to the figure, by increasing its scale and monumentality within the overall pictorial space. As he did with the majority of his works of the Sixties (cf. cats. #13 and 16), Billy outlined the print in black, visually eliminating the white edges of the photographic fiber paper that he found to be distracting.

## 15. EXPLODING PLASTIC INEVITABLE

Two important events occurred in December 1965 that would coalesce into Andy Warhol's audio-visual production, the Exploding Plastic Inevitable (EPI): Andy's introduction to the Velvet Underground by Barbara Rubin and Gerard Malanga; and producer Michael Myerberg's projected transformation of an abandoned airplane hangar in Queens into a new discotheque (see cat. #3). In exchange for Warhol's endorsement of his proposed club, Myerberg agreed to name it "Andy Warhol's UP," and to let Andy provide the entertainment. Consequently, the artist and his collaborators created a revolutionary multimedia show,

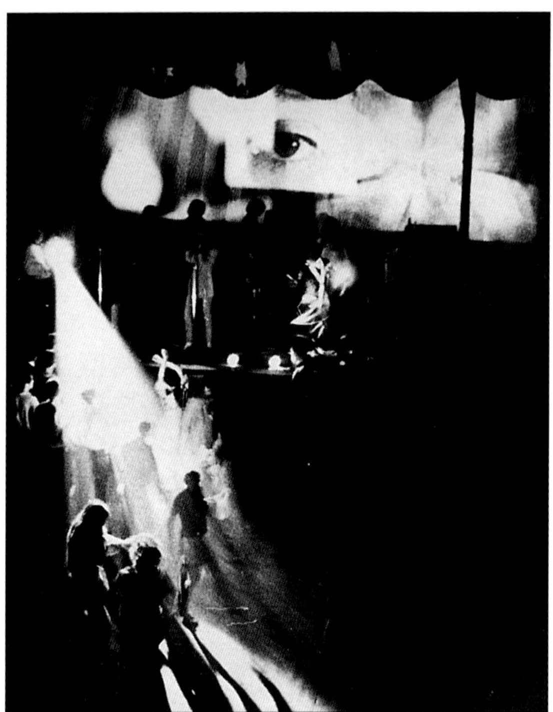

which included the live music of the Velvet Underground and Nico; interpretive dancing led by Malanga; and the projection of lights, colored dye and gel slides, and Warhol films on the walls, the band, the dancers, and the audience. Prior to the scheduled opening of UP in April 1966, Warhol took an early version of his show on the road: first as "Andy Warhol, Up-Tight" at the Film-Makers' Cinematheque on West 41st Street, from 8 to 13 February;[26] then as "Andy Warhol's Underground New York" at Rutgers University, New Brunswick, New Jersey, on 9 March;[27] and then, three days later, at the University of Michigan in Ann Arbor. For the event at the Cinematheque, Factory Fotographer Billy Linich changed his name to Billy Name, "which Andy thought was 'so cute.'"[28]

Back in New York in April, the deal with Michael Myerberg fell through, leaving Warhol the task of finding a new venue. Fortuitously, one night at the Cafe Figaro, Andy and Paul Morrissey were overheard discussing the situation by Jackie Cassen (a psychedelic artist who had worked with Timothy Leary) and Rudy Stern, from whom they quickly arranged to sublet Stanley's *Polski Dom Narodowy*—a big Polish dance hall at 23 St. Mark's Place in the East Village.[29] The rental agreement for the month of April was negotiated on Wednesday, 30 March; on Friday, 1 April, the papers were signed, Gerard Malanga painted the walls white, the Velvets set up their equipment, and the crowds came for that evening's performance. In the meantime, Morrissey and Warhol placed a series of ads in the *Village Voice* promoting the newly named, and quickly re-named, production at the Dom. In the edition of 31 March, the promotion read:

> COME BLOW YOUR MIND/the silver dream factory presents the first/ERUPTING PLASTIC INEVITABLE/with/ANDY WARHOL/THE VELVET UNDERGROUND/and/NICO.[30]

15. Billy Name
*The Exploding Plastic Inevitable* 1966
Gelatin silver print
9 3/8 x 7 1/2

By the next week, the advertisement was changed to:

DO YOU WANT TO DANCE AND BLOW YOUR
MIND WITH/ THE EXPLODING PLASTIC
INEVITABLE/live/ANDY WARHOL/THE VELVET
UNDERGROUND/and/NICO.[31]

Billy Name captured the historic happening at the Dom
from the vantage point of the balcony, high above the
dance floor, where he also took an occasional turn at
operating the lights. His photograph immerses the viewer
in the "mind-blowing" stimuli that bombarded the senses
of the EPI's live audience. The Velvet Underground and
its members went on to use some of Billy Name's

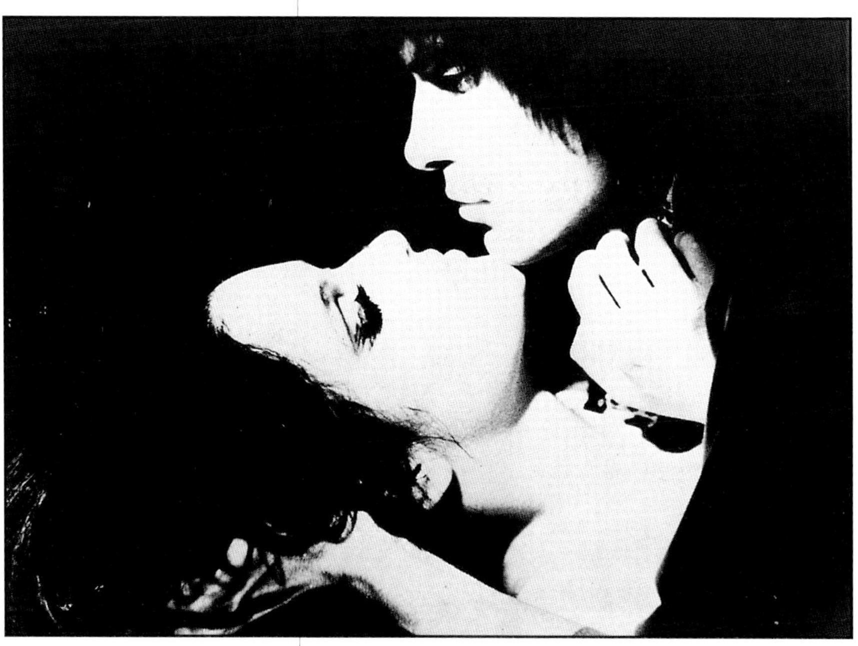

16. Billy Name
*International Velvet and
Allen Midgette in ****
1967
Gelatin silver print
8 3/8 x 12 7/8

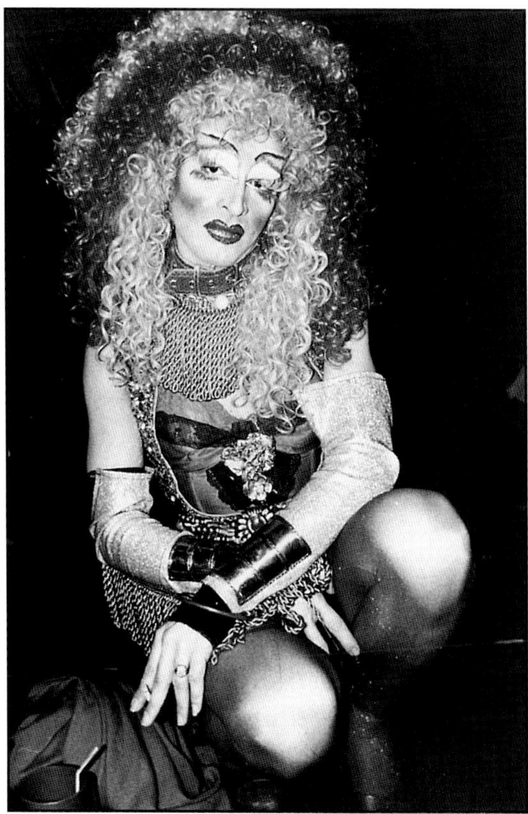

17. Billy Name
*Drag Queen at the Roxy*
1991
Gelatin silver print
14 x 11

photographs for the covers and liners of their subsequent
LPs and CDs.[32] Lou Reed was especially effusive in his
appreciation of Billy: "He's a divinity in action on earth.
He does pictures that are unspeakably beautiful. Just pure
space."[33]

## 16. INTERNATIONAL VELVET AND ALLEN MIDGETTE IN ****

Among the most beautiful subjects Billy Name
photographed at the Factory were Superstars International
Velvet (Susan Bottomly)[34] and Allen Midgette during the
filming of their segment of Andy Warhol's twenty-five-
hour movie ****.[35] His bust-length profile view of the
pair's love scene numbers among the photographer's own
favorite works; he considers it the consummate
expression of his artistic goals. In it, Billy successfully
captures the extreme contrast of pure white and deep
velvety black; the abstract plays of positive and negative
space; the perfect balance of an asymmetrically framed
composition; the crisp focus and linear clarity of form
and contour; and the extraordinary good looks and sex
appeal of the youth movement that dominated the Sixties
and that Andy promoted in his films. All these stylistic
qualities are emphasized by the flattering theatrical
lighting that Billy installed in Warhol's studio;[36] its
powerful effects of chiaroscuro result in the high tonal
contrasts and dramatic figural presence that also
characterize the contemporary fashion photographs of
Richard Avedon and the earlier glamour portraits of
Hollywood stars by George Hurrell.[37]

As with Hurrell's photographs, Billy's still was intended
for publicity purposes, to promote the current Warhol
film and its featured Superstars. In essence, it is the
Factory's up-dated version of Hollywood's "8 x 10
glossy," and it is one of the most popular and frequently
reproduced of all Factory Fotos. The image's subtle off-
axis balance of Midgette atop Bottomly, gazing into her
heavily made-up eyes, is punctuated by the highlights of
her lush hair in the lower left-hand corner of the
composition that sparkle in the darkness and enliven the
otherwise empty space.

## 17. DRAG QUEEN AT THE ROXY

After Andy Warhol's death, Billy Name re-emerged from
the relative obscurity in which he had lived since his
departure from the Factory in the winter of 1969-70.[38] To
everyone's surprise, he showed up in New York for
Andy's memorial service at St. Patrick's Cathedral on 1
April 1987. Subsequently, the Estate of Andy Warhol
located and returned Billy's vintage Factory Fotos and
negatives, left behind in the silver trunk in which he had
stored his belongings at Warhol's studio.[39]

Baird Jones (professional party-giver, curator, and gossip
columnist) contacted Billy and became instrumental in
his active return both to photography and to the New
York art world. He made Billy the gift of his own 35mm
camera, and threw a series of parties at various clubs in
Manhattan, at which Billy was the featured guest. As a
result, one significant aspect of Billy Name's

photographic *oeuvre* of the 1990s comprises scenes of nightlife in the city.

In his glittering portrait of a *Drag Queen at the Roxy*, Billy's masterful tonal range, sharp focus, three-dimensional perspective, and monumentality of form convey the overwhelming presence of his sitter. The audacious subject, in full disco costume, make-up, and wig, poses for Billy's camera and contemplates the viewer with an uncompromising, direct gaze. The subject matter recalls segments of Billy's work from the Sixties, such as the Exploding Plastic Inevitable's happening at the Dom (see cat. #15) and portraits of cross-dressers like Mario Montez (cat. #14). But, technically, Billy's recent photographs are easily distinguishable from his vintage Factory Fotos: they are printed on Kodak's newer polycontrast rosin-coated (RC) paper, rather than on the organic fiber paper of the earlier period;[40] and his compositions are never cropped (as is the case with cat. #15), but are printed full frame within a standard white border. This method suggests a more confident and mature artist, who now composes his pictures solely through the lens of his camera, with no further compositional adjustment in the darkroom.

## 18. BLACK AND WHITE PHOTOGRAPHY (PER SE)

For those of us who grew up with Billy Name's celebrated Factory Fotos, documenting life in Andy Warhol's circle in the 1960s,[41] his recent conceptual photographs come as a surprise. Absent are the familiar faces, the verité subjects, and the eccentric camera angles that are the hallmarks of Billy Name's Pop style and the "straight photography" he continues to practice (e.g., cat. #17). Here the artist has forsaken the use of camera, film, and figurative expression in favor of a minimalist abstraction, albeit one whose evolution can be traced back through his past three decades of activity: his training in the New York avant-garde of the late 1950s and early 1960s; his enduring fascination with Zen philosophy; and the most salient qualities of his better-known objective images.

Billy Name's conceptual prints are the latest manifestation in a relatively long history of cameraless photographs,[42] whose appearance often paralleled contemporary developments in painting and other media.[43] And so it is with Billy Name's foray into the medium, which takes its inspiration from modern painting, rather than photography. His monotone photographs owe a debt to such color-field, minimalist, and monochromatic painters of the Fifties and Sixties as Ad Reinhardt, Josef Albers, Barnett Newman, Frank Stella, and Robert Rauschenberg—those radical reductivists whose works filled the avant-garde galleries and modern museums, and most impressed the young Billy upon his arrival from Poughkeepsie to New York in 1959. But Billy's conceptual prints are even more radical than their predecessors in paint, and in a largely untested medium. Here Billy Name reduces photography to its bare essence: the presence, or absence, of light on sensitized paper, with no variations in texture or modulations in tone. In these aspects, Billy Name's *Black and White Photography (Per Se)* most nearly recalls Andy Warhol's "blanks"—the flat, monochromatic

18. Billy Name
*Black and White
Photography (Per Se)*
1993
Gelatin silver prints
14 x 22

canvases conceived as companion pieces to his figurative silkscreened paintings.[44] The significant distinction between the two, of course, is that Andy never intended his blanks as independent works of art, but merely as the other half of a diptych.

In his conceptual extremism—the isolation of the Warholian blank—Billy Name brings us into a Zen-like state of contemplating nothingness, or as near to nothing as an existing work of art can be. True to his Pop background, Billy's conceptual prints still retain the properties of empirical objects—a rectangle, a photograph with a border—and therein lie the Zen paradoxes and balance. It is not coincidental that the tenets of Zen should be encompassed in Billy Name's work. During his early years in Manhattan, he was employed at the bookstore Orientalia, where he avidly pored over the writings of Eastern authors and philosophers. At the same time, he associated with the Zen-inspired downtown community of performing, literary, and visual artists, including Ray Johnson (see cat. #11) and La Monte Young (the minimalist composer with whom Billy collaborated on avant-garde theatrical productions as lighting designer at Judson Memorial Church and as chorus singer in the Theatre of Eternal Music).[45] Both Johnson and Young had indirect connections with the veritable epicenter of the minimalist/Zen arts movement in America, in the musician and composer John Cage. Johnson was a student of Josef Albers at Black Mountain College (1945-48), where Cage would teach summer sessions in 1948, 1952, and 1953. Young, as a graduate student at Berkeley, was deeply affected by Cage's theories and later, at the New School of Social Research in New York (Fall 1960), attended a continuation of John Cage's electronic music class taught by Richard Maxfield.

The ubiquitous impact of Cage would be reinforced for Billy in the second half of the Sixties, when Andy Warhol became manager of the Velvet Underground. One of its founding members, John Cale, previously had formed The Dream Syndicate with La Monte Young, and was himself profoundly inspired by the avant-garde freedom of John Cage. Among Cage's most notorious accomplishments was the incorporation of lengthy periods of silence into his musical presentations.[46] This tendency he succinctly summarized with the paradoxical declaration, "I have nothing to say and I am saying it." In John Cage's minimalist music, we hear silence; in Billy Name's conceptual photographs, we see nothing: the medium is different, but the aesthetic is the same.

While Billy Name's experiments in such reductivist principles find their fullest expression in his conceptual black and white prints, there is a strong element of abstraction that runs throughout his *oeuvre*. The pure intensity of lighting effects seen in such classic Factory Fotos as *International Velvet and Allen Midgette in ***** (cat. #16), with its deep velvety shadows and blindingly brilliant highlights, reveals an artist intrigued with the darkness of black and the lightness of white. Thus, it is not too far a leap to his current *Black and White Photography (Per Se)*, founded on the same aesthetic principles, but now with all vestiges of objective representation removed. Despite their monotonality, Billy's conceptual photographs are not monotonous. Their glossy surfaces produce plays of reflected light that lend a sensuality to the rectalinear regularity of their compositions. The sleek, saturated black and white tones epitomize the flawless elegance invoked in Mies van der Rohe's oft-quoted dictum, "Less is more."

## 19. SELF-PORTRAIT FOR EVERYBODY

When Billy Name left the Factory c. 1969-70, he returned for a while to his native Poughkeepsie, then spent some time in Washington, DC and New Orleans, and eventually hitch-hiked across country to California. In San Francisco, he visited the poet Diane Di Prima, a friend he had known since his early days in New York. Afterwards, he lived a virtual hermit's existence, and, during this time, began his fascination with concrete poetry and conceptual sculpture.[47] Since his return to Upstate New York in 1977, he has continued working in these media.

19. Billy Name
*Self-Portrait for Everybody* c. 1988
Broken mirror assemblage
5 1/2 x 5 1/2

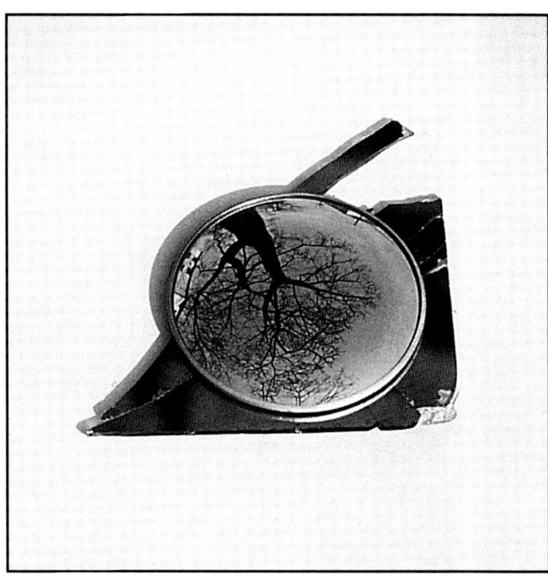

*Self-Portrait for Everybody* is, perhaps, the piece that best summarizes Billy's sculptural *oeuvre*, reflecting the myriad influences that have shaped him as an artist. The broken mirror assemblage pays homage to his association with the artists of Black Mountain College and Judson Memorial Church, his affinity for Eastern philosophy, and, above all, his long-time collaboration with Andy Warhol.

When Billy came to New York in the late 1950s, he immersed himself in an avant-garde art scene that included such visionaries as Merce Cunningham, John Cage,[48] Ray Johnson, and La Monte Young. Their ideas are evident in *Self-Portrait for Everybody*. For example, the element of random experience, so integral to Cage's compositions,[49] is the essence of Billy's sculpture, which changes its appearance with every new observer. (Even Billy's name, which he chose after several years in the Warhol circle, suggests that we fill in the blank with our own). This invitation to participate is reminiscent of Johnson's interactive New York Correspondence School of Art. Johnson's medium was the United States Postal Service, his art the mailing of ephemera and collages, often with instructions to circulate the correspondence to a third party after adding something to the piece.[50]

It was Johnson, of course, who introduced Billy to Andy Warhol, the quintessential collaborative artist of our time. Billy covered the walls and pipes of Andy's headquarters with silver foil and Mylar,[51] and, in Warhol's words, "brought cans of silver paint and sprayed everything with it, right down to the toilet bowl."[52] Warhol went on to say that "Billy loved reflecting surfaces—he'd prop broken bits of mirror here and there and paste little sections of them onto everything,"[53] as did his friend, the dancer Freddy Herko, who made flowers out of broken mirrors.[54] The mirror was, indeed, a *leitmotiv* at the Factory. Among the songs Lou Reed wrote for the Velvet Underground, produced by Warhol, was "I'll Be Your Mirror."[55]

It is also significant, in light of Billy's abiding interest in Zen, that the mirror is a recurring theme in Eastern thought. In Shinto mythology, the mirror is an attribute of the sun goddess Amaterasu, who gave a looking glass to her grandson Ninigi no Mikoto, telling him, "My child, when thou lookest upon this mirror, let it be as if thou wert looking on me."[56] Many years later, the Zen master Shunryu Suzuki wrote:

> You are independent, I am independent;
> each exists in a different moment. But
> this does not mean we are quite different
> beings… I am a part of you.[57]

Thus, with *Self-Portrait for Everybody*, we become Billy, adding our faces to his and to those of everyone in the universe.

## 20. CONCRETE POETRY: TONE POEM

The term "concrete poetry" came into common usage in the mid-1960s, to describe an international movement that espoused "a poetry of materials" or poetry "at one with not only its symbolic but also its material form."[58] One of its American exponents, Mary Ellen Solt, described three types—the visual, the verbal, and the kinetic—all of which share "a concentration on the physical material from which the poem or text is made.[59]

But even in the Sixties, the notion of concrete poetry was not new. The Dadaists, in the early decades of the twentieth century, broke away from the traditional ways in which language had hitherto been used in art[60] (primarily as text for illustration, or as explanatory inscription). Raoul Hausman claimed, "In 1918, I introduced typography as a picture element and I created my poster poems," which are "phonetic poems, composed according to the sound of the letters."[61] The element of sound was also important to Marcel Duchamp, Dada's most famous exponenet (and Andy Warhol's favorite artist). In Duchamp's goateed version of Leonardo da Vinci's *Mona Lisa*, the inscription "L.H.O.O.Q." is a phonetic pun that reads, in French, "Elle a chaud au cul," or, roughly translated, "She has a hot ass."[62]

Random occurrence was another significant aspect of Dada, as when printed words were cut up, shaken up, and recomposed according to the laws of chance:[63] László Moholy-Nagy referred to such poems by Kurt Schwitters as "verbal collages."[64] This method of construction also recalls the Dadaist use of "found objects" in the creation of cleverly named "readymade" sculptures, such as Duchamp's *In Advance of a Broken Arm*, composed of a common snow shovel. Similarly, in the 1960s, the artistic movement Fluxus sought to deconstruct established notions about fine art by using commercially produced and found objects.[65] Its practitioners, who included Yoko Ono, Ken Friedman, Mieko Shiomi, Nam June Paik, and Charlotte Moorman, were inspired by Dada, concrete poetry, and the "chance operations" of the Zen-influenced artist/composer John Cage, in their mingling of high and low aesthetics.

Fluxus came quickly on the heels of the closing of Black Mountain College, a school, and more significantly, a community of artists and composers that had included Cage, dancer/choreographer Merce Cunningham, architect Paul Williams, and Ray Johnson (see cat. #19). Johnson developed his mail art during the 1960s, sending the hand- and mechanically-produced collages and communiqués that prompted Nicolas and Elena Calas to write: "Ray Johnson is to the letter what Joseph Cornell is to the box.[66] Not surprisingly, Johnson admired Cornell,[67] whose enigmatic boxes, with their snippets of news clippings, maps, and found objects, paid tribute to the movie stars and ballerinas he loved.

Billy Name began his exploration of concrete poetry after his mysterious departure from Warhol's Factory and his relocation to California in the 1970s. Physical illness, economic worries, and a longing for domestic stability made this a difficult period for the artist. He recalls:

> I did some analysis and I realized that
> what I was using as my modus operandi was
> something I was taught in high school—
> pronouns. My prime operator was the first-
> person singular pronoun "I." What does "I"
> stand for? You can say it stands for me as
> a person or a human being, but these are
> categorical factors. What am "I" really?
> What is the basic operator? Not really
> considering myself to be real, I figured
> I'd have to make something up, because I
> couldn't accept all of these definitions.[68]

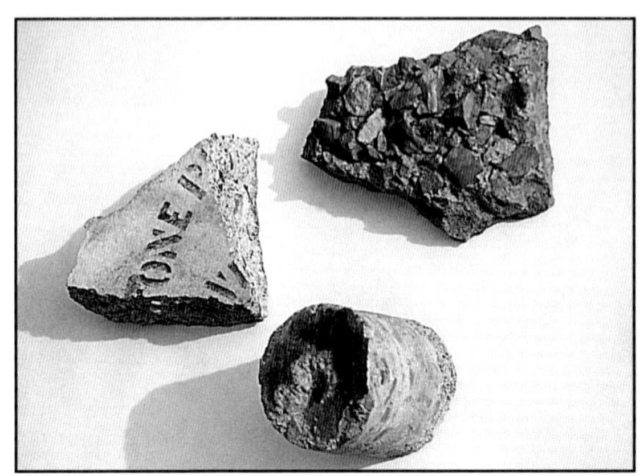

20. Billy Name
*Concrete Poetry: Tone Poem* c. 1989
Concrete found-object assemblage
5 x 10 x 13

This intense self-examination helped to shape the next phase of his artistic development:

> So I started playing with sound and I
> recalled the vowel system: a, e, i, o,
> u. I decided to make a concrete poetry
> canon out of the sonic system. What
> would be the best, strongest sound to
> use? The rankest sound? And I said,
> well, "rank," of course, is rank, but
> stronger than rank is "krank," simply
> because it's a stronger sound. So for
> a, e, i, o, u, I did krank, krenk,
> krink, kronk, krunk. And I did it as
> a bank canon, so there's the bank
> krank, the benk krenk, the bink krink,
> the bonk kronk, and the bunk krunk.
> So it's a concrete poetry sonic canon.
> And if you go over to my neighborhood,
> all the kids call me Krank.[69]

In *Concrete Poetry: Tone Poem*, Billy synthesizes his sonic canon with found-object sculpture, resulting in an appropriately literal art form. The sculpture, reminiscent of the "readymades" of Marcel Duchamp and the "signs" of Joseph Cornell, consists of broken pieces of concrete, each with a different shape and texture, which Billy found at a construction site near his home. There are three components: one a cylinder; one a jagged slab; and one imprinted with the suggestive letters "… TONE P….," from which Billy inferred the phrase "Tone Poem." Here, the hard sounds of the "Bank Krank" are not present in the words themselves; they have been transferred to the material on which they are inscribed, thus producing new ways of seeing and listening.

# ULTRA VIOLET (b. 1935)

Isabelle Collin Dufresne was born to a wealthy family in Grenoble, France. In 1953, the young convent-educated beauty came to New York, where she spent a decade in the artistic milieus of John Graham, John Chamberlain, and Salvador Dalí, with whom she began her painting career. Through the grand master of Surrealism, she first made the acquaintance of Andy Warhol in 1963, changed her name to Ultra Violet, and became one of Warhol's most visible and memorable Superstars. As an actress, Ultra Violet has appeared in such films as John Schlesinger's *Midnight Cowboy*, Milos Forman's *Taking Off*, Norman Mailer's *Maid Stone*, and Andy Warhol's *I, a Man*. As a writer, her best-selling autobiography, *Famous for 15 Minutes: My Years with Andy Warhol*, has been published in more than a dozen languages; her play, *You Are Who You Eat*, was performed in Czechoslovakia in 1992 (both in its original English version and in a Czech translation) and at the Theatre for the New City in New York, 1994-95. As a visual artist, her mixed-media works have been exhibited in over 70 venues throughout the world. In 1990, she published the manifesto of her new artistic movement *L'ULTRATIQUE,* which aligns art with spirituality, and focuses on the themes of apocalyptic angels, the color spectrum, and the sphere. Ultra Violet presently divides her time between her studio in Nice and her penthouse apartment in Manhattan.

21. Marcel Duchamp backstage with Ultra Violet and Taylor Mead at Charles Ludlam's *Conquest of the Universe* 1967
Photograph by Wynn Chamberlain
Not pictured

## 21. CONQUEST OF THE UNIVERSE

Mid-November 1967 marked Ultra Violet's off-Broadway debut in New York's Playhouse of the Ridiculous Repertory Club. She appeared in Charles Ludlam's *Conquest of the Universe* along with a roster of regulars from the Factory, including Taylor Mead, Mary Woronov, Ondine, Beverly Grant, and Frankie Francine. The press release for the absurdist play, directed by John Vaccaro, described it as:

> a paramoral study of these space-intoxicated times… [in which] the intergalactic voyager meets in the kings and queens of far-flung planets doppelgängers of Earth's everyday psychoses.[1]

Warhol had some early connections with the Theatre of the Ridiculous; his first scriptwriter, Ronald Tavel, with whom he had collaborated in 1964-65, became its premier playwright in the summer of 1965. And Andy was in sympathy with the outrageous sensibility and artistic integrity of the Ridiculous:

> Now it was clear that there were two types of people doing counter culture-type things— the ones who wanted to be commercial and successful and move right up into the mainstream of society… and the ones who wanted to stay where they were, outside society. The way to be counter culture and have mass commercial success was to say and do radical things in a conservative

format [like *Hair*, which became a long-running hit on Broadway]. The other people—the ones who didn't care at all about mass commercial success—did radical things in a radical format, and if the audience didn't happen to get the content or the form, then that was that.[2]

While *Conquest of the Universe* was not destined for the level of mainstream success enjoyed by *Hair* (which, Andy noted, had been in rehearsal downtown at about the same time), critical opinion of both the play and its cast was not unkind. For her performance as Natolia, the Middle-English-speaking Queen from Saturn, Ultra received rave reviews. Michael Smith, writing about this "pop fantasy future" in the *Village Voice,* called her "brilliantly funny" amidst "an explosion of talent that leaves the mind in tatters."[3] Marcel Duchamp, whom she had invited to attend the show on 21 November, was likewise impressed. Ultra's co-star Ondine recalled his reaction:

> …Duchamp was *most* intrigued by it. He said [that] it was the best theatrical evening that he has ever had. He was just flipped-out over it. He *adored* it, and he wanted to come backstage and be filmed with the cast…[4]

Duchamp's praise came as no surprise to Ultra Violet; one reviewer, lauding this "very entertaining casserole of zaniness," remarked that *Conquest*'s "colorful chaos is a direct descendant of Dada."[5]

## 22. I, A MAN

One night at Elaine's, the trendy uptown restaurant at Second Avenue and 88th Street in Manhattan, Andy Warhol promised Ultra Violet that she would be the star of his new movie *I, a Man*.[6] In reality, she was one of a total of eight women featured in the film, which consists of a series of encounters between them and their leading man Tom Baker. Ultra's other appearances in the Warhol films include a minor, seated part as a member of the family in *The Life of Juanita Castro* (1965); a *Screen Test,* shot on 6 February 1966; a few reels of the 25-hour movie **** of 1966-67 ("Courtroom," "High Ashbury," and "Mondo Ultra," filmed at her new, unfinished apartment at 860 United Nations Plaza); and a segment of *Tub Girls* (1967), in which Viva had the lead role. But *I, a Man* was of special importance because it was conceived as a feature-length movie for theatrical release.[7] Consequently, it would be seen by an audience larger than the usual downtown art crowd. Furthermore, as a result of Paul Morrissey's participation, it received a significant amount of post-production editing, which gave it a somewhat more polished, commercial look than Warhol's earlier underground films had had.

The movie, compiled from a number of individual reels, was shown in at least four different versions. For its debut at the Hudson Theater in New York on 24 August 1967, the feature ran approximately 100 minutes.[8] The cast consisted of Tom Baker, Bettina Coffin, Stephanie Graves, Cynthia May, Ivy Nicholson, Valerie Solanas, and Ingrid Superstar; it did not include Ultra Violet or Nico. Early in 1968, when it played at the Cinematheque-16 in Los Angeles, the total running time had increased to 110 minutes, and Ultra Violet and Nico were listed in the cast.[9] Later that year, the footage was re-edited to its present 95-minute format, which still contains all eight of the actresses. Warhol also included each of the uncut reels of *I, a Man* in the sole full-length screening of his 25 hour epic ****, on 15-16 December 1967.

Ultra's unscripted segment called for her to flirt with Baker. In it, she is soft-spoken, refined, coquettish, and feminine; hers is a dramatic contrast with the scenes of the more raucous and aggressive American-born women in the cast. The pair begins to kiss, the camera zooms in for a close-up, and we are exposed to the kinetic, glistening interlace of their darting tongues. Then the camera cuts to an obviously edited insert. It shows a profile view of Ultra Violet before a plain white background, *sans* Baker, with her tongue fully extended. Andy would later comment on her "incredibly long tongue,"[10] and Ultra herself noted:

> [It] is obscenely long. I can extend my
> tongue a full six inches. It has been
> photographed many times as a rare specimen.[11]

## 23. MIDNIGHT COWBOY

In the spring of 1968, British director John Schlesinger approached Andy Warhol about appearing as himself in an underground party scene for his forthcoming movie *Midnight Cowboy*. The Hollywood feature, based on the novel about a male prostitute by James Leo Herlihy, was to be shot in New York that summer. Andy declined Schlesinger's offer, but suggested Viva for the role of the avant-garde filmmaker. In addition, the casting list called for a stereotyped assortment of party-goers, including male and female hippies, a "poetic fag," high fashion and social types, hustlers, drag queens, "2 dike ladies," student activists, black nationalists, a "fag hag," a painted nude in a coffin, "1 super star," and the "Warhol/Morrissey film group."[12] Taylor Mead and Paul Morrissey numbered among the movie's extras, and Ultra Violet was typecast as the Superstar. She also appeared in a black-and-white film-within-the-film shot by Morrissey and screened as part of the party scene. The bedroom of Ultra's own apartment at the United Nations Plaza was used as the set for the subsequent sex scene between stars Jon Voight and Brenda Vaccaro.

Although she was recognized in the Sixties for her outrageous purple hair, Ultra notes that, for her two weeks of shooting (beginning on 28 June 1968, at Manhattan's Filmways Studio in East Harlem), "Hollywood logic requires that I wear a blond wig."[13] Warhol, who was in Columbus Hospital at the time recovering from the near fatal gunshot wounds inflicted by Valerie Solanas on 3 June, also expressed his disenchantment with Hollywood's recreation of New York's artistic underground:

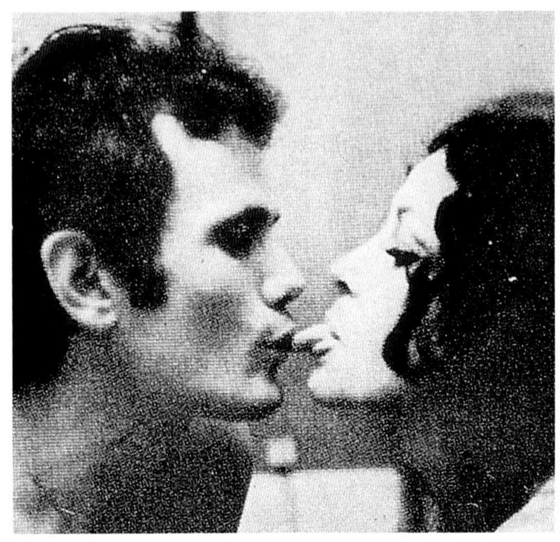

I had the same jealous feeling thinking about *Midnight Cowboy* that I had had when I saw *Hair* and realized that people with money were taking the subject matter of the underground, counter culture life and giving it a good, slick, commercial treatment…. I thought, "Why didn't they give *us* the money to do, say, *Midnight Cowboy*? We would have done it so *real* for them." I didn't understand then that when they said they wanted real life, they meant real movie life![14]

Criticisms notwithstanding, *Midnight Cowboy* won three Academy Awards in 1969, for Best Picture, Best Screenplay, and Best Director. Ultra witnessed firsthand the contrast between "John Schlesinger's firm-handed direction" and the "disorder" of the Factory's more radical, independent filmmaking.[15] In the end, the Superstar acknowledged that things turned out better than they had hoped for, in that she and Viva did have a scene with lead actors Dustin Hoffman and Jon Voight—they were not totally isolated from the "Hollywood luminaries" and the main movie. And Warhol and Morrissey, who felt that Schlesinger had appropriated his subject matter from their earlier film *My Hustler* (1965), were inspired by the success of *Midnight Cowboy* to begin work on a new hustler trilogy of their own. The time was now right for Warhol's productions of *Flesh* (1968), *Trash* (1970), and *Heat* (1971).[16]

## 24. PORTRAIT OF PICASSO

The south of France, with its temperate climate and blazing colors, has been a popular locale for artists throughout the twentieth century. During the summers of 1947 and 1948, Pablo Picasso stayed with his family (then mistress Françoise Gilot and their two children Claude and Paloma) at the villa "La Galloise" in Vallauris—a small town known since Antiquity for its pottery industry.[17] The teen-aged Isabelle Dufresne, vacationing at that time with her family on the Côte d'Azur, made an unannounced visit to Picasso's studio. She recalls:

22. Ultra Violet with Tom Baker in Andy Warhol's *I, a Man* 1967-68
5 x 7
©1967 Andy Warhol Films, Inc. Used with permission.

23. Ultra Violet, Dustin Hoffman, and Viva in John Schlesinger's *Midnight Cowboy* 1969
7 1/2 x 9 1/2
Not pictured

> ...I went to Vallauris, an art center near
> our home, and knocked on the door of Picasso's
> studio. Caught by surprise when he opened the
> door himself, I said dramatically, "Here I am."
> Then I found myself speechless under the
> blazing fire of the master's eye. He invited
> me to look around. I stared at the paintings,
> numb with the sense that I was living a
> moment of history.[18]

After having established her own studio in Nice in the late 1980s, Ultra Violet paid homage to Picasso with a portrait of the artist as a young man.[19] Its summary draughtsmanship (the linear, energetic scribbles of hair and short slashes of whiskers) and arbitrary color (with areas suggestive of three-dimensional modeling) take their inspiration from Picasso's revolutionary abstract style. Her appliqué of metallic foil around the eyes suggests multiple associations and sources: the technique of collage popularized by Picasso and invented by his fellow Cubist Georges Braque in 1909; the injured owl that shared Picasso's studio and became one of his favorite models in Antibes in 1946;[20] the sheets of aluminum foil and silver Mylar with which Billy Name draped Warhol's Factory in the 1960s; and Ultra Violet's own trademark penchant for purple, as reflected in her Superstar pseudonym.

24. Ultra Violet
*Portrait of Picasso*  1991
Mixed media

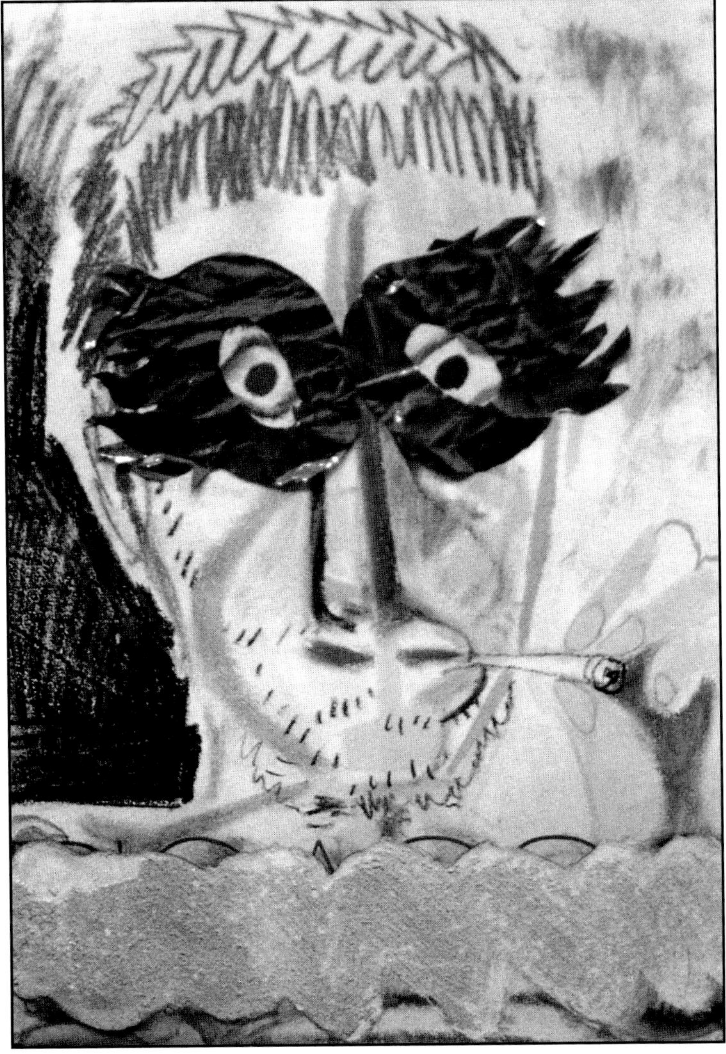

## 25. THEY SOLD ME FOR 30 PIECES OF SILVER

At the age of six, Isabelle Collin Dufresne began her religious education, commuting daily to a Catholic school run by the nuns of the Sacred Heart a few miles outside her native Grenoble. The following year, she began boarding at the Sacred Heart Convent. The strict regimen there, combined with feelings of isolation from her home and rejection by her parents, incited the young girl to rebel "against everything: family, religion, authority, eventually society in general."[21] Consequently, as a thirteen-year-old, she was subjected by her priest and Mother Superior to the Catholic rite of exorcism, with the full consent and cooperation of her parents.

Such traumatic experiences from childhood resulted in Ultra Violet's estrangement from the Catholic church, but not from religion entirely. After decades of youthful hedonism, culminating in the Warhol Sixties, Ultra began to search for "a sense of reason and fulfillment."[22] Her extensive spiritual studies led her back to the Bible, to Christianity, and to repentance for perceived past and present sins. She abruptly ended an adulterous affair with California Pop artist Edward Ruscha, then spent a year in bed recuperating from an ulcerated colon and an emotional breakdown. She re-emerged as a born-again Christian, dedicated to the moral reform of her own life and to spreading the Gospel through her art.

Despite her own conversion from Catholicism, in *They Sold Me for 30 Pieces of Silver* Ultra appropriates a traditional Catholic subject from the Passion of Christ. Her source is the Italian Renaissance artist and Dominican friar Fra Angelico. At the center of the composition is a detail of the head of Christ, reproduced from Fra Angelico's fresco *The Mocking of Christ*, painted for the Monastery of San Marco in Florence (now the Fra Angelico Museum), c. 1440-41. The central image is surrounded by a background of silver, which recalls the silvered surfaces of Warhol's Factory of the 1960s and visually reinforces the bold inscription in Ultra's native French, "Ils m'ont vendu pour 30 pièces d'argent." Both compositionally and didactically, the words of Christ are as important as the image itself. The Christian artist transforms the urban scribbles of contemporary graffiti art (which reached its peak of popularity in the 1980s, with a new generation of Warhol collaborators like Keith Haring, Jean-Michel Basquiat, and Kenny Scharf)[23] into an edifying and clearly legible religious message. Her use of clean-edged, stenciled and applied letters displays the lingering impact of Ed Ruscha and their shared artistic belief in the power of the word.[24] As defined in her artistic manifesto *L'ULTRATIQUE*,[25] Ultra engages in a post-modern, semiotic/letterist crusade, using words and signs in conjunction with the visual arts to herald the forthcoming millennium and to "illuminate our XXIst century."[26]

With her turn to religiosity, Ultra's personal development has followed an evolution similar to that in the subject matter of Warhol's art. She herself has noted:

> Warhol's early work mirrors the American
> Dream [e.g., consumer products and movie
> stars], but it also reflects the reversal

of the dream, as shown in his Disasters
Series; toward the end of his artistic
career Warhol reveals his reconciliation
with his spiritual self [in subjects like
*The Last Supper* and *Crosses*].[27]

She concludes:

> …[Andy] was raised in a very religious
> home. He possibly went away from that with
> his work and lifestyle but near the end I
> think that he returned to that very profound
> spirituality. I think that his message here
> is to take a second look at these images,
> question them, and see what validity they
> might have in our life.[28]

In this respect, Ultra Violet's art of the 1990s represents a
continuation of Andy Warhol's ultimate legacy and
meaning.

## 26. THE ARCHANGEL GABRIEL

With the approaching millennium, angels have
experienced a popular resurgence in the media. For a
period in the early 1990s, Ultra Violet devoted her art
exclusively to their depiction. In a lecture delivered at the
Inaugural Conference of The Andy Warhol Museum in
Pittsburgh, she noted:

> Angels are very fashionable now and I think
> that there is a very good reason for that.
> Looking at the past, the most important message
> from angels was when they announced the coming
> of the Messiah. I feel that we are re-living
> that time and that is why they are coming back.
> They are on Broadway, in books, on television.[29]

Etymologically, the word angel derives from the Greek
"angelos" or "messenger." The Judeo-Christian tradition
identifies angels as the messengers of God, whose
mission is to instruct and to guide humankind according
to the authority of their divine sender. During the Middle
Ages, the orders of angels were codified in Pseudo-
Dionysius the Areopagite's *Celestial Hierarchy* and
Thomas Aquinas's *Summa Theologiae*.[30] Both catalogued
nine categories, or choirs, of angels orbiting around the
central throne of God. These nine then were grouped by
threes into triads. The third or lowest triad, believed to
border on the created temporal and material universe,
consists of principalities, archangels, and angels. Because
these three choirs, according to the Pseudo-Dionysius, are
firmly rooted in the realm of the first heaven, closest to
earth, they are the most familiar to us. The seven
archangels are the most important of them, as they carry
divine decrees to humanity.

One of the archangels mentioned by name in both the Old
and New Testaments is Gabriel, whose function is to
carry revelations from God.[31] It was Gabriel who
delivered that most momentous message in Christianity,
to which Ultra Violet referred, when he announced the
incarnation of Christ to the Virgin Mary (Luke 1:26-38).
Ultra, however, does not depict Gabriel as the angel of the

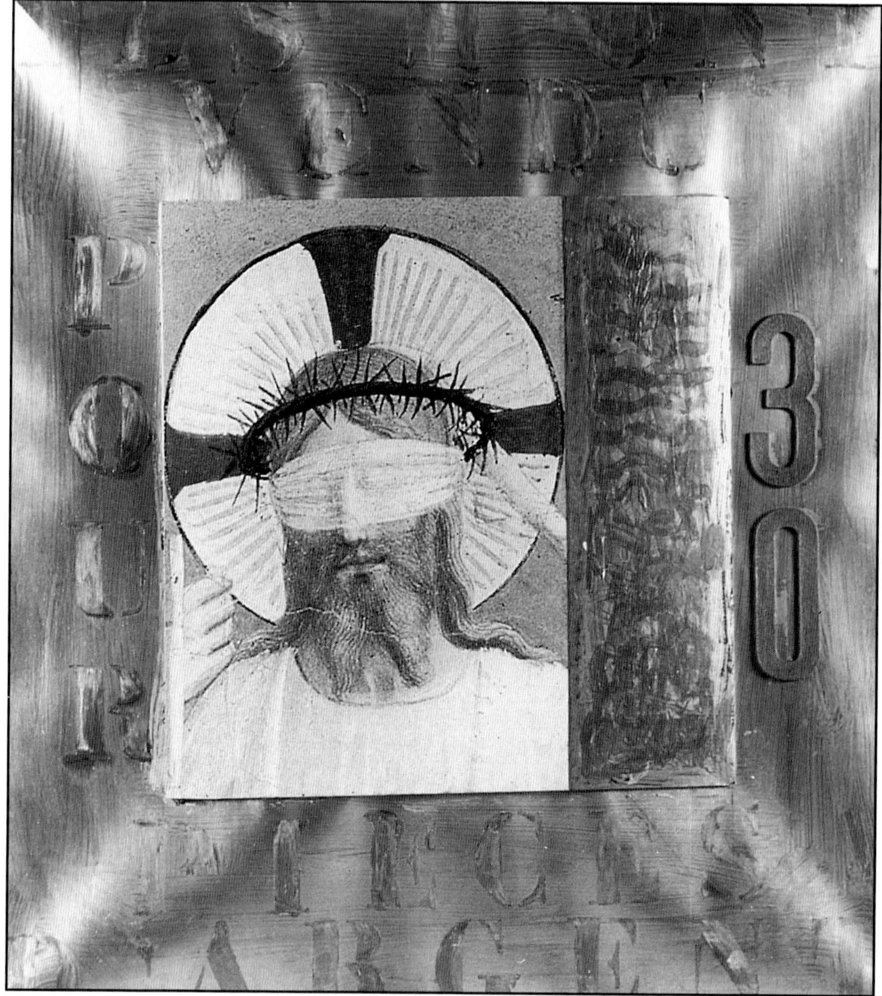

Annunciation, who, traditionally, is shown alighting to
Earth and bearing the Virgin's attribute of the lily. Rather,
she declares herself to be "an apocalyptical courier,"[32]
whose art forecasts her profoundly held belief in Christ's
imminent Second Coming. Her Archangel Gabriel is
resplendent in a painted halo of golden hair and an
applied robe of draped gold Mylar that reflects and
refracts the light and embodies the glory of God. The
actively gathered, three-dimensional material and the
sweep of the surrounding pink drapery suggest the
angel's flight through space as he prepares to deliver his
joyous news.

25. Ultra Violet
*They Sold Me for 30
Pieces of Silver* 1992
Mixed media
35 1/2 x 31 1/2

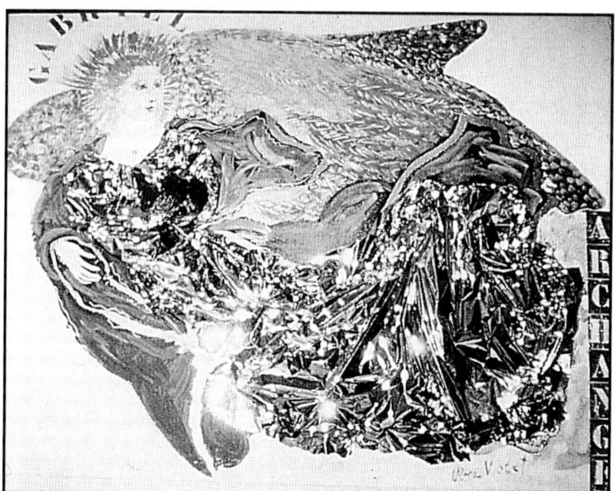

26. Ultra Violet
*The Archangel Gabriel*
1991
Mixed media on canvas
67 1/2 x 89 1/2

27. Ultra Violet
*Angel of Mercy*
*(AIDS Angel)* 1993
Color xerographic
collage on acetate
8 1/2 x 11

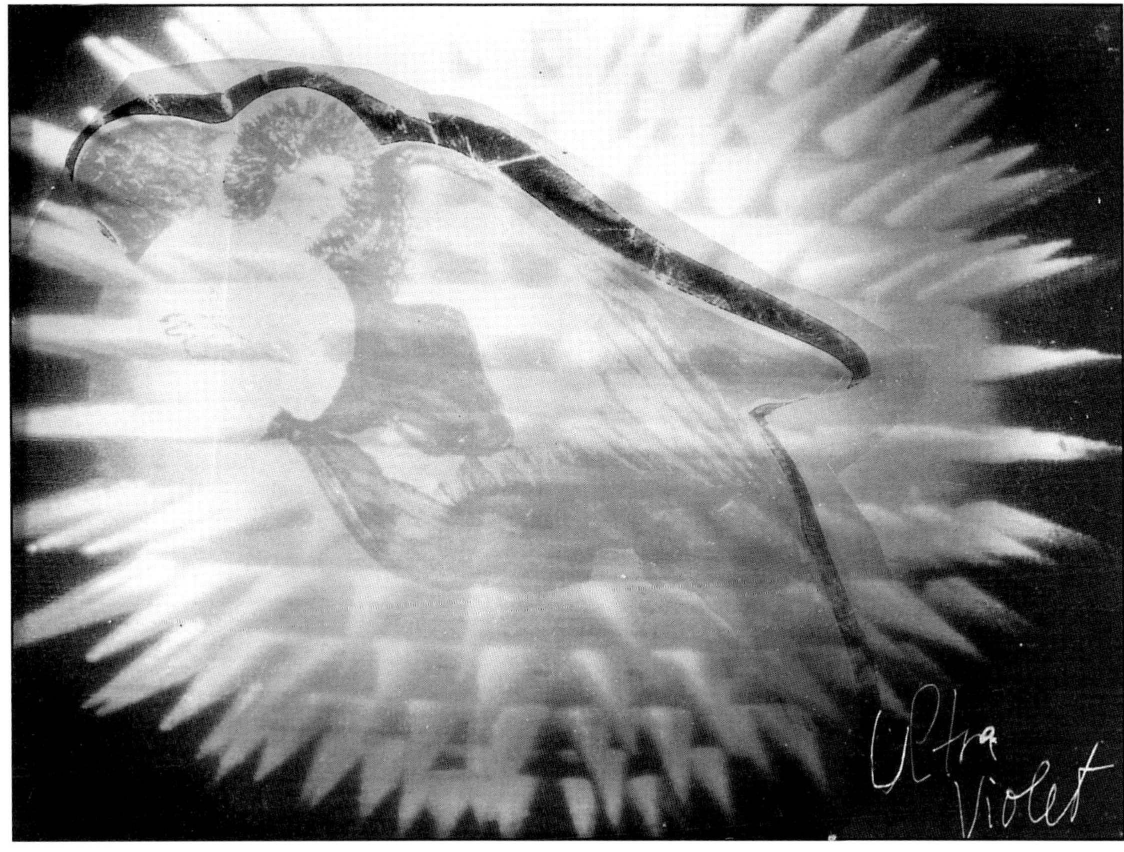


## 27. ANGEL OF MERCY (AIDS ANGEL)

In 1983, the human immunodeficiency virus (HIV) was first isolated from the blood of AIDS patients; in the following year it was identified as the causative organism of AIDS. Since this discovery, the scientific and medical communities have accumulated more knowledge about HIV than about any other virus that affects humankind.[33] But over a decade of intensive research has failed to produce a cure, or even a consistently effective treatment for AIDS. Following the same paradigm used for the control of infectious diseases since the days of Koch and Pasteur (i.e., to identify, then to inactivate, the causative organism) thus far has proven ineffectual.[34] In general, there are very few drugs that can stop a viral infection, and neutralization of HIV in particular has been complicated by its status as a retrovirus—that is, one that places a copy of its genetic material in the DNA of cells, where it can hide from pharmaceutical attack.

AIDS has reached epidemic proportions since the early 1980s; statistics are staggering. The World Health Organization has documented 1,025,073 cases of HIV infection worldwide and nearly six million attributable deaths. But estimates of unreported cases are much higher, with perhaps as many as 22.2 million people infected with HIV since the beginning of the pandemic. It is projected that by the year 2000, 30-40 million people will be HIV+ and ten million people will have died of AIDS-related illnesses.[35] Mario Amayo, Sam Wagstaff, Jon Gould, and Charles Ludlam (playwright of *Conquest of the Universe*; see cat. #21) number among the casualties of the Warhol circle.[36]

Although science has not yet triumphed in its fight against AIDS, Ultra Violet believes that we must not lose faith and cannot discount miracles. In *Angel of Mercy*, she has given visual form to her favorite credo: "By faith miracles are wrought, by faith angels appear."[37] An incandescent burst of color explodes out of a black background in a spikey geometric pattern. It is an enlargement of the human immunodeficiency virus. A beautiful angel (the same image used for *The Archangel Gabriel*; see cat. #26) hovers before it, gently looks back toward the looming virus, and raises a hand in a beneficent gesture of benediction. In Ultra's vision, the messenger of God brings mercy, comfort, and blessing to ward off the threat of HIV and to give hope to those afflicted.[38] The translucency of the acetate on which the image is printed enhances the angel's ethereality and the colors' luminosity, in keeping with the age-old tradition that God is light.

## 28. LET THERE BE LIGHT

The mystery of the origins of the universe has been a common focus of inquiry for the disciplines of science, philosophy, and theology. Just as each religion has its own creation myth based on tradition and faith, so have the scientific branches of astrophysics, cosmology, and cosmogony sought to explain our ultimate beginnings through observable and measurable phenomena. In Western civilization, the two most familiar explanations of how and when the universe began are the Biblical story of Genesis (1:1ff.) in the Old Testament and the Big Bang theory, independently developed by Russian meteorologist Alexander Friedmann (1922) and Belgian clergyman Georges Lemaître (1928).[39] Like the abbé

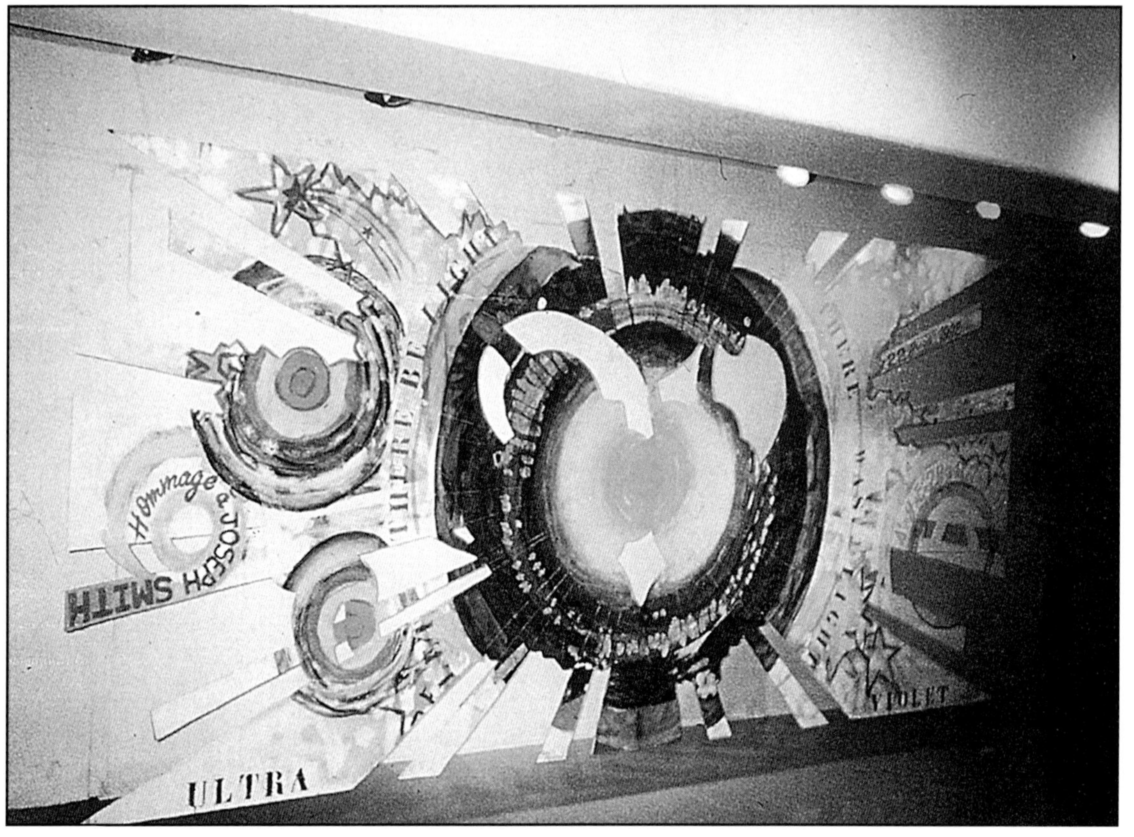


28. Ultra Violet
*Let There Be Light* 1992
Mixed media installation
(acrylic on cut plywood
and colored spotlights)
8 x 14'

Lemaître, who was able to reconcile his Christian beliefs with his scientific theories, Ultra Violet sees no conflict between the scientific and religious creation epics she synthesizes in *Let There Be Light*:

> As aesthetics and ethics coalesce in the
> noblest art form, so can technology and
> theology cooperate as a team.[40]

Ultra's installation consists of a large-scale, wooden panel (approximately 8 x 14 feet) that has been cut out and painted on both sides, resulting in a see-through painting. It is intended to be hung or stood in the middle of an open space, so that viewers can see each other through the cuts in the plywood as they walk around the work. In so doing, the dimensions of time and space are incorporated into the piece, which represents the moment of creation. It depicts swirling color prisms, luminous stars, a mathematical light formula, and the eponymous inscription from the Book of Genesis 1:3: "Let there be light: and there was light." The panel is augmented by spotlights of various colors that emerge through the cut-outs. These projected rays of light emphasize the burst of energy that, in scientific theory, characterizes the Big Bang. But, simultaneously, they represent the Judeo-Christian tradition that God is light, and by extension, all the colors of the spectrum as refracted in the prism. The scientific equation inscribed on the panel defines the relation between the speed of light and the space-time metric, which led to predictions of light ray desplacent (like a prism) near the sun.[41]

Ultra Violet explains her preoccupation with the theme and iconography of light:

> My name Ultra Violet fits me as a glove, for
> Ultra Violet is beyond the... visible light
> prism... I do not know of anything more
> beautiful than light. That's the reason I
> am working in that field. I want to bear
> testimony of the beauty of light and the light
> beyond color... the light that illuminates
> each man that comes to this world and the light
> that is necessary to create a universe....
> Christ said, "I am the way, the light, the
> truth"...I want to bear witness of that
> light of God's creation...[42]

The artist dedicated the installation in "hommage à Joseph Smith" (1805-44), founder of the Mormon religion.

## 29. WHO BUT AN ANGEL CAN STOP A MISSILE?

The late 1960s and early 1970s witnessed incredible strides in the development of new technologies and instruments, most of which were driven by the Cold War and the arms race.[43] The origins of guided-missile weapon systems can be traced back to the radio-controlled, unmanned aircraft in use before World War II, but by the mid-1960s, they had been developed to attain ranges of up to twelve miles and speeds of Mach 3. And while the first electronic computer, the Electrical Numerical Integrator and Computer (ENIAC), was developed at the University of Pennsylvania in 1946, it was not until the mid-1960s that engineers began to investigate the utilization of computers in the field of design. With the invention of the micro-processor in the early 1970s, which signaled an increase in accessibility to non-military and non-engineering users, the age of computer-aided design by visual artists had arrived.

In *Who but an Angel Can Stop a Missile?*, Ultra Violet explores both the creative and destructive results of these recent advances in military and informational technology. Her composition comprises a computer-generated collage of three appropriated elements:[44] a magazine photograph of a United States Marine Corps fighter jet outfitted with an air-to-air missile; an angel; and a color spectrum (cf. cat. #28 for Ultra Violet's abiding interest in the various manifestations of light). The prototypes, extracted from their original context, have been manipulated (realigned and "cleaned up") in the computer. The resulting laser print is an original composition of familiar elements seen in unexpected relationships, which impart a new meaning and message. Ultra's intent here is to depict:

> an aircraft's steel wing that coincides with a
> holy messenger… witnessing their parallel
> trajectories, wishing they had an analogous
> mutual purpose: the *messagerie* of good news,
> alleviating suffering… shifting away
> from military hardware to the usage of life-
> supporting technologies.[45]

And so Ultra's angel guides the jet with a gentle but firm hand, through a sky that is not just blue, but all the colors of the rainbow. Stylistically, her use of a full spectrum of hues ties her to the artistic tradition of the Côte d'Azur, of which Nice (where Ultra's studio is located) is the capital. For example, the Impressionist master Renoir, noted for his colorful "rainbow palette," spent the last years of his life (1903-19) in Cagnes-sur-Mer, west of Nice.[46] Iconographically, in the Judeo-Christian tradition, the rainbow has been a sign of God's covenant with humankind, as it appeared at the end of the Biblical deluge (Genesis 9:13-17). In the New Testament, a rainbow surrounding the throne of God is one of the visions of the apocalypse—itself a dominant concern in Ultra Violet's art and writing. She believes that the "nuclear age is the apocalyptic age" and asks us to ponder the question, "Who can stop a nuclear weapon, but an angel?"[47]

## 30. POLITICALLY INCORRECT

When the Swiss Institute in New York contacted Ultra Violet in February 1995, it was to borrow a painting from her private collection for its forthcoming exhibition on the art of chocolate.[48] She agreed to lend Edward Ruscha's *Well Roughly* to the show,[49] but suggested that she be invited to submit a work of her own, as well. The surprised curator asked Ultra if she, too, worked in chocolate; the artist emphatically reassured her, "Yes, of course!"[50] Ultra then began work on her very first chocolate piece, completed in time for the opening on 6 April.

In keeping with the gastronomic theme implicit in chocolate, the artist created a formal table setting composed of found objects, family heirlooms, personal effects, and noteworthy memorabilia. Among the "recycled" items are a broken ceramic candlestick that has been glued together, a French *chocolatier* (a serving vessel for hot cocoa), pieces of Limoges china, silver flatware, a crystal vase, and a champagne bottle, all of which have been dipped in melted chocolate, sent to Ultra by the Swiss Institute. These pieces are augmented by a candy cigar and chocolate roses, and placed on a tablecloth of rich brown velvet; two chocolate angels hover above the table and its bounty. To break up the solid chocolate tonalilty, Ultra added some lighter elements, which she did not candy-coat: an assortment of sparkling, dangling earrings appended to the dipped silverware; gold foil doilies; and a piece of antique lace passed down through her family over the centuries. The overall effect is one of the elegant good taste for which Ultra Violet and the Dufresne family are known.

The title, *Politically Incorrect*, has several possible interpretations. The cigar and ashtray suggest the dangerous and addictive habit of smoking, which, in the past few years, has been legislated out of such public spaces as domestic airline flights, sports stadiums, buildings on university campuses, and restaurants. Nearby, matches from the Watergate Hotel recall the political scandal that precipitated Richard Nixon's resignation from the presidency of the United States on 9 August 1974. But Ultra Violet explains that her true intent was to focus our attention on the ostentatious waste of food displayed in the exhibition. She considers it a "politically incorrect" affront to stage a show on chocolate in view of world hunger.[51]

29. Ultra Violet
*Who but an Angel Can Stop a Missile?* 1993
Computer-generated print on paper
36 x 24

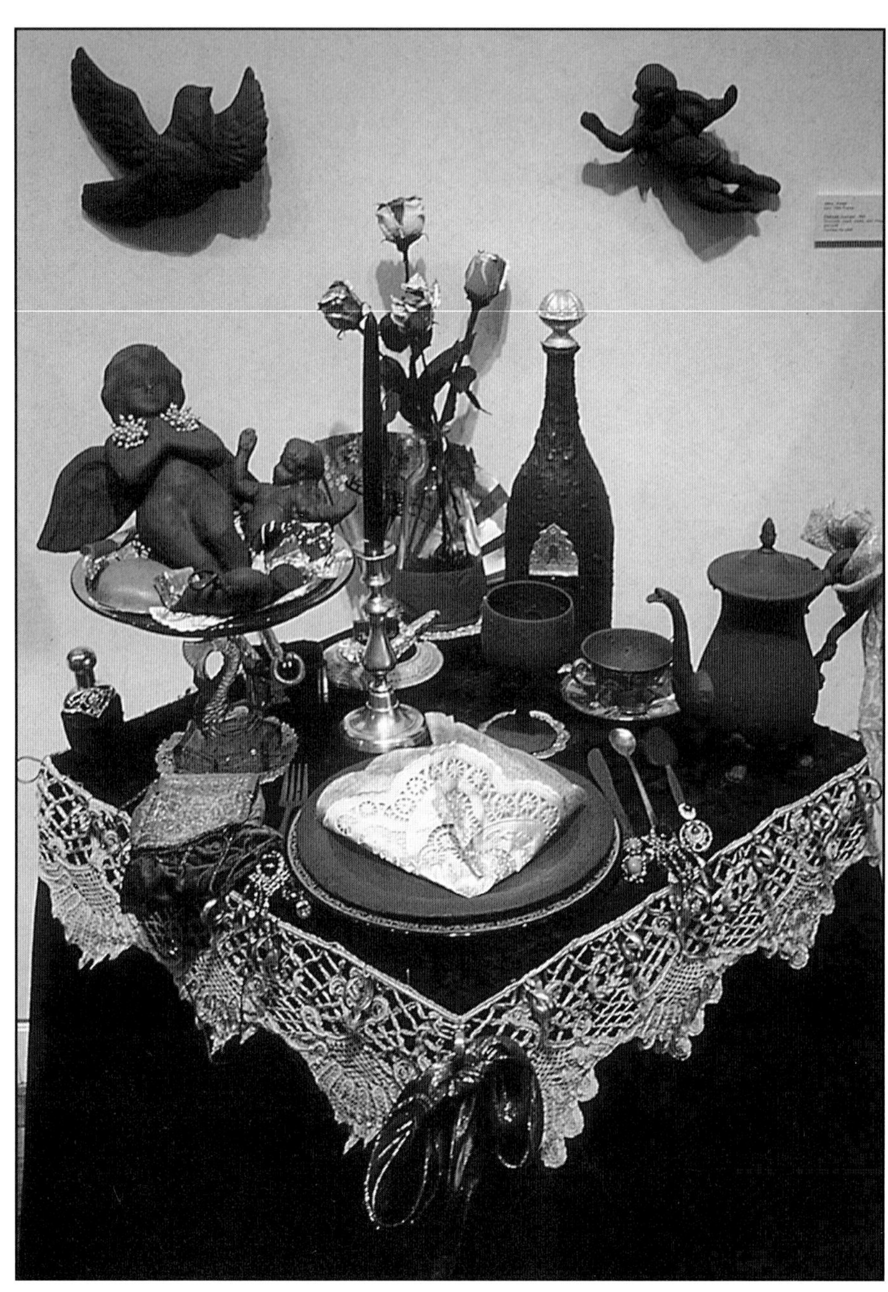

30. Ultra Violet
*Politically Incorrect*
1995
Mixed media installation
(found objects and
chocolate)
6 x 3 x 3'

# ALLEN MIDGETTE (b. 1939)

Before his introduction into Andy Warhol's Factory, Allen Midgette, a native of Brooklawn, New Jersey, had established himself in Italy. He appeared in films by the noted European directors Pier Paolo Pasolini and Bernardo Bertolucci (among them, Bertolucci's *The Grim Reaper* and *Before the Revolution*) and attended the Spoleto Festival of Two Worlds. Through Warhol Superstar International Velvet (the model Susan Bottomly), the actor met the Pop artist and became a featured player in some of his movies of 1967-68 (******, *The Nude Restaurant*, and *Lonesome Cowboys*). Midgette's most famous performance was his impersonation of Andy Warhol on the college lecture circuit—a prank instigated by Warhol and his assistant Paul Morrissey, which remained undiscovered by his audiences for nearly six months. Since Andy's death in 1987, Midgette has revived his impersonation *cum* performance art, and appears unexpectedly at various events as Warhol. He has continued his acting career in off-Broadway productions and films (e.g., *1900*, *Cat People*, and *Heat Suffocates*), and in recent years, has begun to produce wearable art, paintings, prints, and mixed-media assemblages based on natural forms related to his Cherokee heritage.

## 31. BEFORE THE REVOLUTION

Since childhood, Allen Midgette has been involved in performing. He first appeared in school plays in his hometown of Brooklawn, New Jersey, and wryly notes that "the other boys didn't want to try out, so I always got the parts!"[1] He pursued his interest in acting at the University of Miami, where he studied theater, and then at a memorable summer workshop in North Carolina, sponsored by Rutgers University. Midgette soon moved to New York; he continued to study acting with Frank Corsaro of the Actors' Studio. His first professional break came when he appeared in the opening scene of Robert Wise and Jerome Robbins' *West Side Story* (1961). At subsequent casting calls and auditions in the United States, the handsome young actor, with his finely chiseled bone structure, haunting brown eyes, and perfect diction, was frequently faced with the comment that, "You have a really interesting face, but you don't look American and you don't sound American."[2] Consequently, Allen decided to go to Italy, where he had no trouble being cast as an Italian in Italian-made films!

Midgette's circle of friends in Rome included people who knew the radical young Communist filmmaker Bernardo Bertolucci.[3] Upon being shown the American actor's photograph, Bertolucci arranged for a meeting. He told Allen that he would like to use him in his movies, but, unfortunately, Midgette had studied acting and Bertolucci preferred not to use actors—a sentiment that would be echoed in the following years by Andy Warhol. Allen quickly replied, "To tell you the truth, I never learned anything in acting class."[4] So, when a friend of Bertolucci's from Calabria asserted that Midgette looked Calabrian, he was given the key role of Teodoro, a soldier, in *The Grim Reaper* (1962). The same year, Bertolucci's mentor, Pier Paolo Pasolini, cast him in *La Ricotta*. This was followed by a leading role in Bertolucci's *Before the Revolution* (1964).

Bertolucci was just twenty-two years old when he made the movie, which has been described as "an absorbing polemic about European politics and Marxism… youthful idealism and unbridled desire."[5] The title is based upon Talleyrand's famous remark: "Only those who lived before the Revolution knew how sweet life could be." Although the low-budget, slow-moving, New Wave film was scripted and directed, it contained little dialogue, allowed for some physical improvisation on the part of the actors, and was largely shot in single takes—a method Allen Midgette would encounter again with Andy Warhol. With his hair dyed blond, Midgette gave "able support"[6] as the main protagonist's anguished, suicidal friend, Agostino. As was often the case in European films with a multilingual cast, the American delivered his lines in English and was later dubbed in with a voice-over in Italian. In one of the most noteworthy scenes in *Before the Revolution*, Agostino is seen doing tricks on a bicycle. Allen recalls that his performance was largely unrehearsed; he had only been given the bicycle the day before filming. Nevertheless, the entertaining scene, to a great extent extemporaneously choreographed by Midgette, would be cinematically quoted in 1969 in George Roy Hill's classic western, *Butch Cassidy and the Sundance Kid*, starring Paul Newman and Robert Redford.

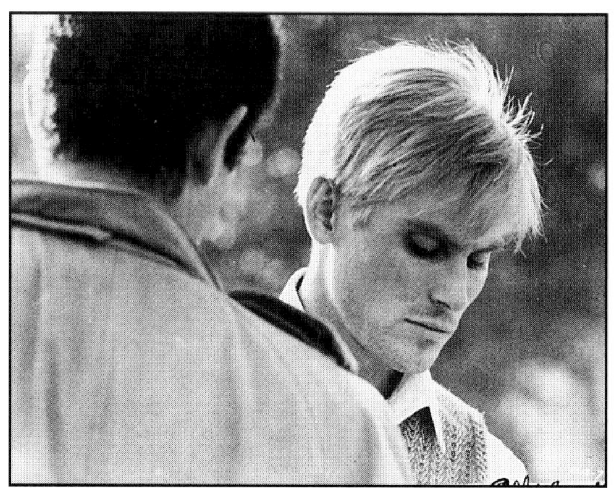

31. Allen Midgette as Agostino in Bernardo Bertolucci's *Before the Revolution* 1964
7 1/8 x 9 3/8
Courtesy of New Yorker Films. Used with permission.

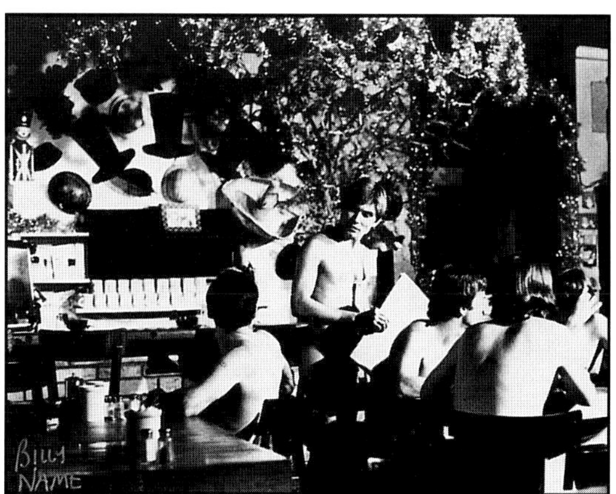

32. Allen Midgette in Warhol's *The Nude Restaurant* 1967
6 5/8 x 9 5/8
Photograph by Billy Name

33. Allen Midgette as Andy
    Warhol  1996
13 7/8 x 9 1/2
Photograph by Gerald
Lyons

## 32. THE NUDE RESTAURANT

In the spring of 1965, producer Lester Persky threw a spectacular party at the Factory for "The Fifty Most Beautiful People."[7] Judy Garland, Rudolf Nureyev, and Montgomery Clift numbered among the guests. Allen Midgette was there, too; it was the first time he met Andy Warhol. Midgette did not return to the Factory until 1967. At that time he was working at a discotheque in New York and his friend, David Croland, was dating the model Susan Bottomly (i.e., Warhol Superstar International Velvet). Bottomly arranged for a meeting between Andy and Allen at the disco. As she had anticipated, Warhol found Midgette appealing and invited him to be in his movies. The actor got a call from Andy a short time later; he and his company of Superstars were going to Philadelphia the next day to shoot a film, in which he wanted Allen to appear. Midgette recalled, "Well, I wasn't doing anything that day, so I said, 'Yeah.'"[8] The cinematic results of the trip were several reels of Warhol's 25-hour movie, ****. Upon their return to New York, Midgette was filmed in additional reels that would be incorporated into Warhol's day-long epic.

One of the episodes filmed in New York in October 1967, at the Mad Hatter Restaurant, featured Allen Midgette as a waiter in an all-nude, all-male cast. That film was the first version of *The Nude Restaurant*, which was to be inter-edited with identical scenes showing the actors fully clothed.[9] A second version, starring Viva and Taylor Mead, had a male and female cast, including Midgette, clothed in G-strings. The latter film was released as a feature-length movie for New York's Hudson Theater; the former, also known as "Restaurant," was subsumed into ****.[10] Typically, the unscripted, unrehearsed movie was largely improvised by its cast. Midgette, who had worked with the young Bertolucci and, thus, had some previous experience with avant-garde filmic techniques (see cat. #31), found this method to be somewhat less than satisfying for a trained actor. He revealed:

> To be honest with you, I did get to the point
> where… I really wanted a part…
> something with lines… some kind of a
> real challenge… I wanted something that
> I could succeed or fail at… It wasn't
> enough to just have people like you and just
> kind of drift along…[11]

Midgette would go on to appear in one more movie by Warhol: *Lonesome Cowboys*, shot in Arizona in January 1968. He was living in New Mexico then, and working with the sculptor John Chamberlain, who accompanied him to Arizona for filming.

## 33. ALLEN MIDGETTE AS ANDY WARHOL

One night in the fall of 1967, Andy Warhol's assistant Paul Morrissey asked Allen Midgette to join him for a drink at Max's Kansas City. Morrissey then asked Allen if he would like to go to Rochester the following day to impersonate Warhol at a lecture he had scheduled for the university there. Midgette at first declined, but was persuaded to go when he was offered $600 for the job.

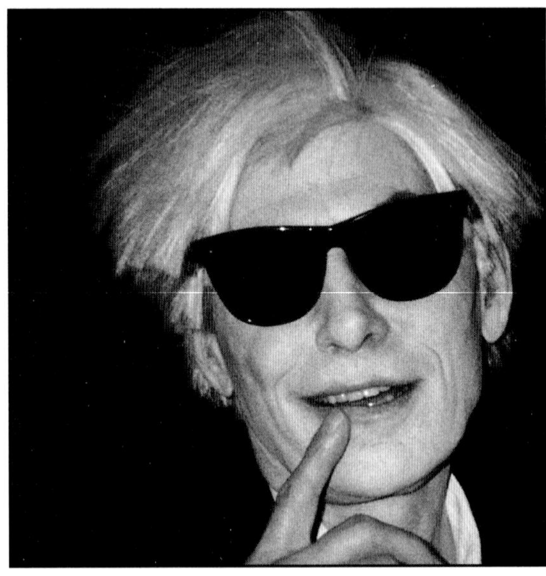

33. Allen Midgette as Andy
    Warhol  1996
13 7/8 x 9 1/2
Photograph by Gerald
Lyons

He spent the night at Morrissey's apartment, so that the men could catch their morning flight to Upstate New York. In preparation for his role, the actor sprayed his short hair silver and heavily dusted it with talcum powder. He applied Max Factor's Erase—the lightest shade of cover-up he could find—to his face and hands, lightly dotted his nose with lipstick, and donned Andy's black leather jacket and dark sunglasses, provided to him by Morrissey. The ersatz Warhol's appearance at the campus gymnasium was followed by an interview with the local television station and a cocktail party. Between questions, a nervous Midgette, who knew little about Andy's personal life or career, repeatedly implored Morrissey to "get me out of here."[12]

Midgette decided to leave New York for San Francisco, attracted by reports of the scene in Haight-Ashbury; Warhol and his current Superstar, Nico, visited him there. A few months later, when Allen called the Factory, Paul Morrissey answered the phone and asked him to return to New York to resume his successful impersonation on the college lecture circuit with appearances in Salt Lake City, Utah, and Eugene, Oregon. It was a windy day in Salt Lake City. When "Andy" stepped off the airplane he was greeted by a gust of wind that blew a white cloud of talcum powder from his hair. Also on the lecture tour, Allen was videotaped as Andy; he did his best to hide his face from the camera, obscuring it with his hands and posture. Finally, at Eugene, Allen's audience included a student who had known Andy and who seemed a bit suspicious of his guest lecturer. Nevertheless, Midgette made it through the day. The deception was not uncovered until about four months later. According to Warhol:

> …somebody at one of the colleges
> happened to see a picture of me in the
> *Voice* and compared it to the one he'd
> taken of Allen on the podium and we had
> to give them their money back. When the
> local newspaper out west called me for a
> statement, what could I say except, "It
> seemed like a good idea at the time."[13]

Meanwhile, Midgette, who had earned a total of $2600 for the masquerade, had already gone off for an extended stay in Mexico.

After Warhol's death in 1987, impresario Baird Jones approached Allen to revive his impersonation after a 20-year lay-off. Midgette began to show up at events in New York City as Andy, frequently eliciting reactions of outrage and consternation. During an exhibition of "Pop Art: Yesterday, Today and Tomorrow" at the club Alibi, a gallery-goer began screaming and hitting him. Jones, the show's curator, insightfully called the altercation "performance art history in the making."[14] At a party for Warhol's *Interview* magazine, incensed advertising director Paige Powell tried to have Allen thrown out; long-time Warhol friend and collector Stuart Pivar was moved to tears. Midgette caused a stir at the Whitney Museum of American Art's press screening of Warhol films and at Sotheby's auction of The Andy Warhol Collection,[15] and was ejected from both. But many of Andy's friends, fans, and family members (including Billy Name and Jamie Warhola) take delight in seeing the beloved Pop artist again, in the man Warhol himself chose to imitate him in the 1960s. Midgette's uncanny performance art, indeed, captures not only the look and mannerisms, but also the attitude and demeanor of Andy Warhol.[16] It is a great tribute to someone who is dearly missed.

## 34. DOUBLE SELF-PORTRAIT

With his move from Manhattan to Woodstock circa 1991, Allen Midgette began to focus his creative energies on painting and wearable art. The small town in Upstate New York had gained prominence in the summer of 1969, when the Woodstock Music and Art Fair, held on 15-17 August, attracted nearly a half-million concert-goers for an advertised "three days of peace and music." The rock festival was quickly immortalized in Michael Wadleigh's three-hour movie (*Woodstock*, 1969), in Joni Mitchell's song ("Woodstock," Siquomb Publishing Co., 1969),[17] and in Abbie Hoffman's manifesto (*Woodstock Nation: A Talk-Rock Album*, New York, Vintage Books, 1969). Woodstock became synonymous with the counter-culture of the Sixties, and a vital arts and crafts community grew up there.

Prior to his relocation, Allen was living at the historic Chelsea Hotel—legendary site of Andy Warhol's epic film *The Chelsea Girls* (1966)—on West 23rd Street in New York. He had some friends in Woodstock, and decided to make the move primarily "for the country, to get away from the dirt and crowds of the city."[18] While much of the art he produced there reflects his love of nature and his respect for the Native American population (cf. cats. #36-39), works like the *Double Self-Portrait* and the *Warhol Vest* (cat. #35) draw upon his association with Warhol's Factory in the 1960s.

Midgette's *Double Self-Portrait* is based on a Factory Foto of 1967 by Billy Name. The close-up head shot of Allen was used as the back cover for *Andy Warhol's Index (Book)*.[19] Its format is appropriate for transformation from portrait to self-portrait, in that the sitter makes direct eye contact with the viewer, as if the artist were looking at himself in a mirror. The theme of the self-portrait, too, is indicative of Midgette's relationship with Warhol; with

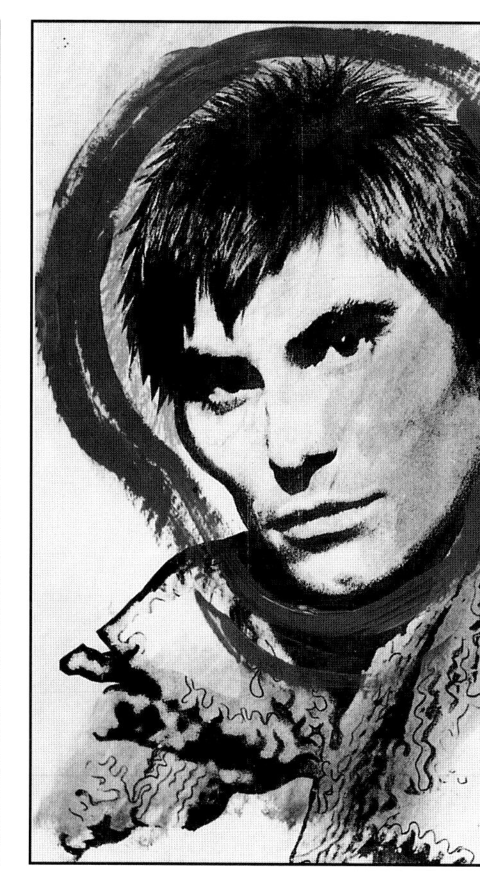

34. Allen Midgette
*Double Self-Portrait*
c. 1992
Acrylic on paper
17 x 11 each

the exception of Rembrandt,[20] few painters in history have been as fascinated with their own visage as Andy was with his.[21] Warhol attributed this to an idea he elicited from the art dealer Ivan Karp:

> You know, people want to see you. Your looks are responsible for a certain part of your fame—they feed the imagination.[22]

Surely this observation may be applied to Allen Midgette's strikingly handsome face, as well.

The technique of replication also ties Midgette to the Warhol circle. His composition employs the mechanical reproduction of Billy Name's photograph through xerography, in two-fold multiplication. The identical pendants are then painted by hand (not silkscreened), resulting in two uniquely colored images. Allen's self-identification with Andy, whom he was chosen to impersonate in 1967 (see cat. #33), is implicit in the diagonal color division of his face in the likeness on the left—a design derived from Warhol's *Self-Portrait,* in three-quarter view, of 1967 (Collection James Warhola). But Midgette's manual execution is more painterly in style and his brushwork much looser and more spontaneous than Andy's photo-silkscreening process.

## 35. WARHOL VEST

The *Warhol Vest* is a visual artist's biography. It documents how Allen Midgette perceived Andy Warhol and the contributions he made throughout his career. On the back, Midgette painted a larger-than-life-size likeness of the renowned Pop artist. The bust-length image of Warhol in a tuxedo, with a real black bow tie attached at the waistband, is based on a photograph by Christopher Makos. It is executed in thick impasto against a vibrant orchid background that continues onto the left front side of the vest [the viewer's right]. The right side has a contrasting white background.

On the vest's front, Midgette has catalogued some of Warhol's most famous images in miniature. The composition, he asserts, was largely intuitive:

> I didn't intentionally pick the images that Andy created—Marilyn Monroe, Campbell's Tomato Soup, Life Savers, banana, and flowers. They just came to me. Like when I think of Andy, I think of the lasting images he gave to the art world, really, to our world.[23]

The pockets display Allen's recreations of two of Andy's most beloved works: *Marilyn* on the left;[24] and *Flowers* on the right.[25] Directly above the flowers is a banana, derived from Warhol's peelable print of 1966, but turned upside-down by Midgette.[26] A can of Campbell's tomato soup, a roll of Life Savers that spills out around the vest, and an advertisement for Van Heusen shirts, featuring Ronald Reagan and promising "won't wrinkle… ever," recall Warhol's beginnings in commercial art and his lifelong *leitmotif* of consumer products.[27] Finally, a dollar sign—which appears on the left side of the vest and

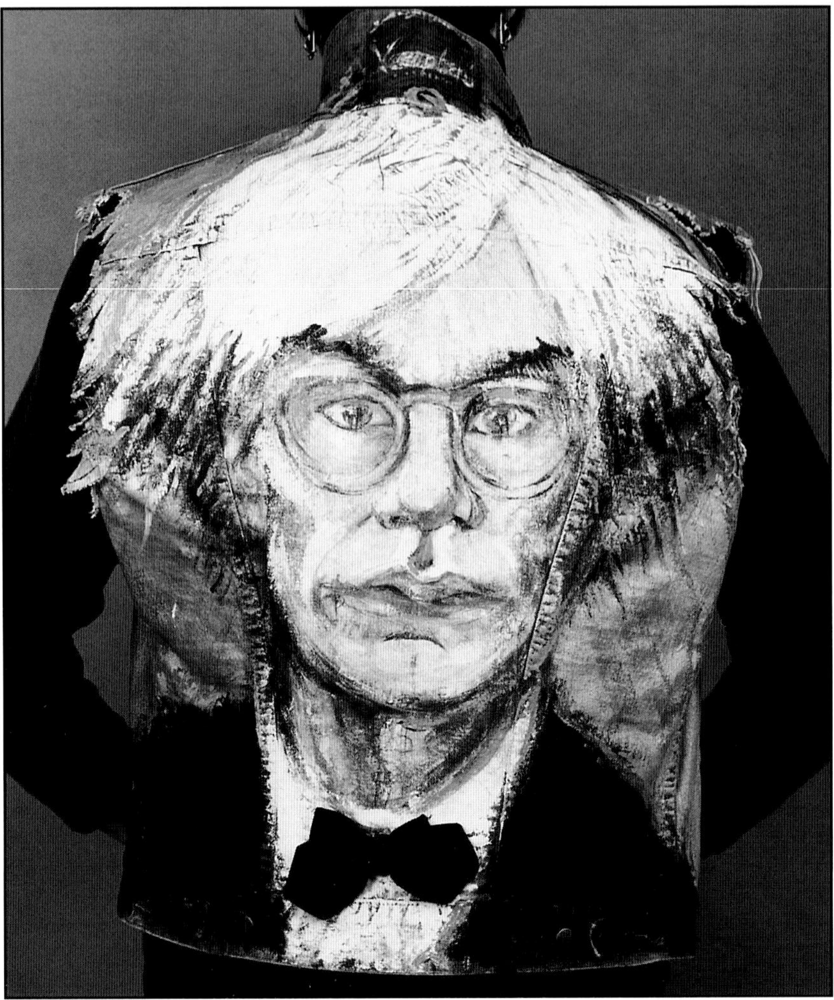

replaces the Campbell's seal on the soup can label—expresses Warhol's well-known penchant for making money.[28]

Unlike Andy Warhol, Allen Midgette was never motivated by commercialism. He recalled:

> I always was interested in art, even as a young boy. I just like to paint, create, let something that is a part of me become an art object that can be appreciated by others.[29]

When asked if he would prefer to see his wearable art displayed rather than worn, Midgette responded:

> Hey, whatever the person wants to do with it is just fine with me. Even if they want to burn it, well, I just created it, they bought it, its theirs. I create art because I just have to; it is within me. I just let the art speak for itself, whether it should be worn or displayed.[30]

## 36. RUSSELL MEANS

In 1976-77, Andy Warhol issued a series of silkscreened portraits entitled *The American Indian;* his model was Russell Means, the Oglala Sioux leader of the militant

35. Allen Midgette
*Warhol Vest* c. 1992
Acrylic paint and fabric
on denim
25 1/2 x 20 1/2 x 2

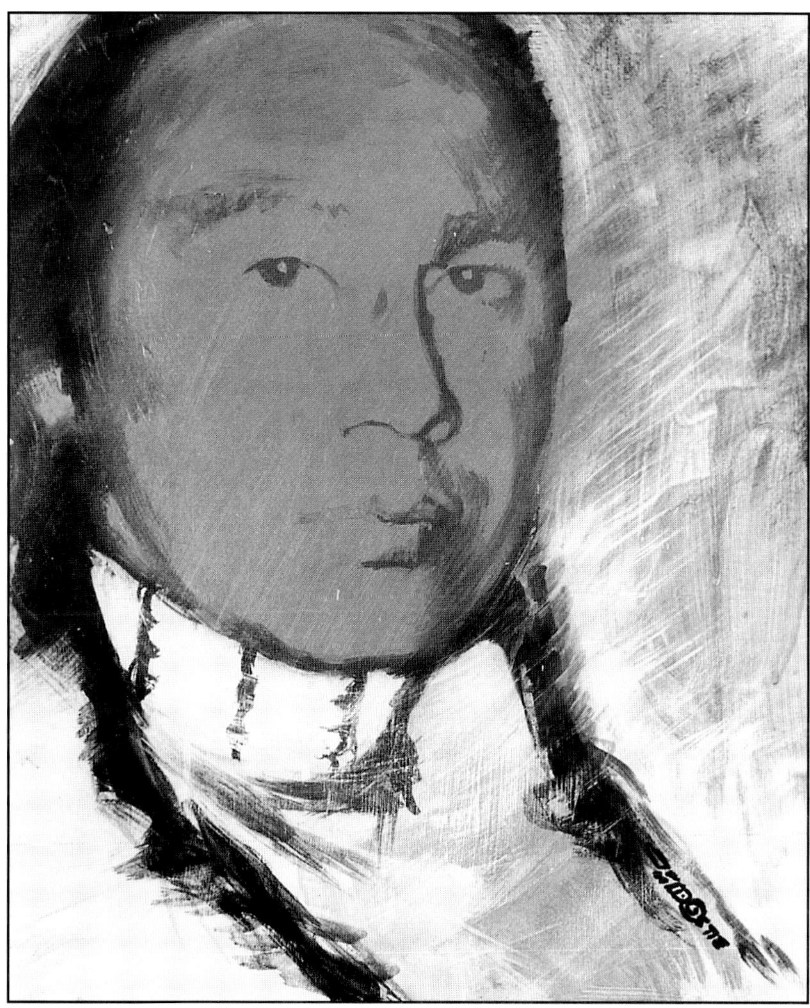

36. Allen Midgette
*Russell Means* c. 1993
Acrylic on canvas
24 x 20

Custer Battlefield, Montana (25 June 1976). In his quest for justice, honor, and equality for his people, Means had received gunshot wounds in three separate incidents,[32] was arrested on several occasions, and was charged with aiding and abetting the murder of Martin Montileaux in the restroom of a bar in Pennington County, South Dakota, on 3 March 1975.[33] On 7 August 1976—the year in which Warhol painted him—a jury acquitted Means of the murder charges, for which Richard Marshall was earlier convicted and sentenced to life imprisonment.

Warhol's portrait of Means depicts the modern Sioux warrior in traditional costume, with a dignified demeanor and a commanding presence; he represents all American Indians, who have suffered, and struggled, and triumphed. Both the sitter, and Warhol's obvious respect for him,[34] led Allen Midgette to create his own series of paintings of Russell Means. Midgette's likenesses of the Plains Indian leader are based on Warhol's three-quarter view, bust-length image of 1976; but unlike Andy's photo-silkscreens, Allen's versions of the subject are painted by hand. His style is simplified, strong, and direct; his emphatic lines, monumental forms, and bold colors convey the power and conviction of the man that he, and Warhol, chose to immortalize in art.

## 37. INDIAN PORTRAIT FEATHER TREE

Hand-made feathers of varying sizes and shapes hang from the branches of a dry, cut tree. Each feather bears the likeness of a Native American male—a powerful chief or tribal elder, a discerning shaman or medicine man— that keeps Allen Midgette in touch with his ancestral past. Midgette feels a special affinity for those magical men of the spirit-faith; his Uncle Gus Burrus (the husband of a great aunt), was a shaman at Cape Hatteras, North Carolina. "I remember as a kid, people were always going to him for cures."[35]

Living in New Jersey as a child,[36] Allen became somewhat disconnected from his genealogical roots:

> When I grew up, we never talked about our Cherokee heritage. It was something to hide. But when I was in the Marines [for an eight-year reserve program, beginning in the 1950s], and afterwards with Warhol, I realized that it was that heritage that made a big part of me—Allen Midgette.[37]

Consequently, the artist was moved by his new sense of pride and awareness to honor his forebears. He recalls:

> The photos and images of the Native Americans came to me through friends from pictures or postcards. I do not even know who most of the Natives are; it doesn't matter. It doesn't matter to me what tribe they are from, what their name is— they are all of my spirit and they influence my art. And it is the spirit of something that I symbolize in the feathers. Actually, the feathers symbolize the religion and creativity of the Indians.[38]

American Indian Movement (AIM). Means had been involved in numerous conflicts in the 1970s, including the occupation of the auditorium of the Bureau of Indian Affairs in Washington, DC (2-7 November 1972), the burning of the Chamber of Commerce Building and Courthouse in Custer, South Dakota (7 February 1973), the 71-day armed siege of Wounded Knee,[31] (28 February -9 May 1973), and the disruption of the bicentennial commemoration of the Battle of Little Bighorn (1876) at

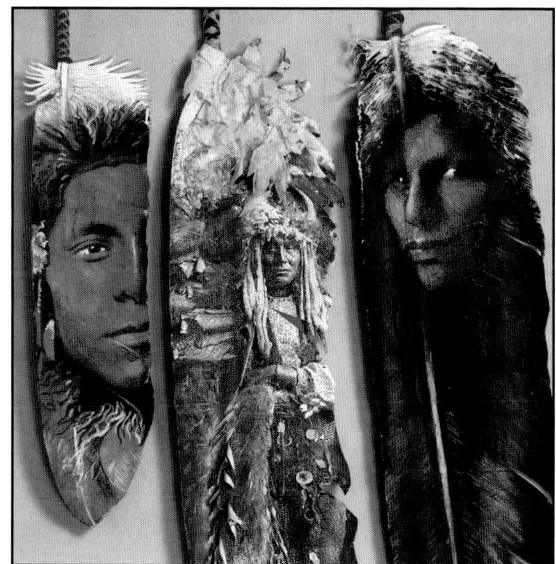

37. Allen Midgette
*Indian Portrait Feather Tree* c. 1993-96 (detail)
Mixed-media assemblage
(detail)

Since 1962, the United States Government established federal laws to protect eagles. Eagle feathers became rare, and Native Americans began to recreate them in their arts and crafts. "That is essentially what I have done, because the feathers are considered holy to the Indian," explains Allen. "I am recreating something holy, of spirit."[39]

Midgette's technique begins with the selection of a portrait for xerography. He then laminates the photocopy with layers of various types of paper, cut into the shape of a feather. Next, the cut and laminated paper is glued to a gently curved and hand-whittled branch of a tree, which serves as the feather's spine. Allen chooses the branch with care: "I want even the spine of the feather to be just right. It must have the right aura to fit the image."[40] After the feather is dry, Midgette painstakingly paints the composition in acrylic. Some of the portraits are executed in full, impressionistic, broken color; others are austerely strengthened with black and white. The obverse side of each piece is rendered naturalistically, in imitation of an actual bird's feather. Finally, Allen wraps yarn and twine around the feather's stem, and hangs it from a stripped and dried tree, which he collected from the former lands of the once mighty Indian nations.

The monumental figures depicted on the small surface areas of the feathers stand alone, as lasting portraits of the indigenous people who were forced to take wing in the last century and to face confinement on bounded reservations. They represent singular men in full dress, or haunting visages that remind us of the on-going struggles and injustices faced by Native Americans, past and present.

## 38. INDIAN SHIELD

The American counter-culture, rebelling against the war in Vietnam, the pollution of our planet, and the inequality of ethnic and sexual minorities, reached new heights of public awareness in the late Sixties, following the phenomenon of the "Summer of Love" in 1967,[41] the televised fiasco outside the Democratic Convention in Chicago in 1968, and the Woodstock Festival in 1969 (see cat. #34). That year, Allen Midgette joined with several like-minded friends to form a commune. The alternative lifestyle of communal living had become extremely popular at the time, as groups of harmonious youths in search of peace, love, and a return to nature pooled their limited resources. During his years in the commune—first at the Delaware Water Gap and later in Santa Fe, New Mexico—Allen trained himself in the art of leatherwork:

> I have been working in leather for about 30 years… Even when I was doing *1900* [Bernardo Bertolucci's four-hour epic of 1977, filmed in Italy], I was working in leather. I really love doing it. It just seems so natural to me.[42]

He began to produce usable objects and clothes, which he gave as gifts, used as barter, and sold for subsistence. Consequently, the present whereabouts of Midgette's early leather designs are unknown.

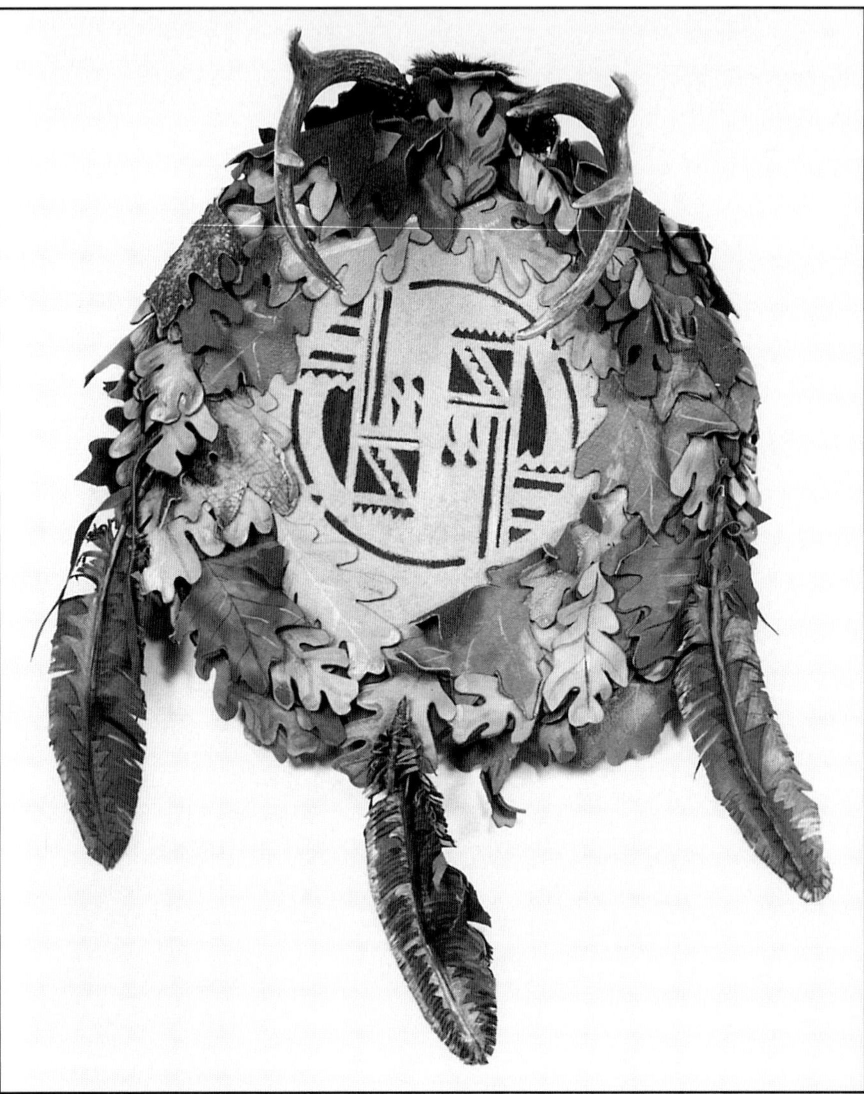

With his move to Woodstock in the early 1990s, Allen not only accelerated his production of leather goods, but also introduced an important new theme into his self-taught craft. According to the artist:

> There is something about being at Woodstock that has made me contemplate my Cherokee roots. I guess that is why I have created a lot of Indian art since I have been here.[43]

Among those many objects inspired by Native American art is the *Indian Shield*. Traditionally, shields were used by the indigenous nations in warfare and hunting, and their designs typically depicted visions of battle, capture, or protection.[44] The set of real antlers that Allen attached to the top of his shield thus recalls one of its original purposes. The symmetrical designs on the shield's body allude to tribal pictographic arts; the dark brown lines against the beige background of leather may be visually associated with Indian sand painting, as well.

Like his Native American ancestors, the artist generally uses materials that are the most easily obtained:

> I use whatever I have available to me. If I find something, I always think… how can I use that? That is just like the Indians. They

38. Allen Midgette
*Indian Shield* c. 1992
Mixed media (leather, antlers, metal, acrylic paint)
25 1/4 x 18 x 11

always used whatever they found in nature. They were very thrifty. Me? I try to buy the best leather, but also, if something just falls into my lap, as with the case of the horns, I use it. In the past, the Indians gathered only what they could use, killed only what they needed. Of course, I don't kill anything, but use it if it happens to come across my path.[45]

Indians frequently used feathers as ornaments and symbols, and Midgette includes this recurrent motif in his assemblage.[46] He also recreates, in soft leather and in a full range of fall colors—orange, yellow, tan, and brown—leaves from the white oak. The spreading hardwood tree thrives from Texas to Canada and is considered the noblest of all American oaks. It is interesting to note here that Native Americans chiefly used the white oak acorn for ground meal for cakes, but leached out the bitter tannin to cure leather.[47] Its leaves have a rounded tip, which conforms well to the circular shape of the shield. Both leaves and feathers cascade down the contours of the Indian Shield, reminding us that all is of the earth, and to the earth all will return.

## 39. LEAF COLLAR

The central motif of Allen Midgette's *Leaf Collar* is the distinctive foliage of the pin oak—one of several hardwood trees growing in the forests of the Catskill Mountains near Woodstock, New York, where he lived from 1991 to 1995. The artist made the most recent of his homes and studios there in adjacent Bearsville, in a converted barn bordered by a creek and surrounded by woodlands. In an interview conducted in that sylvan setting in 1995, he revealed his profound sensitivity to the earth and its cycles:

> I like to be in nature, that is one reason why I live here. I can just go out and understand and appreciate what nature has to offer. When I picked up the leaves to use as models for the collar, I did not just pick any leaf. It had to have the right size, shape, life. I guess that sounds funny, that a leaf, which has fallen from the tree, has a life. But it does, and did, and will…. The leaf at one time offered us shade, oxygen, beauty, food. After it fell, it offered me a sense of appreciation for its beauty and its past…. So I captured it for someone to wear in the leather collar. Then, I returned it to the outside, so that its future could be played out the rest of the way… imminent decay, to be used for hiding places for insects, and, ultimately, it becomes new dirt.[48]

Strata of hand-cut leather leaves are clustered on a flat, V-shaped base that ties at the back of the neck and is tooled with a variety of delicate designs—flowers, lines, waves, circles. Each leaf, though identifiable as a pin oak, is given its own unique morphology and hue. Some are fairly smooth, others have a rough and variegated surface texture; their range in color suggests the varied shades of autumnal brown. The artist is very particular about the type of leather he selects for his fashion designs:

> It has to be the right quality, size, and color. It also must have the right kind of 'soul,' because it did come from an animal. I think that the right kind of leather makes the garment, bag, vest, collar, cape, or whatever I create possess the kind of strong spirit which makes it a dramatic piece of wearable art.[49]

Through such careful observation of natural phenomena in his search for the power and soul of each organic element, Allen realizes his desire to chronicle an object's inherent past, present, and future on earth and to characterize its singular personality. In keeping with the Native American tradition that all things embody aspects of the spiritual world and that "everything in Nature… is inhabited by a mysterious power, which spreads out and influences other beings,"[50] Midgette believes that:

39. Allen Midgette
*Leaf Collar* 1994
Leather
14 x 10 1/4

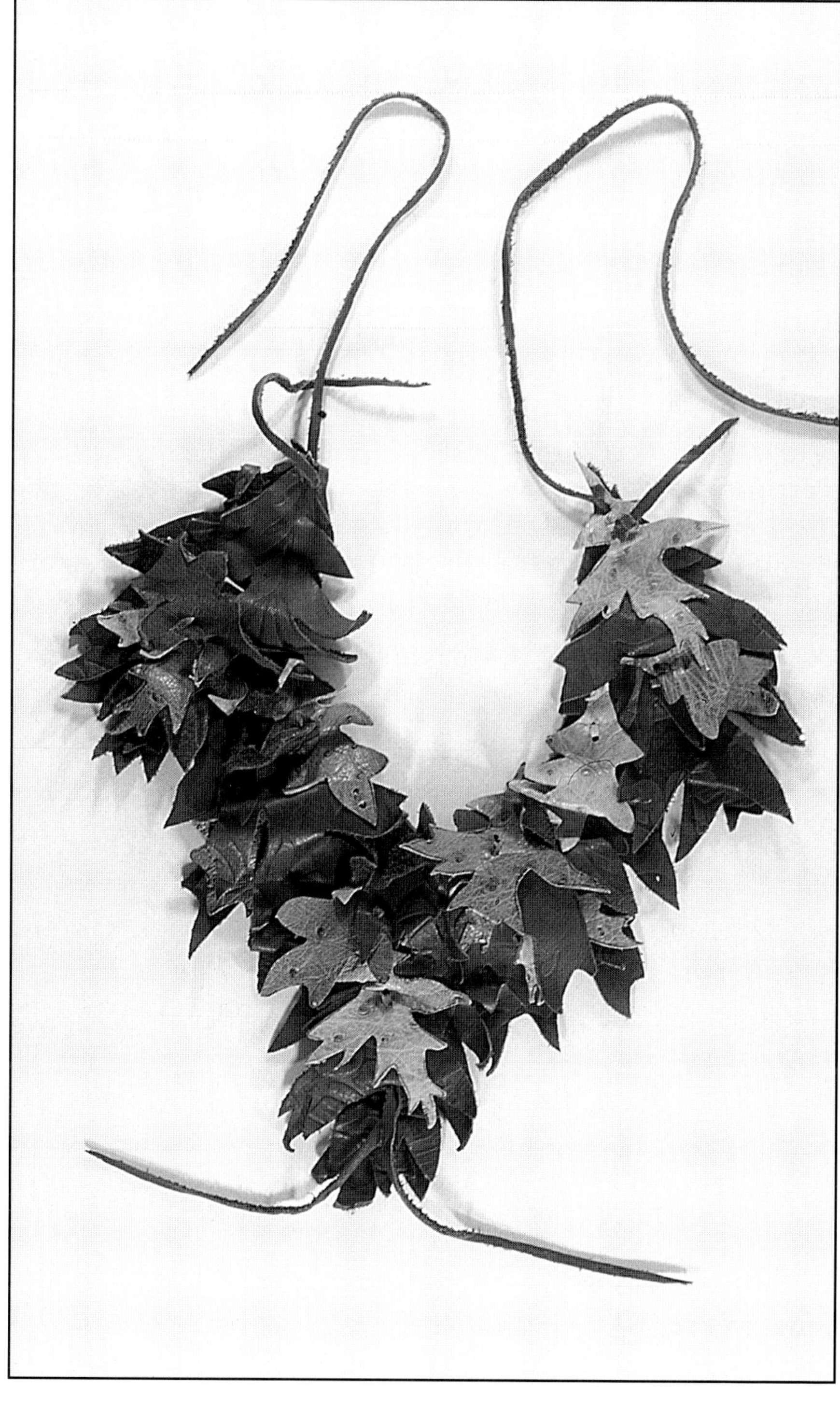

All art should say something about itself.
It is not just something that someone created
to represent an ideal, concept, or feeling.
Art is also about itself.[51]

## 40. KLIMT DRESS

The most extravagantly decorative of Allen Midgette's
fashion designs was inspired by the leading master of Art
Nouveau in Austria, Gustav Klimt (1862-1918).[52] As one
of the founders of the *Jugendstil* and president of the
Vienna Secession (1897), Klimt created a style of
rapturous luxury and sensual fantasy in compositions
filled with brightly colored ornamental undulations,
organic rounded shapes, irregular mosaic-like patterns,
and rich gold accents.[53] His recurrent themes of love,
sleep, and beauty most often revolved around the female,
whom he frequently depicted with long, flowing, and
shining red hair.

In his *Klimt Dress*, Midgette evokes the dreamlike
sensuality and patterned richness of the Viennese artist,
whose work he has always admired. A hand-made fringed
tunic of black suede is covered on the front and back with
colorful swirling designs that emanate from a somnolent
red-haired beauty; the hand-painted composition was
inspired by Klimt's *Fulfillment* (c. 1905-11), from the
frieze he designed for the dining room of Adolphe
Stoclet's mansion in Brussels.[54] The dress is cut broadest
at the shoulders, then tapers to an elegant V below. It may
be worn loosely draped as an overdress, or the fringe may
be tied to create a more fitted silhouette. Small gold-tone
metallic discs are affixed to the ends of the fringe,
echoing the painted golden patterns on the dress and
further recalling the shower of gold in Klimt's *Danaë* of
1907-08 (Private Collection, Austria).

Throughout his career, Klimt promoted the concept of the
"total work of art" and lived in the belief that the arts
should permeate all of life, enhancing it with a
transcendental quality and improving mankind.[55]
Consequently, he himself had designed clothes, and
enjoyed a close relationship with Emilie Flöge, the
proprietress of a fashion house in Vienna.[56] Among their
most noted designs was the Reform Movement dress—a
long smock-type garment with no waistline, which
rebelled against the uncomfortable and unhealthy corset,
and allowed women of the period a new independence
and casualness. Midgette's dress, with its untailored
contours and free-flowing fringe, gives contemporary
women the same graceful comfort and freedom of
movement earlier espoused by Klimt, in whom Allen
appreciated "a certain elegance beyond just being a
painter."[57]

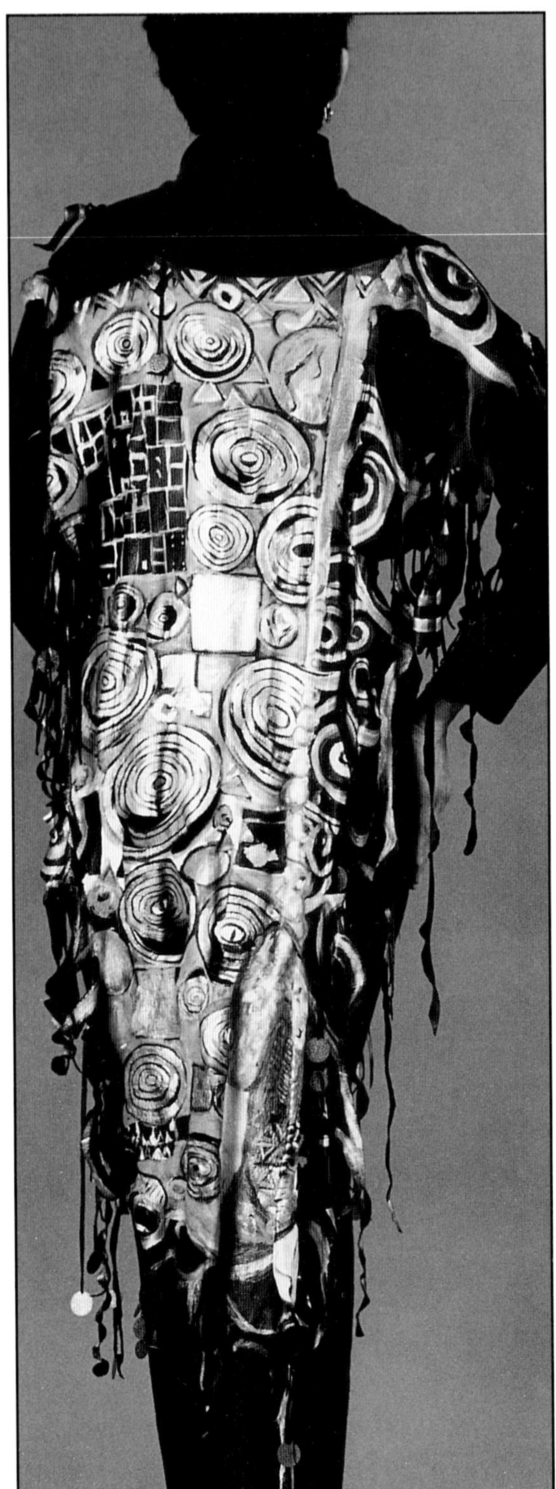

40. Allen Midgette
*Klimt Dress*  c. 1992
Suede, metal, and
acrylic paint
52 x 17 x 4

# CHRISTOPHER MAKOS (b. 1948)

Christopher Makos was born in Lowell, Massachusetts. He grew up in suburban California during the 1960s, then moved to New York. He relocated to Paris for a period in the early 1970s to study architecture and to work as an apprentice to the artist Man Ray. Since that time, Makos has continued to develop his unique style of boldly graphic photojournalism and fine art photography. His works have appeared in *People*, *Esquire*, the *Los Angeles Times*, *Smithsonian*, *Rolling Stone*, and the *Daily News*, among countless other publications. He is the author of two books: *White Trash* (1977) and *Warhol: A Personal Photographic Memoir* (1989), and has hosted his own show, *Makostyle*, on commercial cable television. Makos first met Andy Warhol in 1971 in New York. He became a contributing photographer to Warhol's *Interview* magazine and a close friend and traveling companion to Warhol for the last fourteen years of his life. Presently, Makos maintains an active studio in Manhattan, exhibits his photographs, prints, and paintings throughout the world, and has expanded into cyberspace with his extensive artist-in-residence site on Art Link (http://pathfinder.com/twep/artlink/artist/makos). Christopher Makos may be contacted by e-mail at makostudio@aol.com.

41. Christopher Makos
*Man Ray's Passport*
1976
Gelatin silver print
14 x 11

## 41. MAN RAY'S PASSPORT

In the early 1970s, Christopher Makos left New York City for Paris to study architecture. While there, he began an apprenticeship with the American expatriate Man Ray (1890-1976),[1] whom Makos considers his first great mentor.[2] As a leading figure in both the Dada and Surrealist movements, the elder artist and photographer became known not only for his original "Rayographs"—cameraless silhouettes of actual objects placed on photosensitive paper and exposed to light—but also for the startling incongruities and unsettling edge that characterize such works as his *Gift* of 1921—a flatiron studded with metal tacks.

Clearly inspired by the naked nihilism of Man Ray's art, Christopher developed a bold photographic style in which, as long-time friend and political writer Dotson Rader commented, "Makos uses his camera as a knife."[3] This approach to photography as "an act of violence"[4] is evident in his early work as a photojournalist[5] and in his first published volume of photographs entitled *White Trash* (New York: Stonehill Publishing Company, 1977). Makos paid homage to his teacher by including *Man Ray's Passport* among the plates in that book (cf. cat. #42). The incongruously enlarged reproduction of the inherently small-scale document recalls the jarring paradoxes of the Surrealist/Dadaist sensibility. More than a decade later, Makos reworked the image as a silkscreened print and published it, along with a portrait of Man Ray, in a portfolio commemorating the 100th anniversary of the artist's birth.

The theme of the passport itself holds special significance for Makos. In the years following his association with Man Ray, he would become an avid world traveler, accompanying his close friends Andy Warhol (on the Concorde) and Malcolm Forbes (in his private 727) on "glamorous trips"[6] to such exciting and exotic destinations as China, London, Paris, Milan, the Alps, Spain, and Turkey. His extensive travels with Andy are documented in his second published book, *Warhol: A Personal Photographic Memoir* (New York: New American Library, 1989).

## 42. EARRING BY GILLETTE

After spending the duration of his teenage years growing up in suburban El Monte, California, Christopher Makos made the cross-country trip to New York City in the new Mustang convertible of an acquaintance from Hollywood. Shortly thereafter, he began to meet some of the artists and celebrities whose friendship and patronage he would enjoy in the decades to come. He was introduced to Tennessee Williams by a mutual friend (the writer Dotson Rader). Makos's blond hair, blue eyes, and "waif-like" good looks appealed to Williams, who took Christopher on as a personal assistant and dog-sitter.[7] Makos already had met Lance Loud (of *An American Family*) on the telephone; when Loud arrived in New York to promote his show on PBS, he and Christopher decided to team up as writer and photographer (Makos having been active in the medium since 1966). Their first professional assignment was to cover a concert by the rock band Pink Floyd at Radio City Music Hall for Gerry Rothberg's *Circus* magazine. Subsequently, Makos became *Circus*'s Photo Editor and his work became associated with the most current trends in music and nightlife.

In 1971, Makos met Andy Warhol at the Whitney Museum of American Art, during the Warhol retrospective there. Soon he was hired as a staff photographer for Warhol's *Interview* magazine. Makos recalled, "When I first knew Andy he always used to try to get me to go to these clubs like Max's [Kansas City]."[8] Although he resisted at first, Christopher would spend a significant portion of the Seventies photographing the pre-punk and punk movements he experienced first-hand as an integral part of the New York club scene. Among his many recognizable subjects from that era are Legs McNeil (founder of *Punk Magazine*); rockstars Debbie Harry (of Blondie), Iggy Pop (of the Stooges), Richard Hell and Tom Verlaine (of Television), David Johansen and Syl Sylvan (of the New York Dolls), Patti Smith, David Bowie, Alice Cooper, and Mick Jagger; models Ava Cherry and Grace Jones; and fashion designers Zandra Rhodes and Halston.

Along with the Superstars, Makos documented the anonymous club-goers, their urban milieu, and their ferocious manner of dress. He compiled his visual record of the period in his first book, *White Trash*, published in 1977. *Earring by Gillette* focuses on one of the archetypal images of punk style. The razor, embraced by the punks as a fashion accessory, epitomizes the brutalization and turbulence inherent in the movement, "with its seeming disregard for human and social values."[9] But the obviously clean, smooth-skinned subject, whose gender remains indeterminate in Christopher's photographic close-up, reveals more of a youthful rebelliousness and "an unruly mise-en-scene of punkish posturing and ambisexual allure"[10] than an unbridled brutality. Makos's perceptive framing of the sparkling highlights of his sitter's hair and the elegant line of the neck hint at the refinement of his future work as a much sought-after portraitist to the wealthy and glamorous "inner circle" of the international jet-set.[11]

## 43. ALTERED IMAGE

In 1981, Andy Warhol posed for an extensive series of portraits in drag, comprising both Polaroid self-portraits[12] and fine-art photographs of him by Christopher Makos. According to Bob Colacello, editor of Warhol's *Interview* magazine, the works were a source of controversy at Andy's studio:

> …we had another fight over the latest Chris Makos photos of Andy, drag pictures of Andy looking like the corpse of Candy Darling [q.v., cat. #6]. "But Andy looks like a beautiful young girl in these photos," said Chris. "Yeah, Bob," said Andy, lifting one of them to his eyes to admire his flawless white skin and long blond locks. "What's wrong with these photos? I look really good."[13]

Apart from such quibblings over personal aesthetics, we cannot fail to recognize that the concept of the artist in drag has a significant art historical pedigree, descending from Man Ray's well-known photograph of a cross-dressed Marcel Duchamp as his female alter ego, Rrose

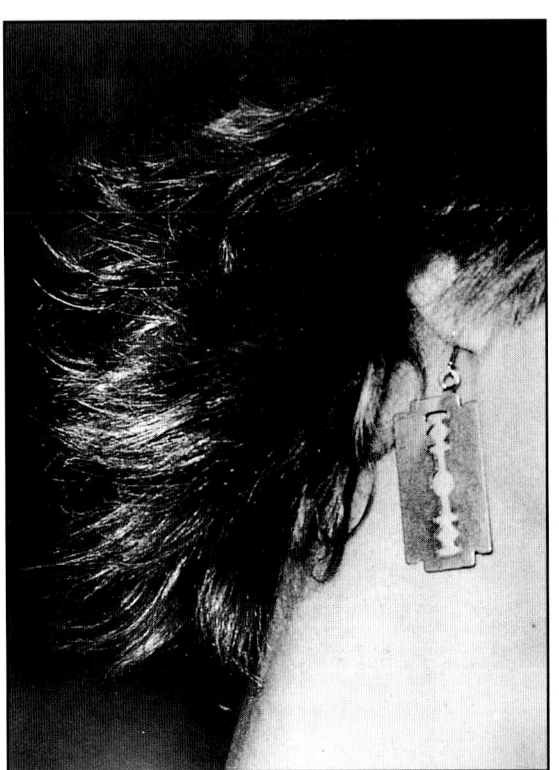

42. Christopher Makos
*Earring by Gillette* 1977
Gelatin silver print
14 x 11

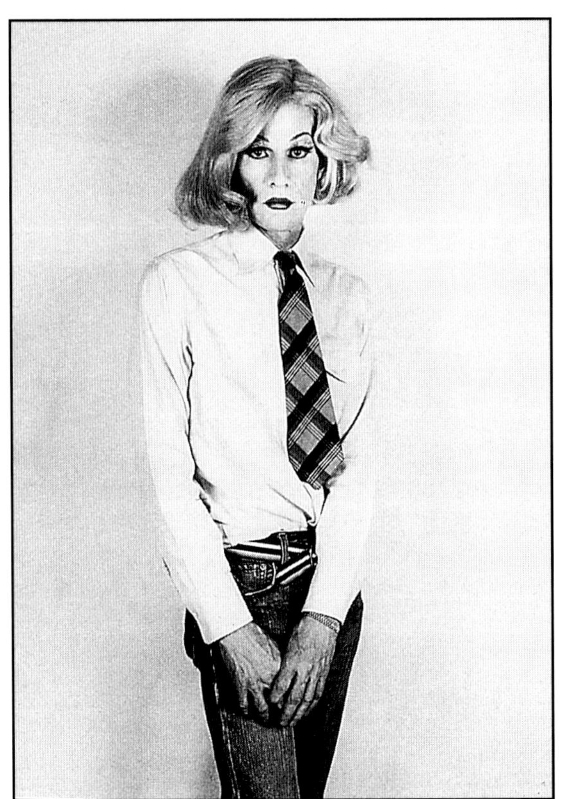

43. Christopher Makos
*Altered Image* 1981
Gelatin silver print
20 x 16

Selavy.[14] It is no coincidence that Duchamp was Andy's favorite artist, and that Man Ray was Christopher's mentor in Paris (cf. cat. #41). Thus, Makos interconnects the Pop artist and his protegé with their revered Dadaist predecessors. Makos further experienced firsthand a profound philosophical similarity connecting the two masters with whom he worked:

> Both Andy and Man Ray… taught me the same thing: "Don't think about making art,

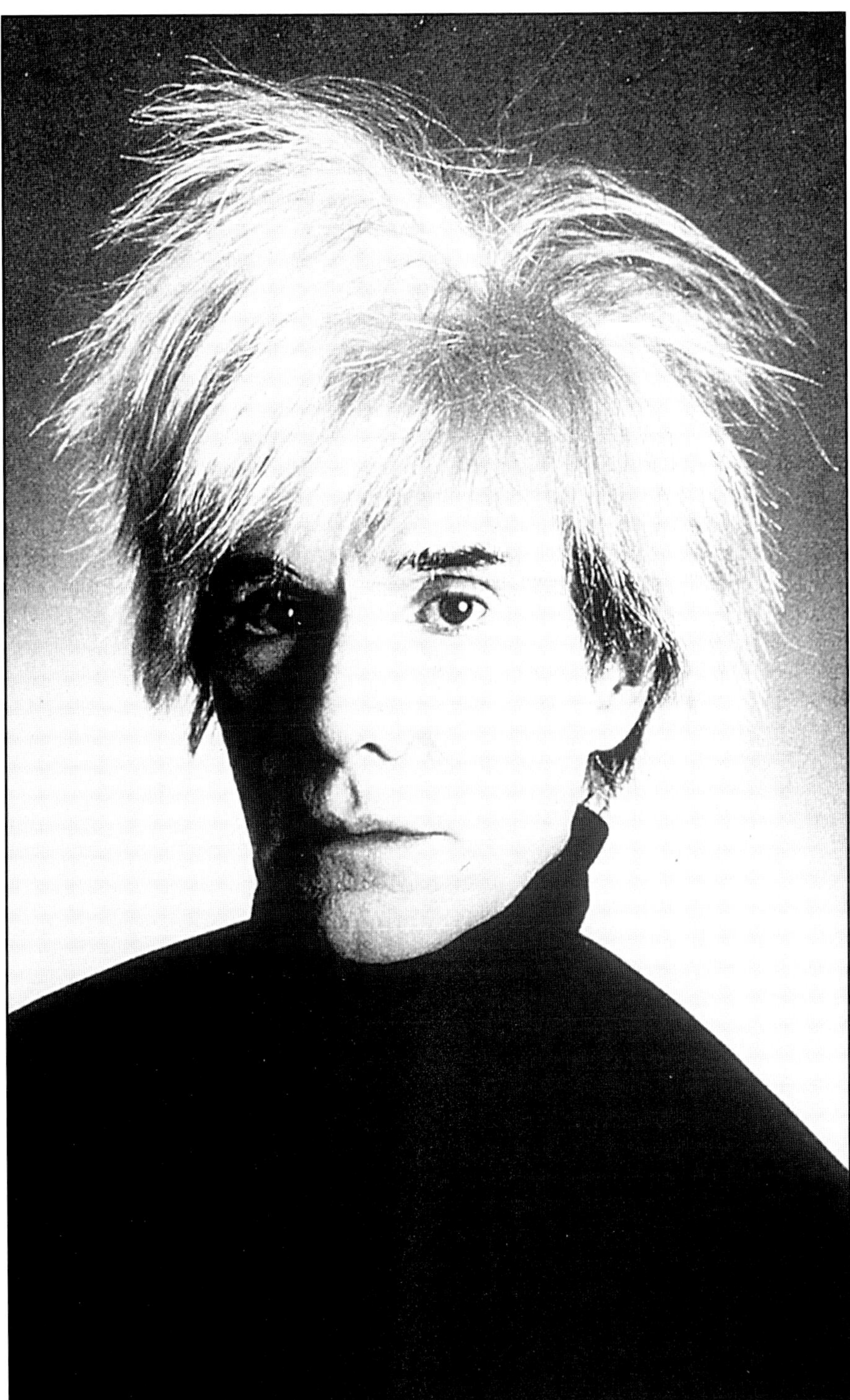

44. Christopher Makos
*Portrait of Andy Warhol*
1986
Gelatin silver print
14 x 11

of Andy's seductive gaze far surpasses that of the earlier image in its bold eroticism.

## 44. PORTRAIT OF ANDY WARHOL

One of the most arresting images of Andy Warhol is the late, bust-length, close-up photograph by Christopher Makos, taken the year before the sitter's death. The photographer describes it simply as "[o]ne of my favourite portraits of Andy."[16] The stark and powerful composition evinces Makos's extraordinary talents as a portraitist. In it, an unsmiling Warhol, wearing a plain black turtleneck and wild silver wig, is turned in three-quarter view, as he looks out at the viewer with his characteristically incisive, direct gaze. Christopher captures all the complexities of his friend's personality; Andy's look is at once penetrating and imploring, resolute and vulnerable. The graduated lighting on the neutral backdrop behind the figure creates a sharp silhouette in its contrasts with the unrelieved darkness of the sweater and the shimmering highlights of the unruly hair. It, combined with the raking light from the right, throws Warhol's head into vivid, tangible, three-dimensional relief.

Makos had done an earlier series of formal head-shots of Andy, in 1981, when Warhol signed on with the Zoli modeling agency.[17] In his diary entry for Thursday, 9 April 1981, Warhol related from Vienna:

> I talked to Vincent [Fremont] in New York
> and he said my headsheet had come in from Zoli.
> Have I told the Diary I've decided to become
> a male model? So then Fred [Hughes] got so
> overwrought—he thinks I'm crazy to start
> modeling. But it's something I want to do
> so I ignored him. Chris [Makos] said Fred's
> just jealous.[18]

Andy's enthusiasm for his new career in modeling was also criticized by Bob Colacello:

> Zoli agreed to represent Andy for special
> assignments, which is agency lingo for
> celebrity endorsements. "Oh, I want to
> be a regular model," said Andy. "I think
> it would be so much fun to go around with
> my portfolio like all the other kids."[19]

just get it done. Let everyone else decide whether it's good or bad, whether they love it or hate it. While they're deciding, make even more art."[15]

The most famous of the controversial, gender-confused portraits of Warhol—Makos's *Altered Image*—was shot on 10 May 1981. In it, Warhol dons a woman's blond wig and make-up, but wears his own white shirt, plaid tie, jeans, and striped belt; his obviously male hands coyly cover his crotch, as he looks directly into our eyes. Warhol's partial transvestism differs from Duchamp's full drag in the photograph of c. 1920-21 by Man Ray, in which the Dadaist is clothed in a woman's dress, hat, and jewelry, in addition to make-up and wig. But the impact

Despite the objections and skepticism of others in the Warhol camp, both artists—Warhol and Makos—realized the value of Andy's name and image as a marketable commodity, based on his celebrity status. But Christopher further recognized that Andy "wasn't insecure about his looks; he knew he had lots of character."[20] In his estimation:

> It was Andy's look that attracted so many
> people. When he was younger, he played
> with the idea of looking older, and when
> he was older, with that of looking younger.
> He was peculiar-looking, and whether or not
> people recognized him as a famous artist,
> they knew he was someone important.

…His last look was as chic as ever, although the overall effect had a lot to do with his general aura. It was as though he'd accomplished everything imaginable in his lifetime…[21]

Through its sharp focus and uncompromising yet tender tone, Makos's striking and insightful portrait of Warhol indeed reveals to us a man who is uniquely captivating. It also shows us how deeply Christopher cared for Andy and how close he came to understanding him.[22]

## 45. PEARLS

Andy Warhol's last exhibition in New York, still running at the time of his death on 22 February 1987, was his show of stitched photographs at the Robert Miller Gallery on East 57th Street.[23] The works shown there were based on an idea given to Andy by Christopher Makos. As a child, Christopher would stitch together dollar bills and pieces of paper on his mother's sewing machine. He recalled:

> I told Andy about it because I knew it would give him an opportunity to repeat images, which is something he was—and still is—known for.[24]

Makos recruited his friend Michelle Loud (Lance's sister, of PBS's *An American Family*) to do the sewing for Andy; a representative from Robert Miller saw the pieces a few years later and scheduled Andy's show. At the opening, according to Makos:

> I was moaning and groaning, and saying jokingly, 'Love your show, Andy.' And he said, 'Oh, Chris, thanks for the really great idea.' …When I got home, there was a message on my answering machine from Andy, saying, 'Thanks, Chris.' And that was it—it was a wonderful thing. I felt so flattered. Everything was perfect then.[25]

In 1993, Makos exhibited his own sewn photographs at Galerie Sho in Tokyo. This exhibition was followed, in 1995, by shows in New York, Chicago, and Santa Fe.[26] Included among the diverse subjects of Christopher's stitched compositions were animals and human figures, statuary and architecture, popsicle sticks and skulls. For the exclusive Fifth Avenue jewelers, Tiffany & Company, Makos shot two close-up views of a lustrous strand of pearls. He employed a softened focus, in harmony with the evanescent radiance of the necklace itself, so that his four joined photographs (with each view repeated twice—upper left/lower right, and upper right/lower left) assume the visual and textural qualities of crushed pearls. Viewed individually, each component in the stitched composition contains the illusion of three-dimensional space and consistent lighting. But through the multiplication of the image, the subject loses its intrinsic perspective and consistency (with one view lit from the right, the other from the left), and becomes a complex graphic design. This random, two-dimensionality of

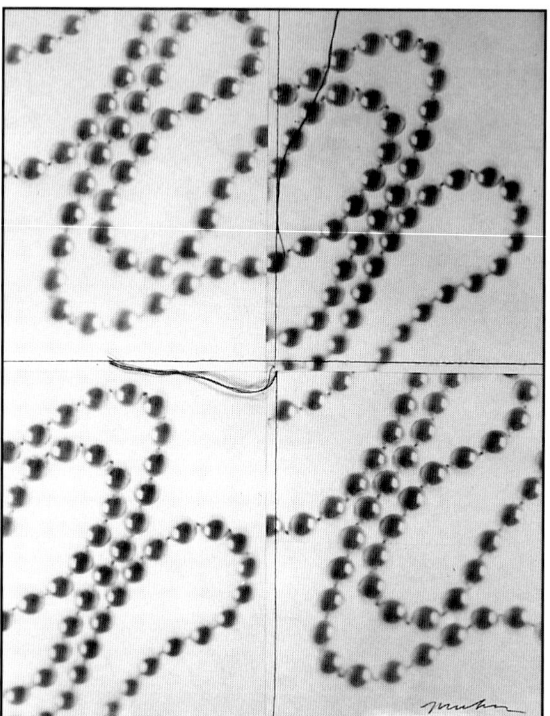

45. Christopher Makos
*Pearls* 1995
Gelatin silver prints and thread
19 1/2 x 15 1/2

pattern is further accentuated by the very visible dark stitching and the dangling ends of thread used to join the pieces—a technique retained from Warhol's earlier group of stitched photographs inspired by Makos.

## 46. DEBORAH HARRY STAND-UP PORTRAIT

Among the many mutual friends and artistic subjects of Makos and Warhol was Debbie Harry, lead singer and songwriter of the rock group Blondie. Makos had known her since the punk heyday of the Seventies; a cropped image of her thighs and hand was used as the cover of his first book, *White Trash*[27] (cf. cat. #42). Warhol silkscreened her portrait in 1980. According to Vincent Fremont:

> They had become friends just as her band, *Blondie*, was becoming successful. She was brought to the studio at 860 Broadway one afternoon and they hit it off… They posed together for a photo session for a magazine… Later when she had her portrait done, Andy and I were producing his TV show, at the time called *Andy Warhol's TV*. As he took Polaroids of her, Don Munroe, the director of our show, video-taped it and we included it in a later episode.[28]

While Munroe video-taped the session of 30 September 1980, Christopher Makos took still photographs. Christopher later returned to the punk rock star as a subject when he featured her in one of his "stand-up" portraits, exhibited at Bergdorf Goodman Men in March 1993.

Makos had invented the compositional format of a sitter standing on a chair before a plain white backdrop as early as the 1970s, and included his early stand-up portraits of Andy Warhol, fashion designer Halston, and Princess

46. Christopher Makos
*Deborah Harry Stand-Up
Portrait* 1987
Gelatin silver prints
40 x 8

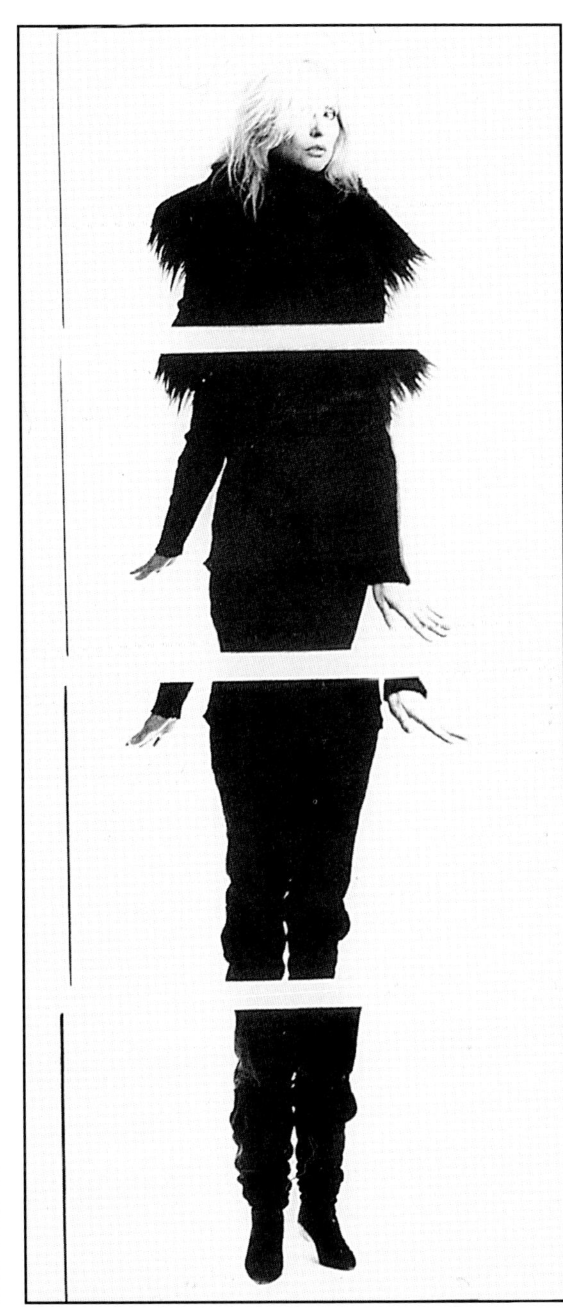

47. Christopher Makos
*Eye and Smile Seascape*
1990
Silkscreen on painted
canvas
18 x 22

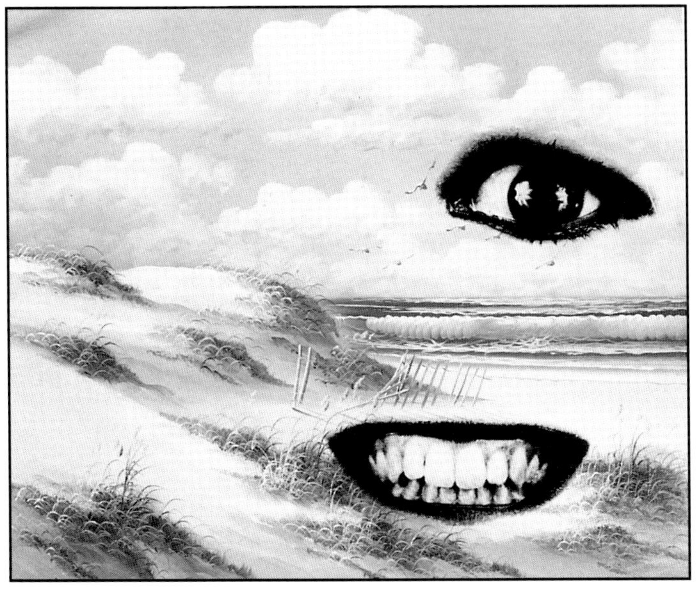

Diane de Beauvau-Craon as fold-out pages in *White Trash*.[29] He shot each of the portraits as a vertical series of three or more frames, which he staggered horizontally so that the sequential parts have no common internal axis. An odd state of tension is felt in this misalignment of body parts; the shattered equilibrium psychologically hints at the potential for the sitter to fall off the chair, or the building blocks of the composition to come tumbling down.

In his later stand-up portrait of Harry—one in a series of sitters done in the late 1980s and early 1990s—Makos has eliminated the chair. The singer, instead, "stands up" on the balls of her feet for added height and stretches her arms and fingers for balance. The individual framing and stacking of the portrait's four sections have the effect of elongating, and thereby attenuating, the figure's proportions; the larger-than-life stretching of the composition is accentuated by the repetition of portions of the body from one frame to the next (e.g., the hands are seen in both the second and third of the four photographs). A long, dramatic silhouette is created by Harry's jagged black outfit, tousled hair, and extended fingers against the stark white background.

## 47. EYE AND SMILE SEASCAPE

Although Christopher Makos gained international recognition as a photographer, since 1989 he has expanded his *oeuvre* to include serigraphic paintings and prints based on his own photographs, using a photo-silkscreening process like the one employed by Andy Warhol. The replication of his compositions in this new medium, on both paper and canvas supports, has resulted in the introduction of color to his original black-and-white images.

*Eye and Smile Seascape* is one in a series of variations on a theme of disembodied facial features. Makos first showed his "Eye Paintings" in November 1989, at Florida's Hokin Gallery, on Bay Harbour Island.[30] In December of that year, as one of his ventures in the world of commercial art, he designed a label for Côte de Rhône wine, which featured the floating eye.[31] That same month, Christopher created *Smiling Sea* to benefit Act Up Action, a fundraiser for AIDS-related causes in New York.

The motif of the mouth recalls Warhol's image of *Marilyn Monroe's Lips*,[32] abstracted from his full-head silkscreen of *Marilyn*, itself based upon Gene Kornman's publicity still for the film *Niagara* of 1953. A single eye has a much longer tradition in the history of art, dating back as far as ancient Egypt and the *udjat*, or sacred eye of the god Horus, a hieroglyphic talisman denoting wholeness and intended to ward off evil spirits. In *Eye and Smile Seascape*, Makos adds a Dadaist dimension by superimposing these *leitmotivs* on an existing painting—a mass-produced seascape signed "R. Wilson"—just as Man Ray (see cat. #41) and Marcel Duchamp employed found objects as the foundations of their art. The unexpected combination of these realistic elements has an unsettling effect on the viewer, akin to Surrealism.

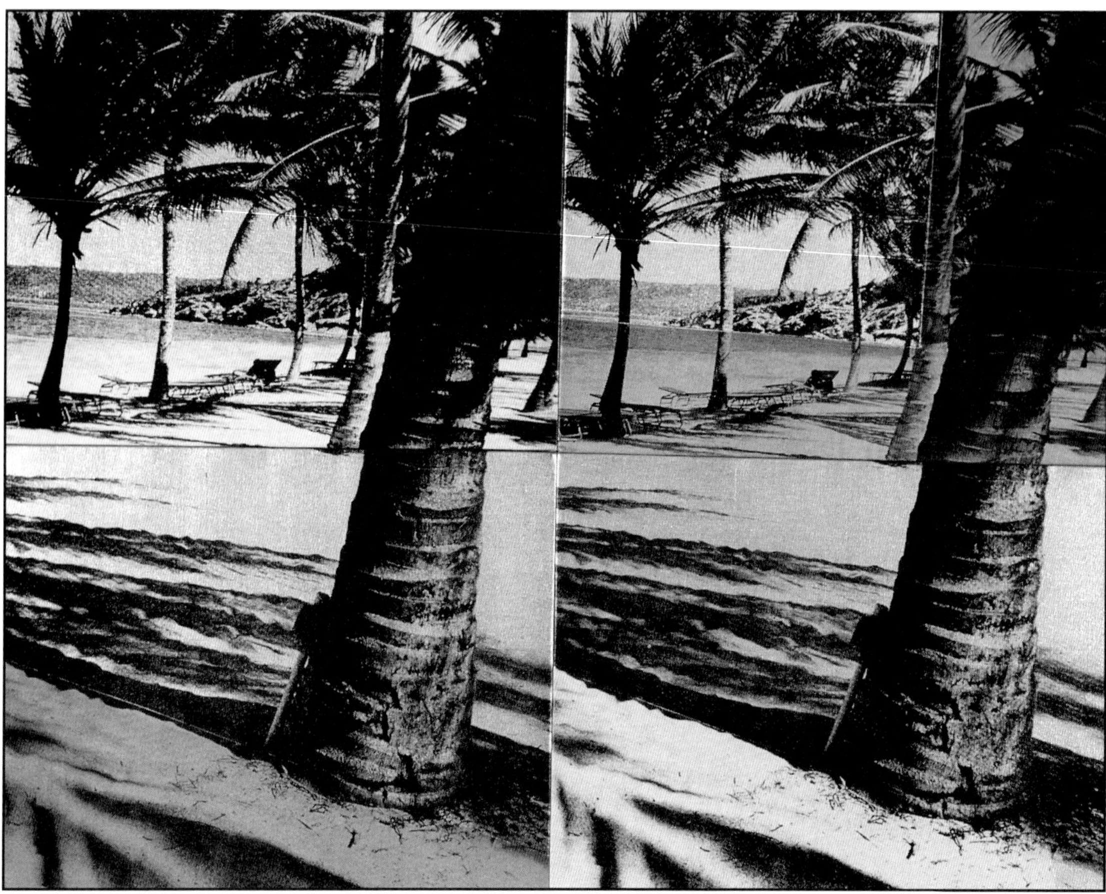



## 48. PARADISE PAINTING

A gentle sweep of idyllic coastline is cooled by rows of majestic palms, their full fronds casting shadows on the sand. The obscured figure of one sole bather is barely visible on a beach chair in an otherwise deserted row of *chaises longues*. The large ringed tree trunk in the foreground is close enough to draw us into the scene. We are seduced by the warmth and quietude of this earthly paradise.

Over the course of his travels, Makos has photographed the myriad cityscapes, landscapes, and tourist sites he visited. From Cologne Cathedral (1980) to the ski slopes of Aspen (1980s), from the canals of Venice (1993) to the Great Wall of China and the Forbidden City (1982), we recognize the major landmarks of our world as seen through the lens of Christopher Makos.[33] What is different here, in his *Paradise Painting*, is that the particular location—a beach on the Caribbean island of Antigua—is less important than the state of mind it evokes. In it are reminiscences of all the paradisaic beaches Makos has frequented, from his youth in California, to his trip to St. Maarten with Andy Warhol in 1983, to his stay in Palm Beach with Ivana Trump at Mar-a-Lago (former estate of Post Cereal heiress, Marjorie Merriweather Post). Perhaps it is the perfect calm, the appealing solitude, the natural beauty that inspired him to select this particular scene for silkscreening.[34] His arbitrary choice of soothing pastel tones augments the mood of total relaxation; his use of metallic paint recalls the glistening sand, sun, and water of this secluded get-away.

The two-part composition is repeated twice, on four joined canvases. It is an original variation on the theme of replication, so popular at the Warhol Factory and in the Warhol circle.

## 49. BACK 2 BACK

Homoerotic subjects constitute a significant portion of Makos's *oeuvre*, as they do of Warhol's. In photographs and silkscreens spanning his entire career, Christopher has focused on the strength and sensuality of the youthful male form and, in so doing, upholds the Classical belief in the compelling beauty of the human body. He reveals:

> To tell you the truth, I have some of the most beautiful young men… pass through my studio, who want to be in my pictures or on my show [*Makostyle*—see cat. #50]… people don't see the amount of physical beauty I see through my lens or coming through my studio.[35]

As a result of this constant exposure, the artist has developed a keen eye for ideal proportion, natural good looks, and sexual appeal, which he prefers to capture in their most ingenuous and unadulterated state. According to Makos, he most often encounters this in a particular demographic type:

> I would say that eighty to ninety percent of the ones who I photograph are usually young, straight men who are not really absolutely straight or gay. But young gay

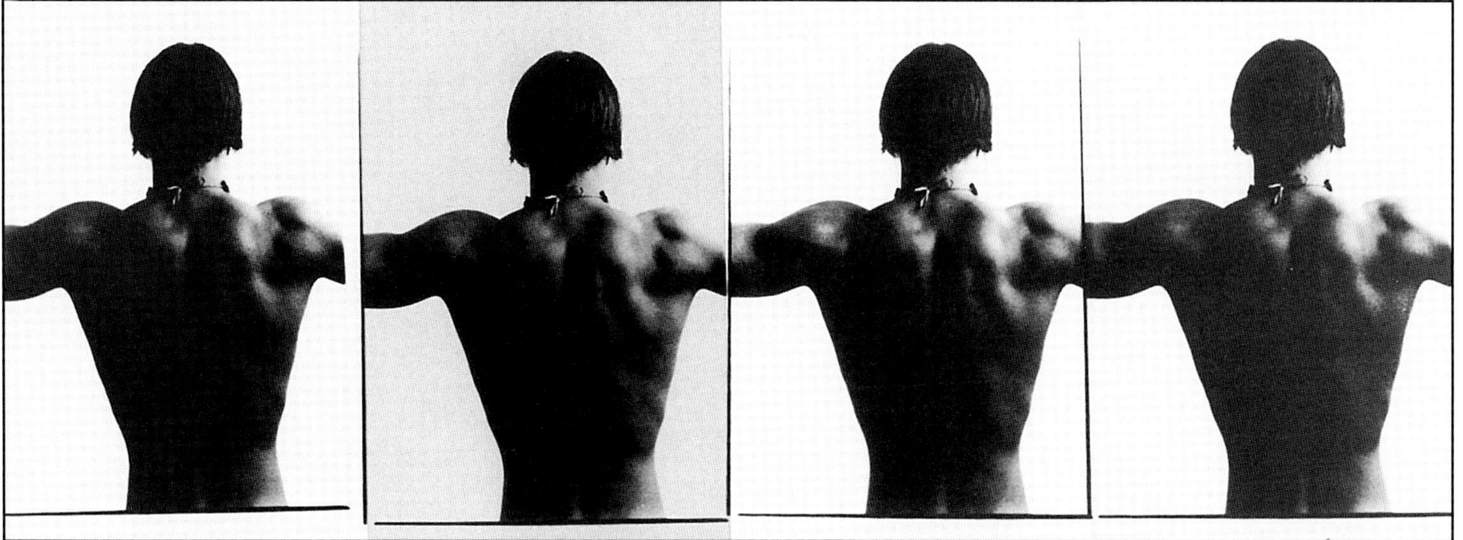

49. Christopher Makos
*Back 2 Back* 1994
Silkscreen on paper
16 x 38

men are usually very self-aware and they've lost some of that naïveté they had when they first came to New York… that innocence you have when you come to a big city can be lost quickly by older men pampering you, giving you gifts, taking you to dinner. Straight men don't experience that. So, visually, to take pictures, you often get a more honest reaction from people who are not so self-aware…[36]

In *Back 2 Back*, Christopher's well-structured model is presented as a contemporary descendant of the ancient Greek athlete, whose physical perfection is to be appreciated and commemorated. The particular identity and sexual proclivity of the young man (Mark Wene) are irrelevant, as Makos's focus is on the aesthetics of his physique; we are not exposed to his face nor to his psyche, but rather to a detail of his heroic anatomy. The format is that of a standing male nude, just teasingly longer than half-length and viewed from behind. The composition is simple and direct; it shows the well-defined musculature of a tapering back, from its broad shoulders to its narrow waist, in an unaffected posture that is balanced halfway between action and repose.

Such works by Makos beg comparison with Warhol's silkscreened series of anonymous nude *Torsos* of 1977 and *Sex Parts* of 1978, although the majority of Andy's images are more blatantly sexual in their collective focus on genitalia and their more strained and provocative postures.[37] A greater debt to Warhol is seen in Christopher's fourfold replication of his composition. In combination with the figure's strong contour lines and outstretched arms, the repeated image becomes a two-dimensional pattern that flows together like a string of paper doll cut-outs.

### 50. MAKOSTYLE

*Makostyle* premiered on Saturday, 4 December 1993. The half-hour show featured Christopher hosting segments shot on location and interviews conducted in the studio with

trendsetters from "all walks of life… from the inner city to the inner circle."[38] The host had earlier done a two-page column called "In, by Christopher Makos" for Andy Warhol's *Interview* magazine. In it, he covered "everybody—from street hustlers to high society, from animals to people and places and objects."[39] Consequently, he approached Marvin Schwam, founder of the Gay Entertainment TV Network, to do something similar on commercial cable television. The result was *Makostyle*, with two episodes taped every two weeks.

The show went national; it aired in New York, Los Angeles, San Francisco, Miami, and Chicago—markets targeted for their large gay communities. Christopher explained:

> Everybody's interested in style… [it] is in every part of our life… [but] the gay community is so full of style. And of course, so much of what we decide is style ends up in the straight community or… the bi[sexual] community. In other words, we pretty much are arbiters of style.[40]

Makos intended that his concept of "what's in" be extended to every element of the show, with each component treated as if it were one of his guests. Every two weeks he had new sets done in a different style, and his wardrobe was provided by the most fashionable shops and designers—Romeo Gigli, Dolce & Gabbana, New Republic, J.M. Weston. He joked that "*Makostyle* is a kind of shallow endeavor, but, you know, as my friend Paul Washington said, 'It's deeply shallow.'"[41]

With *Makostyle*, Christopher shows his indebtedness to Warhol, whose career interests followed a similar evolution in themes and media. From 1979 to 1980, Andy produced a ten-part video program entitled *Fashion*, directed by Don Munroe. Munroe and Warhol teamed up again from 1980 to 1982 for *Andy Warhol's TV*, a series of half-hour videotaped shows modeled after *Interview* magazine. And from 1985 to 1987, the cable channel MTV aired *Andy Warhol's Fifteen Minutes*, a half-hour program directed by Munroe and hosted by Warhol, which featured artists, musicians, designers, and other celebrities currently enjoying their "fifteen minutes of fame."

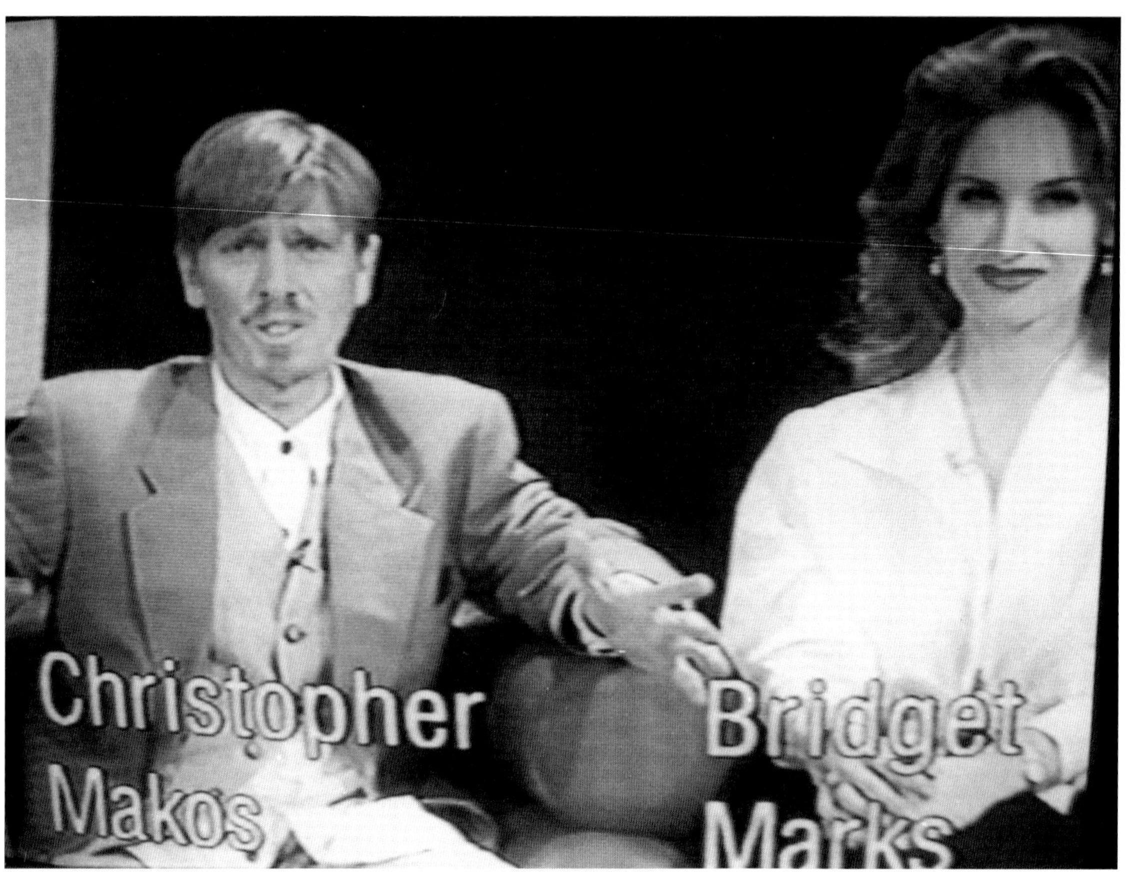



50. Christopher Makos
hosting *Makostyle*
c. 1995
Photograph by
Christopher Makos

# JAMES WARHOLA (b. 1955)

Artist and illustrator James Warhola was born on 16 March 1955, in Pittsburgh, Pennsylvania. He is the nephew of Andy Warhol, whom he remembers with the greatest admiration and affection, declaring that "He was my childhood idol." Jamie received a bachelor's degree in design from Carnegie-Mellon University in 1977. From 1977 to 1980, he studied at the Art Students League in New York with Jack Faragasso, then continued his education by privately studying with Michael Aviano from 1980 to 1984. Over the last decade, he has worked as a book illustrator for several major publishing houses (among them, Berkley, Rocket Books, Warner, Simon and Schuster, HarperCollins, Prentice-Hall, Bantam, and Avon). His designs comprise over 300 covers for science-fiction and fantasy books by such noted authors as Spider Robinson, James P. Blayloch, Esther Friesner, Roger Zelazny, Robert A. Heinlein, and Ron Goulart. Since 1987, Warhola has concentrated on illustrating children's books; his titles include classics like *Jack and the Beanstalk*, *The Brave Little Tailor*, and *The Tinderbox*. Among his latest releases are illustrated versions for children of two Rodgers and Hammerstein songs, *The Surrey with the Fringe on Top* and *My Favorite Things*. Jamie's highly creative imagination produces memorable images with a marvelous sense of humor, color, and detail, in both oils and watercolors. He resides and maintains a studio in Upstate New York, but is an avid world traveler who also serves as consultant to the Museum of Modern Art (the Warhol Family Museum) in Medzilaborce, Slovakia (ancestral home of the Warhola family).

51. James Warhola
*Creature Feature Movie Guide* c. 1982
Oil on masonite
32 x 23

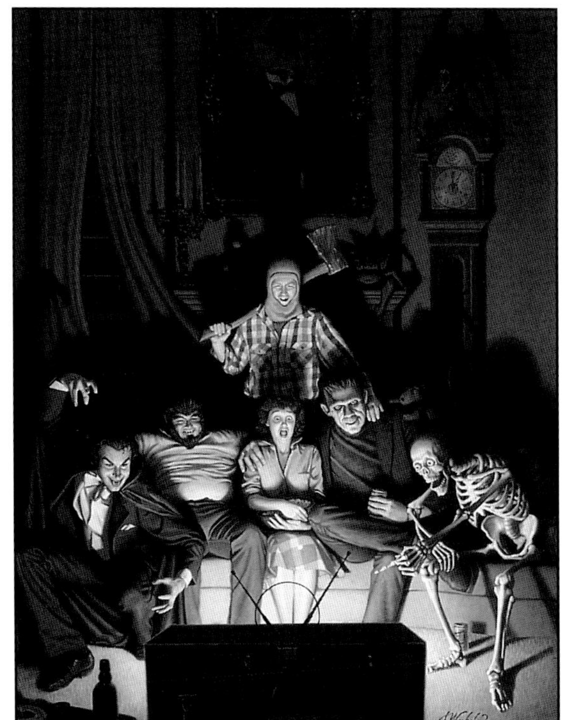





Upon completing his BFA in Design at Carnegie-Mellon University in Pittsburgh, in 1977 James Warhola moved to New York City to pursue a career in art, and to develop and to refine his artistic talents.[1] While working during the day in an art studio, doing freelance design and illustrations for educational publishers, Jamie enrolled in evening classes from 1977-80 at the prestigious Art Students League in Manhattan, then studied privately with the painter Michael Aviano from 1980-84. During these years of study, Jamie learned to master the academic techniques of oil painting. He also learned about the great American illustrators, such as Howard Pyle, N.C. Wyeth, and Norman Rockwell, who were to influence the direction of his career. In 1981, Jamie landed his first professional freelance assignment in New York with Berkley Publishers, as illustrator for the cover of *The Book of Philip Jose Farmer*, a paperback collection of science-fiction and fantasy short stories. Jamie enjoyed paperback illustration because he found it to be the closest to academic fine art in the field of illustration.[2] He also enjoyed fantasy because, as a child, he had always been interested in the Middle Ages in Europe. This love of early Medieval culture made him enthusiastic to illustrate stories about castles, wizards, swords, witches, and magic.

One of Jamie's most successful illustrations from these early years in New York is *Creature Feature Movie Guide*, designed as the cover for the paperback catalogue of the same name by John Stanley.[3] The painting is masterfully packed with details and characters cited in the book. On a sofa in front of a television, a young woman is watching a "creature feature" in the company of an unlikely group of "couch potatoes." With beer in hand and a friendly rat on his shoulder, Frankenstein is joined by a smiling Wolfman, a grimacing Dracula, and a light-hearted skeleton. A bemused Axe Murderer, holding his bloody tool, stands behind the group. A very large bat sits atop a grandfather clock, while a gremlin-like creature from Jamie's vivid imagination perches on a mantel in the shadows. A portrait of the Invisible Man, hanging over the mantel, injects a subtle touch of humor into the composition. By treating the focal point of the television as a *repoussoir* device seen from behind, the viewer is drawn into the painting to participate in an evening of watching TV with this unusual company.

Although Warhola's room is eerie, with shadows dancing on the walls and a curtain flapping at an open window, his mood is decidedly playful. The characters, whom we have come to recognize from the old horror movies described by Stanley, are amused by the scary show. The only obviously frightened viewer is the young woman clutching her bowl of popcorn in the center of the composition. This paradoxical dialectic of the monsters enjoying themselves, while the sole "normal" figure reacts contrary to the rest of the crowd, is a characteristically humorous, Warholian touch.

The inspiration of Jamie's uncle, Andy Warhol, is evident. Not only did Jamie attend the same university as Andy and pursue the same course of study,[4] then relocate to New York and begin his career as an illustrator, but, as in Andy's early works (magazine covers, fashion illustrations, book and record jackets, and artist's books), he displays a similar, light-hearted sense of wit and whimsy.[5] Stylistically, however, Warhola's manner of execution differs dramatically from Warhol's. Andy's illustrations exhibit a loose, free-spirited style; he was primarily a draftsman who produced line drawings that later were "colored in." But Jamie, using a very tight and fastidious brushstroke, produces paintings characterized by a more detailed and finished look. His paint is thinly and smoothly applied with bristle, sable, and fan brushes. From the initial raw umber underpainting to the ultramarine blue glazing of *Creature Feature Movie Guide*, Jamie's color is largely monochromatic and subtle, as a harmonious blue haze pervades the room, which is lit solely by the television. The background details are kept dark in value, not only because of the room's low lighting, but also in deference to the white type that must go across the book's cover.

## 52. THE MAGIC SHOP

*The Magic Shop*, which served as the cover illustration for the novel by Avram Davidson,[6] is another skillful example of how Warhola draws us into his science-fiction and fantasy compositions. Along with the window shopper, who is seen from behind to serve as a surrogate for the viewer, we become absorbed with the contents of the magic for sale in the window. The apparently ordinary man is dressed in a bright gold overcoat and chocolate brown shoes, trousers, and hat, and carries with him an electric-blue striped umbrella. But we soon notice that he is levitating well above the sidewalk! In the shop's window, we see a skeleton holding a deck of playing cards painted in a shocking blue similar to that of the man's umbrella, thus tying the pedestrian to the magical display. A witch's head, an open book beneath a burning candelabra, a blue crystal ball, the floating head of a man pierced with two swords, a rabbit in a hat, a genie's magic lamp, and the pentagonal sign of the devil number among the ensemble of strange objects in the window.

Jamie's striking accumulation of details succeeds in mixing fantasy with a real urban environment, including a fire hydrant and architectural sculpture. In his quest for authenticity, the artist did research throughout New York City and discovered the source for his gargoyles on a building by Stanford White. By placing the items of magic in the window of an equally realistic city structure, Jamie creates the illusion that these objects are a part of our normal quotidian world. But, is the well-dressed window shopper real, or merely an illusion conjured by the magic in the window? Warhola explains:

> I like to create situations that are very fantastic and out of the ordinary—to show things that people can't see and photograph in everyday life.[7]

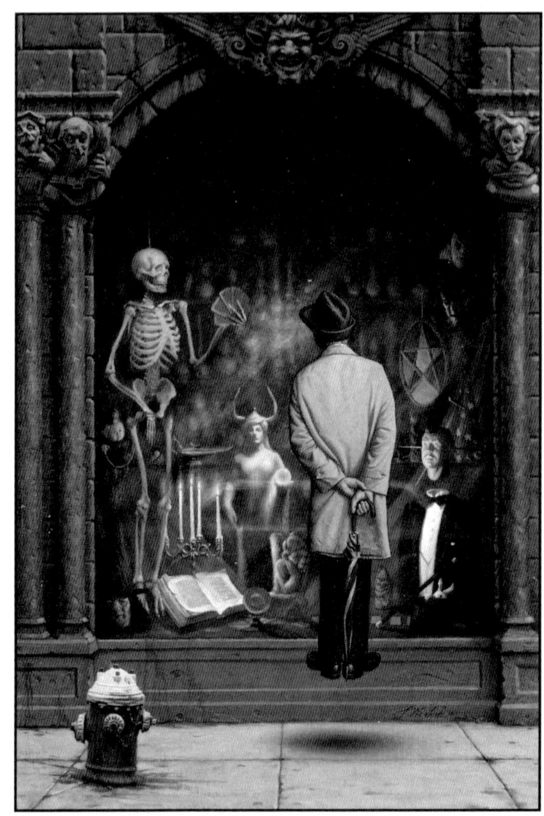

52. James Warhola
*The Magic Shop* c. 1983
Oil on board
30 x 21

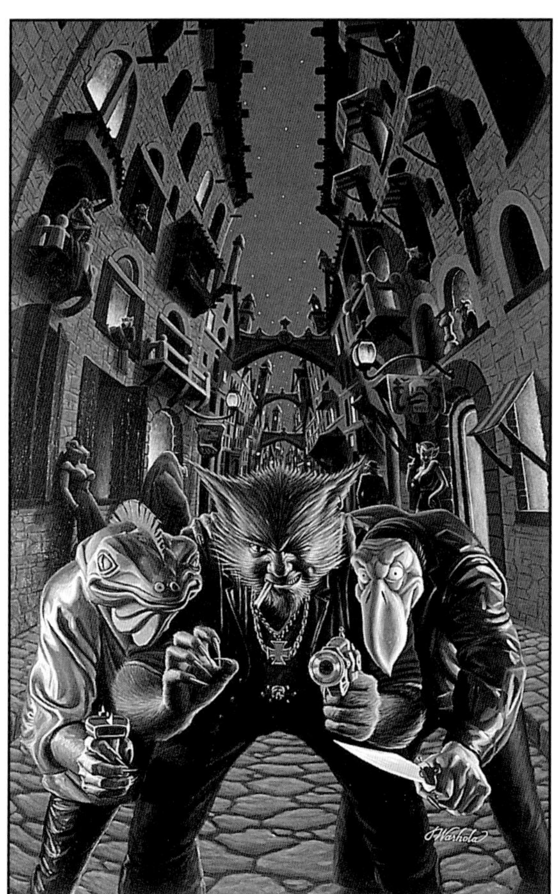

53. James Warhola
*Alien Muggers* 1985
Oil on canvas
32 x 20

In reality, Jamie did photograph an anonymous man from the back, unbeknownst to him, on a city street. He would eventually serve as the model for the hovering window shopper. At the time Jamie photographed him, however, the man was firmly planted on the sidewalk!

Jamie illustrated the cover for Ron Goulart's *Suicide, Inc.*[8] with a painting entitled *Alien Muggers*—the episode of a group of thugs from outer space who attack a human protagonist. In his depiction, three anthropomorphic aliens, with weapons in hand, confront the viewer: a cat-headed figure with a cigarette in the corner of its mouth is flanked by a creature with a large avian beak and another with an electric-green lizard's head. Warhola recalls, "This particular scene was a very minor aspect of the story, but it really summed up the nature of the book."[9]

Almost theatrically, Jamie spotlights the three muggers in a warm ochre brilliance, which contrasts with the deep blue chiaroscuro of the sinister buildings in the background. There is an old European feel to the architecture and the cobblestone street, but with a fantastic element added. The strange, curving perspective, as if seen through a modified fish-eye lens, propels the tightly compacted trio of figures in the foreground into a dramatic close-up. The viewer is so near these beasts as to participate in the action of the scene, both physically and psychologically. In essence, we become the surrogate victims of the alien muggers.

A selection of Warhola's paintings has been issued as a collection of trading cards—a new format for science-fiction and fantasy artists.[10] Jamie chose *Alien Muggers* for reproduction as the series' wrapper illustration.

In addition to the more than 300 covers James Warhola designed for science-fiction and fantasy paperbacks, he has produced independent paintings thematically related to his book illustrations. *Callahan's Place*, painted for the cover of *Callahan's Crosstime Saloon* by Spider Robinson,[11] inspired the artist to create an offshoot series of alien bar scenes that followed in the wake of the celebrated motion picture, *Star Wars*.[12] It exemplifies Jamie's ability to invite us into the world of fantasy in such a convincing way that make-believe situations become real. For the artist:

> Alien bar-room scenes allow so much freedom in the fantasy world. There are endless situations and characters to dream up.[13]

The painting is loaded with both human and anthropomorphic figures gathered in a very ornate, Victorian-style bar; it is a delight for the viewer to discover all the subtle, hidden details in the setting and in the group of colorful characters who populate the scene. The microscopic acuity with which the forms are treated indeed renders them almost believable. Evident here, in Jamie's keen attention to detail and constant striving for accuracy, is the influence of the masters of America's "Golden Age of Illustration:" Howard Pyle; Pyle's student N.C. Wyeth; and Norman Rockwell.[14]

In order to paint his scene realistically, Jamie researched drinking establishments in New York City. He took

54. James Warhola
*Callahan's Place* 1985
Oil on canvas
24 x 30
Collection of Howard
Shakespeare

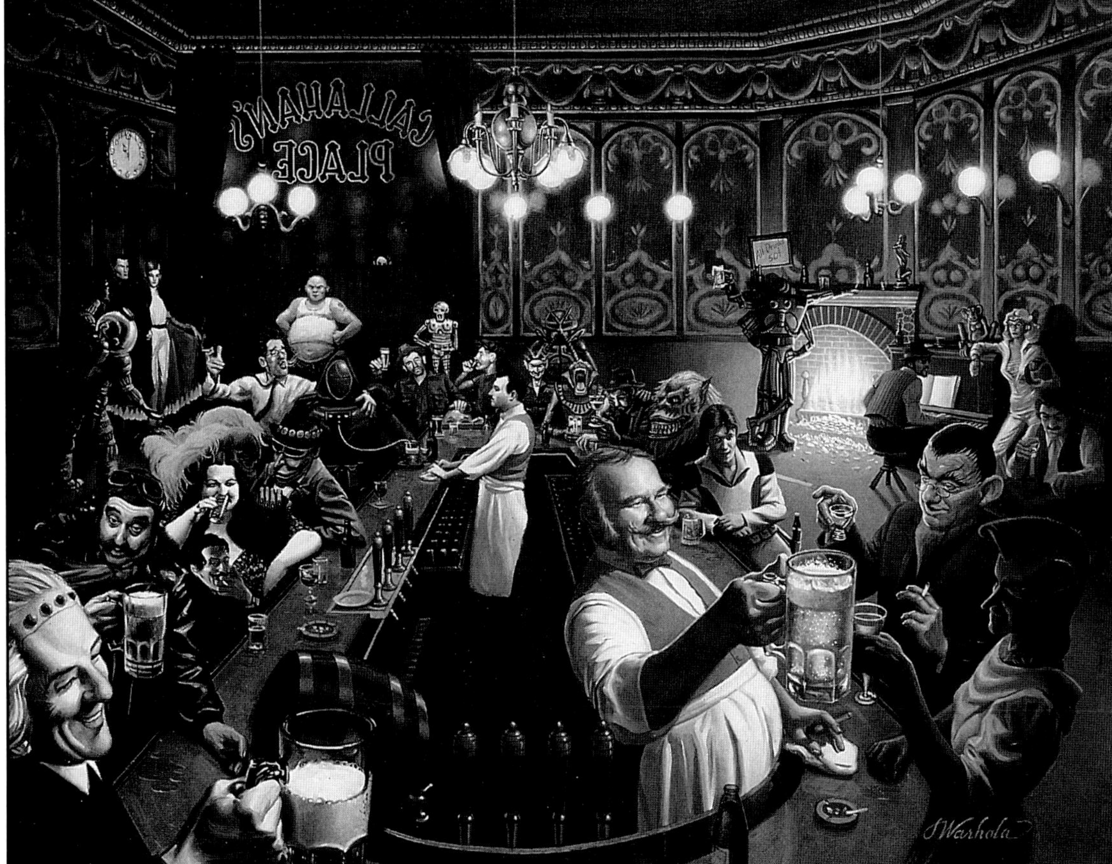

numerous photographs, as Rockwell would have done, before finding the perfect model for his painting at the Cedar Tavern, located on University Place and Twelfth Street in Manhattan. Following the tenets of Pyle, the viewer is thus drawn into participating in the action of this familiar "neighborhood" site, which is based in reality but then altered by the artist's imagination. Our intimacy with the scene is further enhanced by the perspective from which we view it, deep inside the tavern, looking out towards the front window in the background. Jamie's brushwork, too, is reminiscent of the painstaking style of Pyle and Rockwell, and his use of light can be likened to the manner of N.C. Wyeth. Like Wyeth, who emphasized the effects of light in his still-life and portrait paintings, Warhola uses deep saturated colors for the bar's strange patrons, as beautiful old chandeliers and lighting fixtures cast a mellow, golden glow upon the tavern's opulent interior. To achieve his jewel-like luster and reflective surface sheen, Warhola employs his favorite medium of oil. "I love oils because they stay wet and I can work with them and change them," he says.[15]

Jamie's father, Paul Warhola (Andy Warhol's brother), served as the model for Callahan's bartender, who serves up a beer in the foreground. According to the artist:

> My father just loves to be in my paintings. Knowing the ham he is, I gave him a mustache and a toupée, and made him the bartender. Naturally, I couldn't easily photograph the non-human patrons, though I can think of a few that inspired them![16]

## 55. VALENTINE'S SONG

To a great extent, fantasy paintings reflect our need to identify with heroes and with shared human values. To achieve these goals, Jamie selected an intimate, romantic scene and employed a soft and sensuous pastel palette for *Valentine's Song*, his painting for the cover of Robert A. Heinlein's cult favorite, *Stranger in a Strange Land*.[17] The artist felt honored to be selected to illustrate the cover for this renowned book's re-issue by Berkley, New York, in 1987. He says with obvious gratification:

> I am most proud of this painting, because it illustrated a novel long touted as the greatest science fiction story ever written. As with an actor getting a chance at his greatest role, I was an extremely nervous artist working on such a famous book.[18]

*Valentine's Song* departs from what we have come to expect in a Warhola composition in that it is devoid of the abundance of internal and auxiliary details for which Jamie is recognized (cf. cat. #52). The painting consists of only two figures. Valentine Michael Smith, the main character of the book, was raised on Mars and possesses unusual powers. He shares an underwater kiss with Gillian Boardman, whom Heinlein describes as "a competent nurse" whose "hobby was men."[19] The encounter takes place at the bottom of a pool, where Valentine has been sent to hide until Jill comes to retrieve him.[20] Warhola depicts Jill as a beautiful young woman

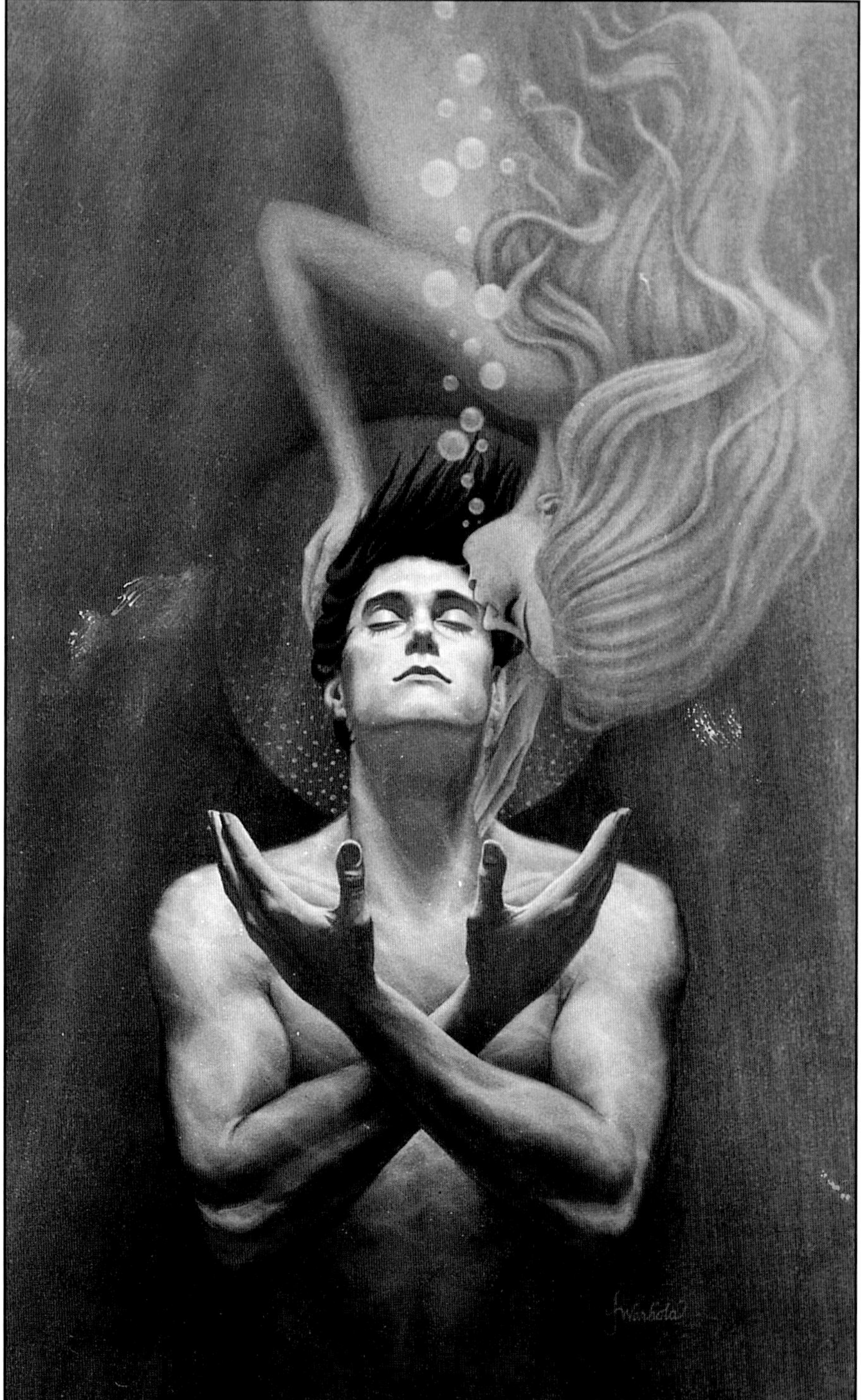

with long flowing hair, suggestive of a mermaid. With his arms crossed and his hands up-turned, the graceful Valentine displays a rapturous expression—at once religious and erotic—that evokes a feeling of reverie in the viewer. The halo-like effect behind his head further contributes to the ecstatic symbolism of the image.[21] Delicate bubbles rise from around the figures' mouths and float through the water, accentuating their vertical alignment and the upward thrust of the composition. The dominant cool aqua tones of the all-encompassing water are punctuated by the seductive violet of the female bestowing the sensual kiss on Valentine, as the plays of light striated across his body echo the wavy curves of her hair. We feel soothed and uplifted by Warhola's pacific, somnolent vision.

55. James Warhola
*Valentine's Song* c. 1987
Oil on canvas
35 x 22

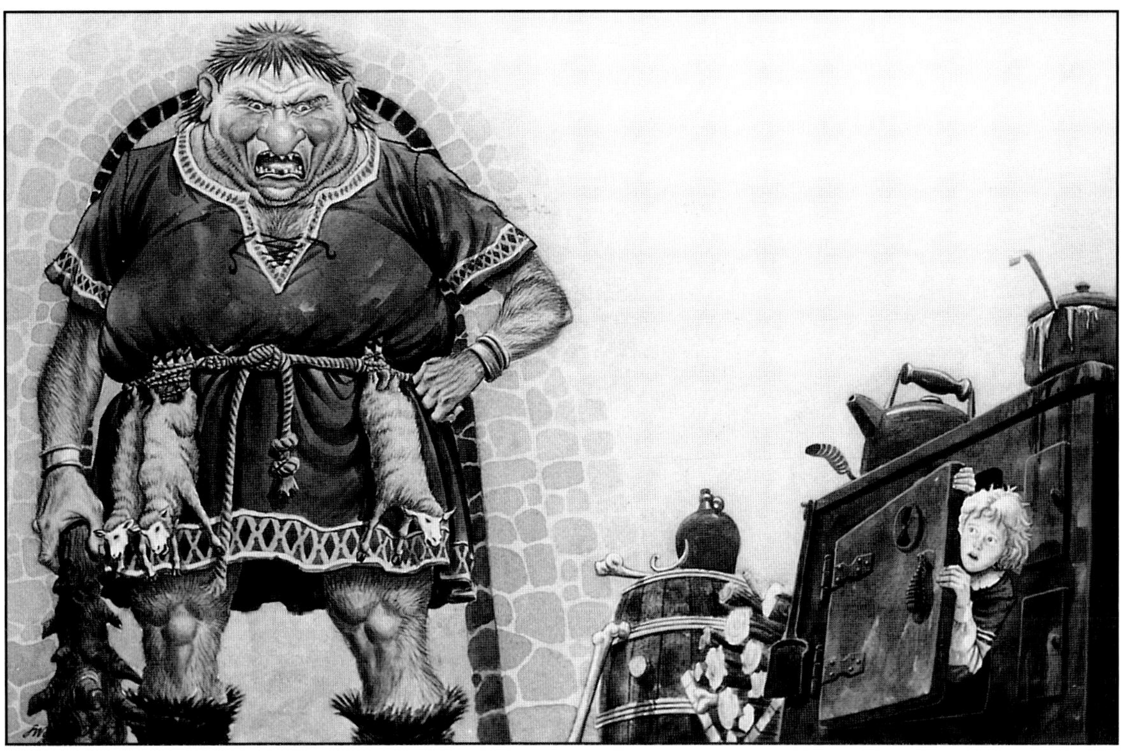

56. James Warhola
Illustration for *Jack and the Beanstalk* c. 1989
Watercolor on paper
14 1/2 x 22

## 56. JACK AND THE BEANSTALK

In 1986, Elaine Groh, an art director from Simon and Schuster with whom Jamie had been working on paperbacks, introduced him to the world of children's books. Jamie first rejected Groh's offer to illustrate a children's book because this type of work is done in watercolor, rather than oil; he recognized that the transition from one medium to the other could be difficult. According to Warhola:

> In oils you can correct your mistakes. In watercolors it's all transparent and you can't fix your mistakes that easily.[22]

Nevertheless, after some reconsideration, Jamie agreed to do his first children's book, *The Pumpkinville Mystery*.[23] The result was a series of watercolor illustrations executed with the same meticulous care and filled with the same minute detail, brilliant color, exciting and sometimes exaggerated characters, and trademark sense of humor and optimism for which his earlier oil paintings had become known.

Since *The Pumpkinville Mystery*, Jamie has created the illustrations for nine other children's books, which range from the retelling of classic fairy tales like *Jack and the Beanstalk*, *The Tinderbox*, and *The Brave Little Tailor*; to the illustration of Rodgers and Hammerstein's songs, *Surrey with the Fringe on Top* and *My Favorite Things*; to delightful accounts of hilarious happenings in *Well, I Never!*, *Aunt Hilarity's Bustle*, *Hurricane City*, and *The Christmas Blizzard*. Jamie explains his philosophy for illustrating books for children in the five- to eight-year-old age group:

> Children's illustration styles can be abstract, realistic, or cartoon-like. As

for myself, I try to keep them realistic, with a light sense of humor, especially traditional tales which could be too serious and a little scary to a young child.[24]

The literary history of the tale of Jack and the Beanstalk began in England in 1807, when it appeared in two publications: the first version was in *The History of Mother Twaddle and the Marvellous Achievements of Her Son Jack*, which was one of John Harris's copperplate books by B.A.T.; the second was in a booklet edited by the philosopher William Godwin for Benjamin Tabart.[25] The latter version is most frequently retold, and served as the basis for Susan Pearson's account of 1989, illustrated by James Warhola.[26] Jamie's richly atmospheric and evocative watercolors retain the folkloric character and enchantment of his nineteenth-century British prototypes. In the example exhibited here, the hairy giant is depicted as an enormous, looming figure viewed from below, as Jack peeks out at him from inside a cast iron stove. Muttering to himself, "Fee-fi-fo-fum, I smell the blood of an Englishman," the rubescent-faced ogre carries a tree trunk as a club and wears a rope belt with three full-size sheep dangling from it around his huge girth. The grotesque and ponderous giant is intimidating, to be sure, but in Jamie's rendition, he seems as unfortunate and laughable as he does scary, and the young reader is assured that the curious Jack will be able to outwit him.

## 57. THE TINDERBOX

*The Tinderbox*, one of the first fairy tales written by Hans Christian Andersen, appeared in *Eventyr, fortalte for Born*, published in Copenhagen on 8 May 1835; it was based on a Scandinavian folktale that Andersen had loved as a child.[27] In author Peggy Thomson's retelling of this time-honored story,[28] a handsome but weary soldier,

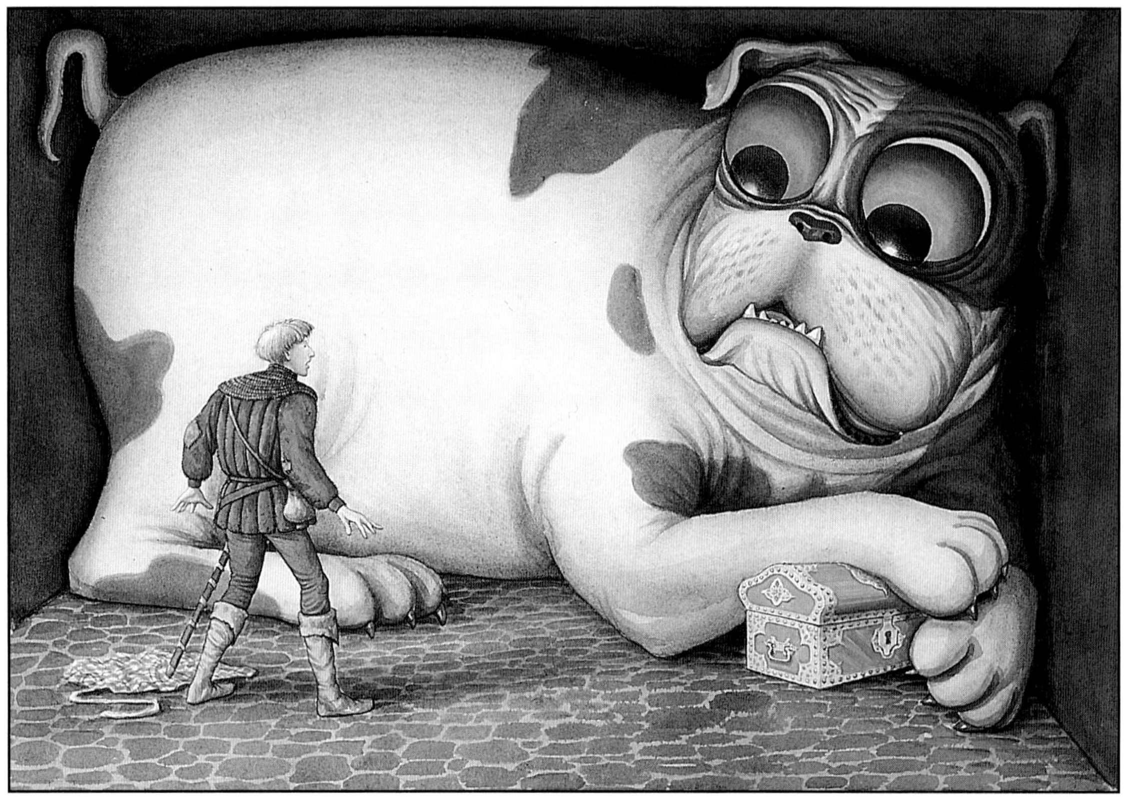



returning home from the war, is confronted by an ugly wart-covered witch, who asks him to retrieve a tinderbox from the hollow of an old oak tree. The soldier agrees to help, and, in the course of his quest, encounters a series of three huge dogs guarding the treasure.

Warhola produces a striking blend of fantasy and humor in his depiction of a confrontation between the soldier and one of the giant canines. Standing on a cobblestone floor, the unexpectedly dwarfed man seems startled by the gigantic spotted dog clutching a red and gold tinderbox in its massive paws. The dog's luminous, electric-green eyes stand out against the artist's otherwise modulated palette and recall the psychedelic colors used by many Pop artists of the 1960s, including Andy Warhol (e.g., the hot pink and lemon yellow of Warhol's silkscreened *Cow Wallpaper* of 1966). Jamie's dog, Zonker, served as the inspiration for his figure, which he rendered as lovable and huggable as his own pet.

## 58. THE BRAVE LITTLE TAILOR

Along with Hans Christian Andersen of Denmark and Charles Perrault of France, the most famous writers of fairy tales were Wilhelm and Jacob Grimm, who issued their collection of folktales in Germany early in the nineteenth century. *Kinder-und Hausmärchen*, published by the Brothers Grimm in 1812 and 1815, collected tales not only from contemporary storytellers and from various local regions, but also material preserved from earlier, even prehistoric, times.[29] The Grimms were careful to distinguish the fairy tale from the legend, in that they considered the latter to be bound to physical places or to historical heroes. By contrast, fairy tales are not specific to any one geographical location or time, and thus possess a timelessness and universality that insure their immortality.

*The Brave Little Tailor*, based on a classic Grimm Brothers fairy tale, was retold by Peggy Thomson in 1992 and illustrated by James Warhola;[30] it marked their second collaboration on a children's book (cf. cat. #57). Jamie's indebtedness to his family's European heritage and his lifelong interest in Medieval castles are evident in his first illustration for the story—a detailed composition of the quaint village surrounding "Ye Lil' Tailor" shop. The half-timber buildings, adorned with shuttered windows and flowerboxes, provide a fitting locale for the townspeople going about their daily occupations. The artist employs a delicate pastel palette of warm apricot hues for the townscape and a pale, moisture-laden blue for the misty turrets of a castle rising in the background. Warhola drew from his own experiences to create this inviting composition. He reveals, "I traveled throughout Europe, doing sketches and taking a lot of photographs of old towns and castles."[31] Among the most noteworthy of his artistic sojourns was a trip to the ancestral villages of the Warhola family in Slovakia in October 1991.[32]

## 59. HURRICANE CITY

In *Hurricane City* of 1993, author Sarah Weeks uses humor in her original story to help children deal with unexpected chaos.[33] Her rhyming alphabet book describes hurricanes, from Alvin to Zack, that blow through the imaginary town. The wild winds, both big and small, blow about cats and dogs, cars and houses, and even an entire family. But everyone successfully deals with the never-ending turmoil, and to a young reader's comfort, no one is hurt.

A child cannot fully appreciate the complete meaning of a story by reading only the words. To communicate the author's ideas, a careful balance between the text and the

58. James Warhola
   Illustration for *The Brave Little Tailor* c. 1992
   Watercolor on paper
   15 x 22 1/2

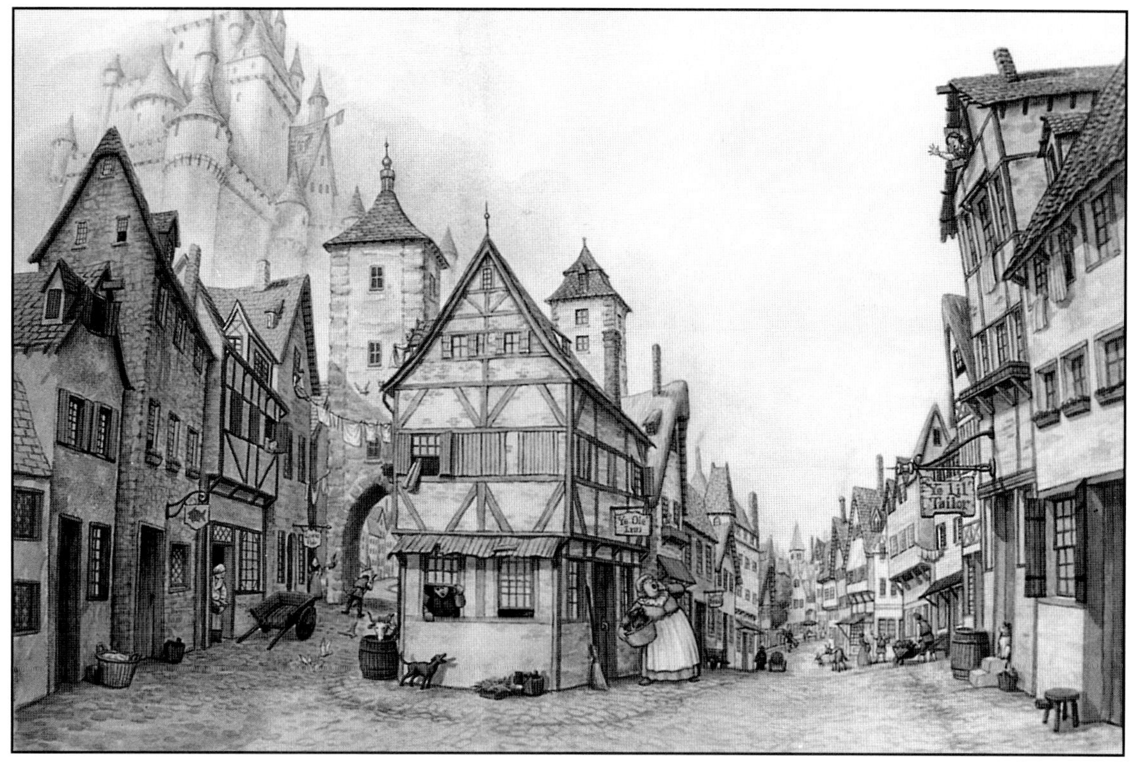

illustrations is needed. A children's book illustration thus recounts the story in a series of readily comprehensible pictures; the precise techniques of composition, color, line, and shape all must communicate the literary intent, as well as the mood of the author.[34] With only short rhymes on each page, Jamie Warhola's illustrations must indeed carry the burden of *Hurricane City*'s narrative.

One of the most endearing illustrations in the book is the depiction for the letter P: "Hurricane Pete rained cats and dogs and cows and geese and fish and frogs." It is a captivating portrayal of brightly colored, cuddly animals tumbling from the sky in a shower of joy. Their exuberant facial expressions and ebullient poses give us a look into their amiable personalities and set a light-hearted tone amidst the meteorological disasters.

The effectiveness of Jamie's illustrations has been recognized; *Hurricane City* was awarded the Nineteenth Annual Georgia Childrens' Picture Book Award in April 1996.

## 60. SOUTHEAST ASIA SKETCHBOOK

Jamie began traveling with a sketchbook in 1976, when he spent two months touring Europe, prior to his graduation from Carnegie-Mellon University. He returned to England in the 1980s, and commencing in December 1989, made a memorable journey to Southeast Asia, visiting Vietnam and other exotic locales. He recorded the sights and experiences of his trip in a two-month visual diary, dating from 15 December 1990 to 10 February 1991.[35]

On each leg of his journey, Warhola was inspired to sketch the people, places, and moments that captured his interest. These range from children in a small village or riding on a bus, to a woman merchant outside a train station, to a man named Tom, whom the artist identified in his diary as "our most loyal guide and friend." He depicted a boat on the beach at Teluk Beheng, Malaysia on 8 January 1991, a serene beach at Hōan Chōng on the 20th, and a narrow street that he described as going "every which way" in Bhaktapur, Nepal on 5 February. Other noteworthy scenes in the sketchbook include views from a cafe where Warhola awaited a train that arrived four hours late, and a canalside in Hue along which he bicycled. All his experiences were rendered simply, yet precisely, on the spot, in either detailed pencil sketches or delicate watercolors. The depth and range of his drawings capture the splendors of the Asian landscape and culture, and impart to us the quiet moods of the local people, for whom the artist clearly feels a profound appreciation.

59. James Warhola
   Illustration for *Hurricane City* c. 1993
   Watercolor on paper
   11 1/2 x 13 1/4

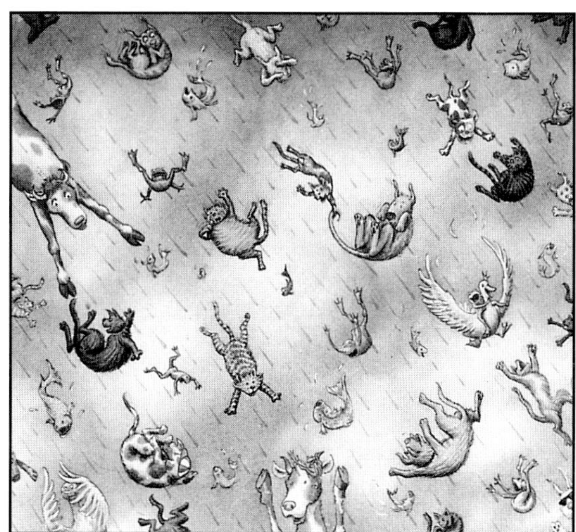

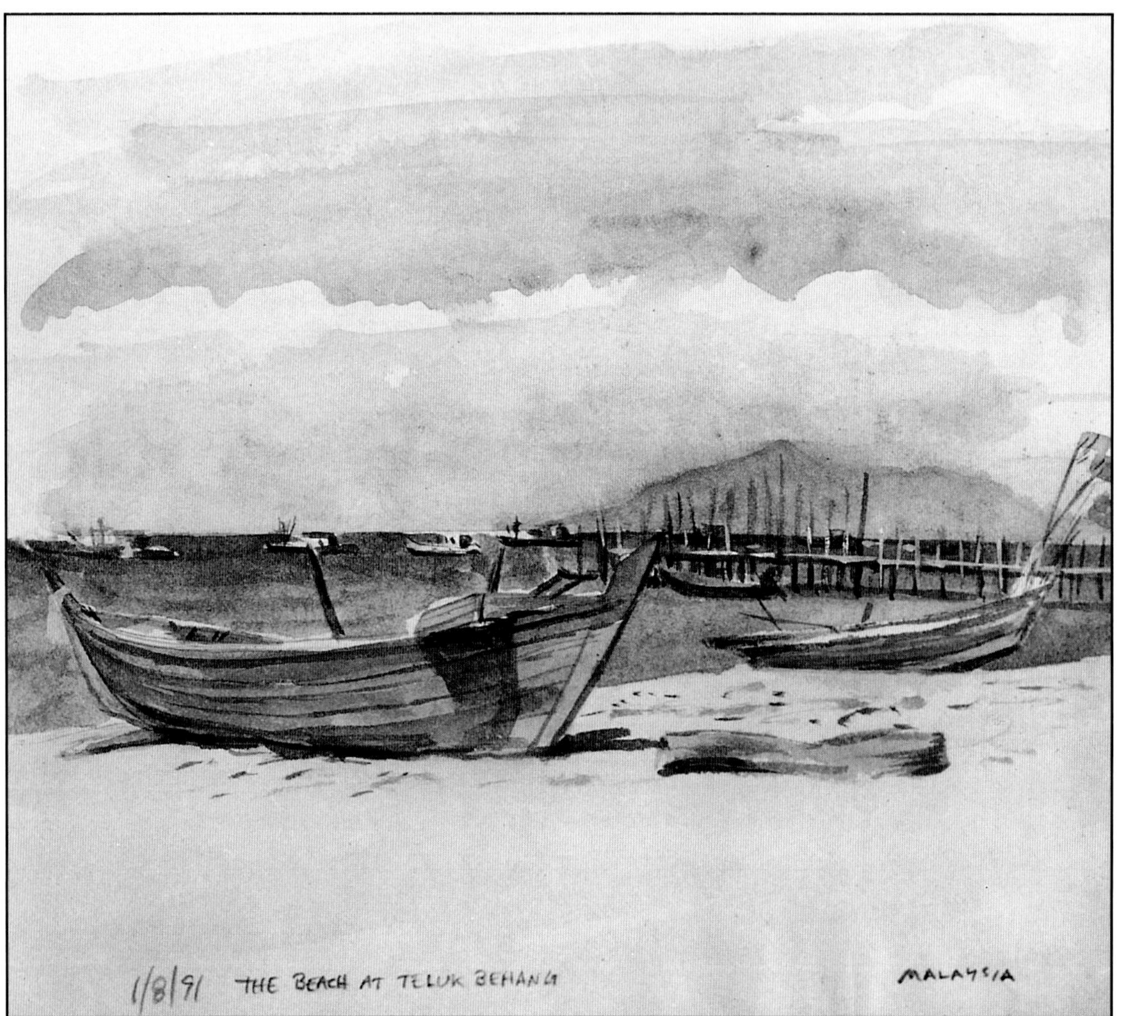



60. James Warhola
Page from *Southeast
Asia Sketchbook*
c. 1990-91
Pencil and watercolor on
bound and unbound
paper
7 x 8

# A MOVIE, IMAGINARY AND TRUE: HISTORY BETWEEN THE LINES by Gerard Malanga

1963—the year is shortly coming to a close. Billy is living in the Lower East Side with a group of young people, aspiring artists and dancers, who are all into amphetamines and one of the things about taking amphetamine it makes you talk a lot or you get obsessed with doing something and you keep doing it without stopping and what happened to Billy was that he started tin-foiling his entire apartment—the walls and ceiling. The wooden floor was sprayed silver too.

Andy and I enter. Here is Billy and Freddy Herko and Johnny Dodd and Søren Agenoux and Ondine…several others flit through the rooms. It's an afternoon get-together…a hair-cut party. (I had already known Ondine and Søren—at least a year before I met Andy—through parties given at a loft on Bond Street John MacDermott and "Mr. Clean" were renting.)

When Andy and I moved into the Factory (November '63) Billy arrived one day to visit and Andy said, "Well, maybe you'd like to paint the place silver?"

■

On a grey, chill morning 1969, Billy Name is seen at the Factory writing a note for Warhol, which reads "ANDY—I AM NOT HERE ANYMORE BUT I AM FINE LOVE, BILLY." He then locks up, descends by elevator, leaving behind a place and people he called home for five years. He mingles with the morning rush-hour traffic, not to be seen or heard from again. SLOW FADE-OUT. CUT to black and white. Billy, in head-shot close-up, looks directly into the camera. He begins reminiscing on his past life living at the Warhol Factory 30-seconds into the shot and then a slow FADE-OUT, synchronized to a voice-over dissolve, begins to merge with a muted color FADE-IN, flashing back to October 1966. Billy, with aerosol in hand, is spraying an empty factory space silver, wrapping the support-columns with silver tinfoil. Splintering sunlight adds to the already thick, dusty atmosphere. In the background, a record of a Maria Callas aria from Puccini's "La Boheme" mingles with street noises. The camera slowly swivels on a 180° pan, taking in the entire width and depth of the space. Off to one side, a beautiful fashion model in Khadejha print dress—Benedetta Barzini—is seemingly lost in concentration applying make-up in front of a stained and cracked mirror fixed above a seedy wash basin. In a far corner, Andy and Gerard, uninterrupted by a sudden outburst of conversation off-camera, are preparing to silkscreen a canvas. CUT to close-up of the work at hand. The Factory is a buzz of seemingly disconnected activities. Everything appears genuinely mundane on the surface, but beneath lurks an incredible surge of creative energy that will change the course of American culture. A new history of art is in the making. These people are unaware of the consequences.

■

Michael Katz, a photographer living on East 7th Street in the Lower East Side, has arranged to make a group portrait of some of his friends and their friends. As I recall it was at Ondine's urging that I be included in the picture. I had hung out with a few of those present, shared their amphetamine, was welcomed into their group—what I referred to at the time as the 'dawn patrol.'

I'll attempt to identify as many as I can remember of those present. John Daley, this writer, Michael Smith, Ondine, Norman Billiard Balls, Billy Name, Charles Stanley, Dorothy Podber, Binghamton Birdie, and Freddy Herko. Today there are only a few faces to join past and present. First Freddy died. Hallucinating that he could fly, Freddy took a balletic leap through the window of Johnny Dodd's 4th floor flat on Cornelia Street in the West Village, landing on the hood of a parked car. Charles Stanley also a suicide. John Daley has since died… Norman Billiard Balls… Ondine… and now I hear Michael Smith too. Johnny Dodd, Jimmy Waring, conspicuously absent from this picture, also dead. And Søren Agenoux. I never knew what became of John MacDermott or Mr. Clean.

■

January 1992, Billy comes to visit. We're now "country neighbors" he tells me. So are Allen Midgette and Jamie Warhola. Upstate New York, the Berkshires of western Massachusetts, about 45 miles as the crow flies through distance and time—a reality "separate" from Manhattan's misty, white pre-dawn light. Over dinner Billy confesses that he—not Andy as I'd always assumed—had, "out of jealousy," crossed out my name on the photo-ready mechanical for the *Index Book*'s title page, 1967, at which time I'd been living in Rome.

And I'm thinking Goethe: Not everything that history offers us has actually happened. And what has actually happened has not happened the way it is presented, and what we know to have happened is only a very small part of what actually happened.

■

This photograph may not be—etc.
This photograph, like so many others, dissolves.
Other photographs take its place.
A whole trunkful.
Other times, other faces.
The future looms.

*Gerard Malanga is a poet, photographer, filmmaker, and archivist. He was one of Andy Warhol's most important collaborators in the 1960s.*

# BILLY NAME (A PORTRAIT)

by Robert Heide

I first met Billy Linich, who later became Billy Name and who now sometimes refers to himself as Billy Goat, at the San Remo Bar in the early 1960s. 'The Remo,' as the regulars called it, was actually called 'The San Remo Cafe' for some reason or other, and had a separate dining room where excellent Italian food was served. It was located at 93 MacDougal Street at the corner of Bleecker Street; and the bar was a popular hangout for oldtime Village characters like Maxwell Bodenheim and Joe Gould, as well as for celebrities like Tennessee Williams, Edward Albee, W.H. Auden, Leonard Bernstein, Ned Rorem, Simone Signoret, Shirley Stoler, Judith Malina, Julian Beck, and others. It also attracted the beat crowd, including Allen Ginsberg, Gregory Corso, Peter Orlowsky, Jack Kerouac, and Taylor Mead, who were then reading their poetry in the MacDougal Street coffee houses. Arty, theatrically inclined, and ambitious gay young men were part of the colorful atmosphere that was an integral part of the dazzling crowd that frequented this watering hole with its bright yellow lights, Art Deco bar, and polished wood booths. One night sipping a Stinger at 'The Remo' with Edward Albee, Ron Link came in with Billy. Ron (who later directed many of Tom Eyen's plays, some of which starred Divine, Jackie Curtis, Candy Darling, and Melba LaRose, Jr.) and Billy were working in those days as waiters at Serendipity 3, the uptown-boutique-restaurant. Billy was startlingly handsome, lean, wiry, with a strange intensity that was instantly appealing. He was very inquisitive about my interest in Existentialists like Jean Paul Sartre, Albert Camus, and Heidegger. At that time many young Bohemian writers and poets were emulating the intellectual world of the Left Bank in Paris; and if you were not reading Sartre's "Being and Nothingness" or Gertrude Stein's "The Making of Americans" you were listening to the recordings of Juliette Greco or Edith Piaf. Cocteau's movie *Orphée* with Jean Marais and Eduoard Dermitt depicted intellectual French café life and on MacDougal Street in the Sixties it was not unlike the scenes depicted in the movie. Juliet Greco the singer was also in *Orphée* and I recommended that Billy go see it, as well as *Les Enfants Terribles*. There was a wildness in the air then, a yearning to be free, a desire to experience everything and to challenge and to push life to its limits. In this sense Billy and I became fast friends and developed a dynamic and intimate relationship, albeit short-lived. Billy had a childlike sensitivity that was coupled with an inner strength and determination. A play of mine called *Hector* was produced at the Cherry Lane Theater along with a play called *Pericles* by the poet Kenneth Koch and Jean Cocteau's *Marriage on the Eiffel Tower*. Nick (or Nicola) Cernovich, who had been the lighting designer for the Living Theater and James Waring's dance group, had directed *Pericles* and *Hector;* and Nick was very 'interested' in Billy when I introduced them to one another. Nick felt, as I had, that this was someone who possessed unique and special qualities. While Billy and I had discussed Sartrian concepts like 'The Non-Being of Being' or 'The Being of Non-Being' as well as the need to choose 'Being Against the Non-Being-Nothingness,' Nick was a follower of Zen mysticism. When Billy went off to live with Nick, one aspect of the relationship was

Zen teacher and Zen student, Nick being the older, more practiced and formidable of the two. They both worked at the Zen bookstore; and Billy began reading Zen books and following the Eastern way. Somehow at that time I could never wed the idea of Nothingness (Existential) with Emptiness (the Zen term), although I am sure from today's vantage point that they are both the same in principle. Billy ran with Zen-scavenger Pop-collagist Ray Johnson and his girlfriend Dorothy Podber, who were exponents of 'the real' and 'the surreal' in art as well as in life. Once this bewitched pair presented me a clock with no hands on its face and inside the clock they had placed a dead rat sprayed gold. I thought this 'prank' to be very Marcel Duchampian in character; but they were more or less followers of John Cage.

When Nick Cernovich married in Judson Church Billy was present but seemed ashen, almost as if it were a funeral rather than a wedding he was attending. Nick had been going to a psychotherapist who somehow convinced him that he needed to resolve his sexual conflicts; and for Nick a heterosexual marriage seemed to be the answer. Although Nick was smiling at the wedding, he also seemed nervous and gaunt as he left Linich in the lurch in the church. Following this scary sacred event Billy really began to run wild; and seemed to be having a good time of it. He moved to the Lower East Side, got into the hallucinogenic scene and played 'Surfin' Bird' type music at his parties. There always seemed to be a lot of mescaline or LSD or speed around and I remember still the blanked-out staring eyes of John Daley, Freddy Herko, Walter Dainwood, and Søren Agenoux at some of these all-night all-day parties. Everyone was as thin as a reed; and no one bothered to eat. At one of these parties I saw a white ghost in a grey wig that at first looked like an apparition. Wearing dark glasses and standing absolutely still as if frozen in space and time, I realized that it was not the ghost of Alexander Hamilton in a powdered wig, but Andy Warhol. Previously I had met Andy through Edward Wallowitch, the photographer who had given Andy some of his photographs to use on his silkscreens.

"Oh, hi!" Andy said, acknowledging my presence, "Do you know Billy? What do you think of him?"

I could see that Andy was fascinated by Billy and was attracted also to the manic energy of the young men in the room. Shortly after this, Billy Linich, 'christened' Billy Name by Lord Andy, was at Andy's factory all the time and soon he was living there. He painted it silver and covered everything in Reynolds Wrap just as he had his own apartment in the East Village. Billy, like Gerard Malanga, became a fixture at the Silver Factory, making silkscreens with Andy and giving him ideas.

"Oh, what'll we do today?" Andy would ask.

"How about cow-wallpaper?" Billy would chime in.

"Yeah, that's a good idea," Andy cooed.

Billy also appeared in the early films and like Andy, his new mentor, he always had a camera slung over his shoulder. He would snap and click away as Andy filmed whatever was going on. Andy and Billy had a common bond in their understanding of Zen Emptiness and Zen Repetition as a concept in art. Andy once said he would like to have painted a bowl of fruit or a vase filled with flowers like one of the old masters; but what he remembered as the primary icon of his childhood was a can of Campbell's Tomato Soup. Andy's mother always kept her pantry filled with Campbell's Soup; and even in his later years would open up a can for Andy, heat it, and serve it along with a tunafish salad sandwich on Wonderbread toast.

At the Factory, at parties there and elsewhere, Billy and I often looked at one another and would burst out laughing at the absurdity of it all. At one point I knew Billy, heavily into drugs, moved into the Factory closet and barely communicated with anyone. Had he found Nirvana? Nobody knew where Billy was at, mentally speaking. Andy feared Billy would kill himself, and did not want anyone to disturb him. One day I was told Billy ran off; and for a long time no one knew where he had gone. It turned out he went back home to Poughkeepsie in an attempt to clean up his act.

Following Andy's memorial at St. Patrick's Cathedral on April 1, 1987, at the party at the old Billy Rose's Diamond Horseshoe, a large man in a lumberjack's shirt came up to me and grabbed my hand, squeezing it painfully. At first I did not recognize him and he said, "It's me, Billy."

It seemed like a miracle. He somehow had survived whatever ordeal he had been through; and there he was at the funeral party co-mingling with the strange mixture of latter-day Warhol friends like Calvin Klein, Claus von Bulow, Debbie Harry, Yoko Ono, and some of the old-timers who had also survived, like Jane Holzer, Brigid

Berlin, Gerard Malanga, Taylor Mead, myself, and others. After the party Billy and I headed for the Village and stopped at Jean's Patio on Greenwich Avenue to talk and to reminisce. Since that time Billy has emerged a new, stronger, more confident self; and the spark of an old friendship is still burning. When a trunk of old Factory photos that had disappeared was later returned to Billy, these were to become important historic and artistic documents; and out of these and other photographs the genius of Billy Name is finally being recognized in galleries and in published book form.

Recently I saw a photo of myself taken by Billy at the Factory on the set of *Dracula*. In this Warhol movie and in the Billy Name photos I am wearing a hat that reads "Suicide" on it. Jack Smith played Dracula (also called *Batman/Dracula*) and there I am opposite another of the great legends. I knew Andy had filmed my play *The Bed* and I remember writing the *Lupe* scenario for Edie Sedgwick, but had forgotten all about *Dracula*. What were we all on when we made that one, I asked myself. In it too is my old cohort Ron Link who now lives in L.A. He also has little recall about making this Warhol movie. So are we all Warhol Superstars now? Did we have our 15 minutes of fame in a Warhol film? In any case, I can thank Billy Name, a giant Buddha of a man and an artist in the truest sense, for bringing it all back home—full circle!

*Robert Heide is a playwright and writer. He was a friend of Andy Warhol's and contributed scenarios for two of his films,* The Bed *and* Lupe.

# TRAVELING WITH THE G

by Ira Cohen

It was hard to begin, full of surprises, an on-going journey without an end. This is about unexpected affinities, wayward mirrors and above all about friendship, a double feature of stars on a binary axis. Gerard thinks Mutt and Jeff, I think Rasputin and Lord Byron, unlikely brothers, a pair of funny buglers, almost never meeting between "Reveille" and "Taps". It took years before we ever had a real conversation, like we were working different shifts. When I arrived, he was just leaving. When he showed up, I was already on my way. I remember the first time I saw him. It was in the mid-Sixties at Paolo Lionni's pad on 11th Street. Piero Heliczer and Angus MacLise were in the wings. Gerard came in with blond hair. He was bringing something over or taking something away. I was just cruising, wondering who is this guy anyway. We probably said Hello and Goodbye. I thought he was a hustler: Who knows what he thought I was, maybe an uncashed bank draft returned from Tangier. I didn't recognize him then, couldn't figure him out. I knew he was involved with Warhol, which for me made him suspect right away. But then he was also connected with Angus, whom I had recently met with Araby in Paris around the Conrescarpe near a building on the Rue Mouffetard, which had a plaque that said Dante had lived there. Piero showed up in Tangier where we cast clothespin oracles together on the roof of my house in Dar Baroud sitting on sheepskins. Raphael says it's like crocheting. Maybe I thought of Gerard as a young Mme. DeFarge. I know he still thinks of me as a collector of Peacock jewels. We're talking 25 years here and of course we were all young men in the time that Jack Smith called his golden period. Gerard, though younger than me by seven or eight years, was always precocious. Though I didn't really know his work, I knew he had made a mark as a poet and editor and as a performer too. He was also making films, maybe just beginning as a photographer. I had done *GNAOUA* in Tangier, a magazine which featured Burroughs, Gysin, Jack Smith and Irving Rosenthal, was getting out the Jilala record (Moroccan Sufi trance music), *The Hashish Cookbook* (a collabaoration with Rosalind under the pseudonym of Panama Rose) and *The Great Society*, another magazine with Bobby Richkin. Gerard was the Grand Vizier at Warhol's Factory. I was standing around at Jack Smith's with an elephant tusk in my arms, attracted by the glamour and the glitter, preparing to move into my own loft on Jefferson Street, where I initiated the Universal Mutant Repertory Company and began The Great Mylar Adventure. I was the prodigal returned, while Gerard was carefully laying a foundation for the future. The truth is I never returned. Somehow I took the Casbah with me, wore it like a hat, its brim covered with burning candles.

Now during this period born of Film Culture and Renaissance dreams, I had only peripheral contact with Gerard, maybe saw him do his whip dance at the Electric Circus or saw him pasted in the corner of Charles Henri Ford's Dakota salon, where Andy also came with powdered wig and putty nose, and we all ogled each other while Charles pulled the strings. Yet we were already creating our circle without even trying. *Magnetic lines of force attract & repel/while we spiral around the sun/trifling w/psychic gravity* was how my poem began. But the thing of it was that we were all on the same trajectory, a kind of post-beat multimedia electronic shamanism. A common vision pulled us all into unique collaborations. Maverick magicians, we sought to express ourselves in many ways and I, too, went from editing and poetry, to photography and filmmaking. Although I didn't quite realize it at the time, I can see now that Charles Henri was our natural precursor, a living ancestor and Aquarian catalyst (*Can't you hear those feathered feet stamping in the abandoned subway of history?*) During this period Charles and Gerard were constantly together. It was Charles who first introduced Gerard to Andy. I can remember Charles and Gerard coming over to check out the Mylar chamber. Charles too was all things and knew everybody, a surrealist high priest who played with a full deck on a multiple stage.

In another time, and I'm talking about the Seventies, Charles and I became really close friends. That was in Kathmandu and Angus was there keeping it all together with his music. What I am now to Charles or to Timothy Baum in the way of friendship, Gerard was then. I see how many experiences, how many friendships we shared, have overlapped. What is the common denominator, our preoccupations, something not quite definable in our personalities? The things I most value in Gerard are his loyalty and integrity, the way in which he always comes through, his ultimate responsibility. He likes to call himself an archivist. I call him Keeper of the Flame. For me it is the AKASHIC RECORD and the main catalogue is in my head. Gerard is nothing if not methodical. My method is closer to madness. Where can I go from here? Like Gerard knows the histories, the lineages, how important a role has been played by Robert LaVigne or Billy Batman, Peter Hartman or Johnny Dodd. He is in fact a witness and a repository—and he takes care of business.

Now I'd like to jump around like our lives, be my own man, let memory guide my steps to the moment we met in Dharamsala in a Tibetan restaurant. He was dressed in white, I was all in black. He was printing poems on light—did I say he, we, were light gatherers and that it was raining? I was printing books in Nepal on rice paper. I think it was then that we really recognized each other. He was traveling with Eileen Taft, also in white. I was with Petra, also in black. Like two pilgrims going around the same stupa counter-clockwise to each other we knew we were yet on the same path. And we went our separate ways, meeting once more in India somewhere on Connaught Circle in New Delhi. From a single stone cast into the water the circles continued to fan out. Gerard returned to New York, where he maintained himself precariously, staying in the scene, but not of it. First and foremost he remained a poet with a conscience which, grounded in fidelity to his own work and that of his friends, imposed upon him a certain isolation common to his calling. He who had enjoyed the rank of Warhol's Prime Minister became a Minister without Portfolio, an unofficial chronicler of his time. I remained in Nepal and India, where in the company of our mutual friends Angus and Hetty MacLise, Charles Henri Ford, and Petra Vogt (former member of the Living Theatre and resident Kali), I continued the Universal Mutant agenda publishing books under the imprint of Bardo Matrix and immersing myself in the study of Tantra. It was a magical time and we lived in gardens of our own mythology, where we pursued the ancient arts of cloud watching and shadow reading. And so I spent years in the fabled land of Shangri-La, where it sometimes seemed as if we would go on forever, but there in the land of the gods we finally came face to face with our own mortality. Gerard had been writing to me and to Angus, asking for contributions to the special Piero Heliczer issue of *Little Caesar*, which he was editing, when Angus's candle blew out. Somehow it was Angus whom I thought of as *Strider*, a kind of Indian Scout or Hermetic Messenger, who was the natural connection between all of us. Angus who went endlessly down the years and through the long nights from my place to Don Snyder's, over to Sheldon Rochlin's and to Tony and Beverly Conrad's 42nd Street loft, out to Jerry Joffen's in Brooklyn for a pick-me-up, past LaMonte and Marion's and over to Jack's place. Angus was even with Gerard at the Factory when Andy was shot. And now in Kathmandu I watched his body go up in flames, his pyre tended by friends and a gathering of Tibetan monks. When I looked into his cracked skull and watched the magnificent coils of pink brain slowly turn into indescribable nothingness floating away on the air, I knew it was the end of an era.

It was not long after Angus's death that I was to leave Nepal for Greece and then Amsterdam, where I met up with Gerard at One World Poetry Festival in 1979. Our correspondence over Piero's *Festschrift* and the special feelings we shared in regard to Angus's death had already served to bring us closer than we had ever been before. Ironically it was Angus once again, even in death, who provided the essential link. From the very first moment of our meeting in Amsterdam we were on a common wavelength. Gerard was planning the Angus MacLise Archive and together we conceived *Operation Angus*, which was completed by Gerard in New York for the Dia Art Foundation, bringing together the definitive collection of Angus's writings, music, calligraphies, and other related materials. We became charter members of the Amsterdam Dawn Patrol, staying up all night and singing to the sun as it rose over Rembrandt canals in the red-light district. Then I decided to document the festival with Caroline Gosselin by making life masks of all the poets and photographing the process. Gerard assisted in every way he could, giving encouragement and documenting the documentation. By the way, photographing with Gerard turned out to be a rare pleasure, a collaborative adventure untainted by elbows and competitive problems almost unavoidable when two photographers try to occupy a single space. He wrote a poem called "Genealogies," a cat's cradle of shared connections which was printed in Eddie Woods' magazine, *INS & OUTS*, with some 21 photos I supplied, making the poem into a true collaboration of words and images, conceptual photos and all the words we repeated to each other from day to day. We traded photos, scrapbooks, information, and let's call it love, rounded off with respect and reciprocity. When Gerard left and I remained in Amsterdam we stayed in contact through the mail. I decided to send Gerard a postcard everyday for at least a month. And before I was finished (and I'm still not finished) I must have sent him 60 or 70 postcards filled with every thought I would never otherwise have written down, a kind of accordion-foldout

of Dutch Treats, Cardboard Dreams, Funny Fragments, Odes to Glibness—and of course it was Gerard who called it forth and in this way he became my ear and I the stoker of his archival mania.

And now I sit here in New York City writing something called "Traveling with the G," getting at the essence of what it's all about, the G and me. Am I the I, the witness (eye) to Gerard's Gee? We have given readings together, shown our films together, made a completion of sorts from opposite sides of a field, meeting in the middle, which is where we started from. Now we talk on the phone—a recent conversation about Jack Smith just before he died was recorded by Gerard and condensed into an article of faith. When I bring back photographs from Japan or Ethiopia I show Gerard the contact-sheets. I hardly know anyone else I trust who knows how to look at a contact-sheet. Gerard takes everything *al dente*. I remember when we went to the Sterling Lord Agency in search of Kerouac's legendary scrolled manuscript of *On the Road* and I photographed Gerard making photographs of the text, or going to Albany to see Robert Creeley named official poet of New York State, passing a single top hat back and forth until it landed on Creeley's head unofficially crowning the day. In Afghanistan they say *Malang* when they refer to a man who is God mad, in other words, divinely obsessed. I once met a *Malang* who ran every day some ten kilometers from Balkh to the mosque of Sidi Ali in Mazar Sharif and back again. Then at a Mexican grocery store in San Francisco I discovered a tuber called a *Malanga*. It had the shape of a lingam covered with hair and smelling of the earth from which it came. Does this tell me anything about Gerard, that he is divinely obsessed, that he is of the earth, that he generates, that he is stubborn and will persist? Gerard is on the ball and the ball is always revolving. It takes a special kind of balance to stay on the ball without falling off. I remember Gerard jumping down on the subway tracks for a nickel because he needed the nickel to get home. If I am the madman, does that make him sane? I remember Gerard spending his last few coins on a small can of stringbeans and going home alone on New Year's Eve. Is that vanity or is it self-sufficiency? Gerard, who has been around and seen it all, remains for me an innocent, an easy mark; and yet he is as precise a jeweler as anyone I know, a connoisseur of diamonds. The life of the artist is not easy and to meet another artist who will pick you up when you are down, who knows how to laugh at life's absurdity, that is rare indeed. One of Gerard's favorite expressions— "That's funny"—he always says in his most serious tone. It never fails to bring a smile to my lips. Yes, Gerard, it really is funny and it is serious at the same time. You are a tender mirror and I don't know anymore if this piece is truly about you or maybe it's about me. I guess it's about the two of us and implies something further about how relationships work, the importance of an other.

What if you really are Napoleon? Let the cameras roll and on with the movie! *We begin in exile and go back past Waterloo to discover the origins of our common aspiration.*

*Ira Cohen is a poet and photographer. He has been an important presence in New York's literary avant-garde since the 1950s.*

# A VIEW FROM THE SEVENTIES: REFLECTIONS ON THE PHOTOGRAPHY OF MAKOS, MALANGA, AND NAME

by Sur Rodney (Sur)

It was the beginning of New York City's New Wave in art, cinema, and music. Performance art was becoming popular, taking on a new attitude. Never clearly identified or labeled, the scene was somewhat punk, or pre-punk, but it was constantly mutating, without any structured political edge. This wasn't London—we didn't have a Queen—but we did have the Mudd Club and CBGB's. And it was the night clubs that were the incubators and centers of popular art and creative social life. In the midst of it all, the photographers—both inside and outside of this cultural New Wave—were its documentors and image makers, popularizing its new and rediscovered celebrities and exposing them to the mainstream American public. At the time, c. 1978, I was creating my own scene by producing photography exhibitions in a basement gallery in Soho. It became a focal point for my introduction to a number of artists/photographers and performers, prior to my association with the Gracie Mansion Gallery.

One of the most notable and active photographers of this era was Christopher Makos, whose works betray a fascination with the club-goers, celebrities, and fashion athletes of his generation. His photographs of the Seventies were based on image modeling; they provided ideal material for the media and, consequently, they flooded the popular press and had a major impact on giving a face and a style to the New Wave. Makos's success and recognition for modeling icons of the American popular culture of the 1970s, '80s, and '90s are well deserved. His visual documents will remain the most familiar images of our social history and taste for generations to come.

My primary preoccupation in 1978 was with finding contemporary artists who were experimenting with the photographic image. It was during this period that I was introduced, through a phone call, to Gerard Malanga. Gerard was interested in presenting a photographic wall installation in a show I was organizing at the time. He was known, of course, for his involvement with Warhol's Factory, while he continued to strengthen his own renown as a poet. His most famous photographs documented his central participation in those worlds of art and literary culture. But Malanga's poetic contribution to my exhibition—a head-shot of a female model cut into quarters, then naturally draped from supporting push pins—produced a unique vision from his extensive photographic archive. It would signal the direction his photography would follow in the future.

Upon Malanga's arrival to install his artwork, he presented me with a newly released book of his poetry entitled *100 years have passed*. What most immediately fascinated me about his book was the photo reproduced on its cover, credited to Billy Name (aka Billy Linich). The photo credit was written in the form of a brief bio, the closing line stating that the photographer's whereabouts were unknown. The mystery of Billy Name and the mysteriousness of his photographic image remained with me for years. I found a surreal quality in his style, created by the unusual contrast of subject to background and the graphic effects of his lighting. The picture read more like a Xerox than a photograph; it possessed a dreamlike sensibility. I wanted to see more. My interest in the photography of Billy Name stood firmly on the impact of this one image. Years later, c. 1989-90, I was finally to become acquainted with the photographer and his artistic concerns through a mutual friend.

Billy Name's photographs are about light and shape. For me, the ones I find most interesting have me examining something to be learned about photographs, invisible barriers, and their place in time—both the shutter speed's and the viewers'. When Billy Name takes a picture, he operates on his senses feeling—how he senses and feels through the camera, and how the physical form of the camera responds to his method. His results are not truly realized until worked in the darkroom. It is here that the greatest events come into play: the resolution of these images composed with the available light of the environment (exposure); the way in which the photograph is printed (chemistry); the choice of paper (texture); and how it is cropped and/or framed (composition). In the final product, the actual subject of a Billy Name photograph is less significant than the abstract qualities of photography.

All three photographers—Christopher Makos, Gerard Malanga, and Billy Name—are important for their contributions to documenting the social history and popular culture of which they were, and are, an integral part. They remain of interest for the ways in which they participate in the experimental aspects and artistry of photography, be it image modeling (Makos), poetic vision (Malanga), or abstraction (Name).

*Sur Rodney (Sur) is an archivist and writer; he lives in New York.*

# A RECOLLECTION BY GEORGE WARHOLA

as told to Maria Warhola

I sat on the bed watching him dress. I did that on most any evening when he was getting ready to go out for the evening—all evening. It was grand theater. He would bathe, then shave. I particularly liked the way he shaved, very methodically. And then the cologne; there were several hundred standing like soldiers at attention on the dresser, on the floor, in the bathroom. But the most memorable of all was the 10-gallon bottle of Chanel No. 5. He liked that one best of all. Then came the pantyhose. He liked them because they kept him warm. Always the best blue jeans, a turtleneck sweater, a shirt (maybe a tie), and the best tailored jacket (wool, of course), the best shoes. After all of that, as I lay on the bed—that big bed—staring at the huge Twombly with all of its circular movements and the Lautrec cyclist speeding off to the edge of the canvas, I would ask him where he was off to. He wouldn't answer immediately, making me even more curious, and then answered, "Oh, just out!" Always a let down. But I knew it would be someplace exciting, perhaps too exciting. Then he would say good night. I would not see him until the following afternoon. I remember these moments as though they were yesterday. I was only twelve then; my uncle, Andy Warhol, was 38.

This was just one of many evenings that I would recall as a child and then later on as a young man. My summers were spent in the home of my uncle and grandmother, Julia. Those years were happy ones. This was the beginning of my uncle's career, and I could see his genius even then. I know I was only a child, but his constant creativity was never put aside. There were so many canvases and paintings all over the house, one never knew when he would stop or slow down his creative process. I don't imagine he really ever did.

There was another child observing and learning about the world of art, of creativity—my younger brother, James Warhola. He became a part of my many observations of Uncle Andy. He too would watch in amazement the creative genius of our uncle; only with Jamie, it continued on in his own work. As a young boy he would participate in a program for young people that were interested in art, just as Uncle Andy had done when he was a young boy. It was called the "Tam O'Shanters." James never wavered in his outlook on life and what his future would hold: to create on canvas, or paper, or any material that came to hand.

Now he is the one who will carry on the work (his own, of course) through his life-like illustrations and other works of art. The legacy was created by our grandmother, Julia Warhola, with her many drawings—her cats, her angels, and the many other little drawings she would put down on paper in that wonderful world of imagine. My uncle continued on in his own creative way, seeing the power of color. And with a simple image, such as a flower, he could produce a symbol of art that would change the world's perception forever of him and of what popular art would come to mean.

James will continue on in his own vivid style of "let's imagine." The legacy has been handed down: the past, our grandmother Julia and our Uncle Andy; the present, my brother James. The future, we'll have to wait and see on that one.

*George Warhola is President of Warhola Recycling. He is the nephew of Andy Warhol and older brother of James Warhola. He and his wife Maria live in Pittsburgh.*

# 'OUR MOVIES':
# ART-MAKING, PERSONALITY, AND SOCIAL SPACE IN WARHOL'S FACTORY

by Callie Angell

It is hard to imagine Andy Warhol alone with his movie camera. With one notable exception, every single reel of the literally hundreds of movies which Warhol turned out in the 1960s is obsessively and exclusively devoted to the seemingly inexhaustible project of capturing other people on film. The one exception to this rule is *Empire* (1964), Warhol's notorious eight-hour shot of the Empire State Building, but even this single-minded study was the product of an organized and deliberately collaborative effort in which Warhol actively involved a number of other people for creative input, technical support, and practical assistance. The *Empire* crew included John Palmer (who had the idea for the film), Jonas Mekas (who rented the Auricon camera for the weekend and served as cameraman), Gerard Malanga (who brought the fourteen rolls of film needed for the shoot), and Henry Romney, who admitted the expedition of downtown filmmakers into his offices in the Time-Life Building on a Saturday night so they could set up their equipment and conduct their all-night surveillance of the skyscraper.

*Empire* remains one of the best-known and singularly outrageous statements of Warhol's career as an artist; it is also a film that would not have been made without the active participation of collaborators who were more than willing to lend their support to the realization of Warhol's personal cinematic vision. This life-long ability of Warhol's to engage, utilize, embroil, and rely upon other people in the process of producing his own work is one of the most difficult, even controversial issues in current discourse about his creative achievement. Did he simply use other people for his own ambitious, artistically selfish ends? Did he effectively "erase the author" by interjecting the input of others into the fabrication of his art works? These issues often seem to find their most direct expression in the Warhol films themselves, the production of which systematically attracted, relied upon, and documented the shifting social populations and multiple subjectivities that passed through the silver Factory in the Sixties.

In Warhol's mind filmmaking seems to have been an activity that was always both creative and interpersonal, a collective enterprise that allowed him to enlist and to enthrall other people while simultaneously producing, with extraordinary efficiency, a constant stream of uniquely Warholian motion pictures whose subjects were invariably the people thus gathered around him. This socially creative process was at the heart of the Warhol Factory as well: just as Warhol's on-going film productions and movie screenings functioned as main attractions in drawing people from a wide range of different cultural and class backgrounds to his studio, so the fertile social ground of the Factory provided the raw material for Warhol's cinema. In fact, Warhol's characteristically underdetermined approach to filmmaking—which relied heavily on unscripted, unrehearsed "situations" shot with an often unmoving camera on full-length, uncut camera rolls— was deliberately designed to transpose the uncontrolled, confrontational interactions of the Factory scene onto film, into what was, in effect, an entirely new kind of cinema. The uniqueness of Warhol's films, in other words, depended to some extent on the unique social environment of the Factory itself, and on Warhol's ability to structure his film productions so they emerged as almost seamless expressions of their own charged social space.

It is hard, at this late date, to reconstruct exactly what it must have been like at the Factory in the 1960s. The varied, often contradictory, sometimes mythologized recollections of those who were there reflect not only the transformations to be expected in any individual experience which has been filtered through memory, but also represent the diverse subjectivities operating at the core of the Factory itself, which could seem a very different place at different times and to people of different backgrounds. For example, Jane Holzer, who was a socialite from New York's Upper East Side, reported that she eventually left the Factory in 1965 because she was alarmed by what she perceived as the growing presence of "too many crazy people… using too many drugs…. The whole thing freaked me out, and I figured it was becoming too faggy and sick and druggy."[1] This is in stark contrast to the recollections of Warhol's scenarist, Ronald Tavel, who, accustomed to visiting Jack Smith and other friends in "Amphetamine Gulch" on the Lower East Side, where police raids and arrests were expected hazards of "underground" life, found the Factory a reassuringly protected and distinctly "uptown" environment, where you were safe from the threat of police harassment and could meet real movie stars like Montgomery Clift at parties.[2] The Factory's mid-town location on East 47th Street perfectly reflected the ambiguity and power of its function as a social and cultural clearinghouse: Warhol's studio was uptown to the downtown crowd, downtown to the upper class, legitimizing for the underground, and excitingly illicit for the proper, an environment that seemed to promise freedom and an absolute absence of judgment for the numbers of disenfranchised teenagers, homosexuals, drug users, and other countercultural types who passed through its doors. The silver Factory appeared like a new fault line in New York's cultural geography, an anxious, pressurized matrix where the city's numerous aesthetic and social worlds met and rubbed together under the watchful, enabling gaze of Warhol and his movie camera.

Warhol's oddly egalitarian version of stardom, in which literally anyone could become not just a star but a "superstar," simply by stepping in front of Warhol's camera for a four-minute *Screen Test* or a 33-minute sound reel, was one of the key undercurrents stirring the energizing atmosphere of social anxiety at the Factory. This was a star system that undermined the exclusivity of fame while underlining its impermanence: if anyone could become a star, then any star could be replaced at a moment's notice. The turn-over at the Factory could be harrowing: rivalries, jealousies, political intrigues, and interpersonal tensions flourished in this environment, and served as catalytic subtexts for a number of the Warhol films.

The purpose of Warhol's filmmaking—which was not to find good actors but to discover interesting people who were good at being themselves in front of a camera— complicated the challenges facing his potential stars. Without scripts to learn (or, occasionally, with scripts which they were *prevented* from memorizing), without direction, and without the reassurance of rehearsals, reshooting, or even editing, they often found themselves obliged to "perform" convincingly as themselves in front of Warhol, his camera, his assistants, and a large and sharp-witted audience of invited friends, press, idle superstars, and envious hangers-on. In this chaotic atmosphere of narcissistic intrigue, knowing scrutiny, and enigmatic levels of artistic intention, it was hard to discern what was really going on. What was Warhol really trying to do in his films? What did he want from you? How could you be "successful" when it was so unclear what the rules were?

For the most part, Warhol's closest associates and most successful stars tended to be those who could discern and appreciate the seriousness of the art-making that was going on, sometimes almost imperceptibly, in the midst of this provocative environment, and who were willing to lend themselves to its chaotic, psychologically complex process. Despite the rewards of Warhol's attentive camera or his often gratifying requests for input and assistance, this dedication seems to have required a certain amount of selflessness. Although Warhol constantly asked everyone around him for ideas for his art and movies, he was often deliberately unforthcoming about his real artistic intentions, and in fact consistently relied on others' misapprehension of his work to introduce elements of chance and realism into his films. As he later explained, "Something that I look for in an associate is a certain amount of misunderstanding of what I'm trying to do."[3] Warhol's filmmaking, like the silkscreening of his canvases, not only required the practical assistance of others, but incorporated the failings and unpredictability of that human presence both as content and as visible sign of its own fabrication.

Warhol's closest associates, therefore, were those who were not only willing to help the artist with his own work, but also willing to expose themselves to an extraordinary degree in that process. Underlying the personal risks of this dedication was the recognition of a vastly expanded concept of what art and the process of art production could be: in devoting yourself to the collective realization of Warhol's artistic vision, you accepted the fact that Warhol's creativity might actually incorporate or be expressed through the medium of your own personality; that you might find your personal strengths and foibles—special talents, beauty, a moment of juvenile narcissism, even the details of your sex life—evoked (or provoked), exposed, and preserved in the eternal register of the Warhol films. However gratifying this process might be (and Warhol could be extremely flattering as a cameraman), it was incredibly demanding as well, and seems to have had a lastingly definitive effect on its subjects, who sometimes seem condemned to forever negotiate their identities in relation to their former associations with Warhol and the traces of their past selves that were appropriated and immortalized in his art.

The bravery and pain of this self-exposure in the name of art were no less than what Warhol demanded of himself, especially in his careful creation of a public persona which was constructed as a projection of the most uncomfortable aspects (shyness, inarticulateness, physical fearfulness, self-consciousness) of his own personality. Warhol's closest colleagues understood this challenge and, in addition to their performances in Warhol's films and their practical assistance in his work, also made important personal contributions to the realization of Warhol's more innovative statements in such untraditional aesthetic fields as publicity and social space. Thus, Ultra Violet and Allen Midgette both lent their identities to the expression of Warhol's controversial public image as an artist and underground filmmaker: Ultra Violet as a superstar who was better known for her public appearances in Warhol's company than for her actual film roles; and Midgette as an alternate and important version of the Warhol persona, touring college campuses in the guise of Warhol himself, complete with silver wig and white make-up.

Gerard Malanga and Billy Name were both key figures in the creation of Warhol's studio; it is safe to say that, without them, both the Factory and the Warhol films would have emerged as very different entities. As Warhol's only paid studio assistant, Malanga provided the reliable labor which enabled Warhol to continue efficiently to produce artworks and films in the midst of the Factory's multiple distractions. This practical assistance was augmented by Malanga's gifts as a social catalyst: Malanga specialized in finding interesting people (poets, actors, painters, students) to come by the Factory and to meet Warhol, and thus played a major role both in enriching the social mix at Warhol's studio and supplying the artist with the raw materials for his filmmaking.

Billy Name was the designer and sole resident of the Factory and also its "foreman," an unpaid, unspecified function which seems to have required both Name's constant presence and his considerable abilities as a creative facilitator. Name usually designed the lighting for Warhol's film productions, and also, as Warhol's official photographer, documented the Factory scene with a vast number of extraordinary photographs. Name's spiritual residence seems to have been a key element in the Factory's psychic identity in the Sixties; indeed, the enormous shift that took place in Warhol's art and film production at the end of the 1960s was marked not only by the studio's relocation to Union Square and the shooting of Warhol by Valerie Solanas, but also by the departure of both Name and Malanga, who ended their association with Warhol at the end of the decade.

Warhol continued to surround himself with assistants and colleagues for the rest of his years, but the level of artistic engagement he required from others was never as intense as it had been in the 1960s; nor did he ever again focus so obsessively on his own associates as subjects for his art. It was perhaps inevitable that such creative and deeply personal involvement in the artist's work would ultimately prove unsustainable both for Warhol's associates and for Warhol himself. On another level, like most of Warhol's achievements, the silver Factory remains unsurpassed as a groundbreaking experiment in the practice of art-making, a social and cultural watershed whose lasting impact on the fields of cinema, contemporary art, gay history, music, performance, and cultural studies—as well as on its participants—has yet to be fully assessed and comprehended.

*Callie Angell is Adjunct Curator of the Andy Warhol Film Project at the Whitney Museum of American Art and consultant to The Museum of Modern Art on the preservation of the Warhol films.*

# PLATES

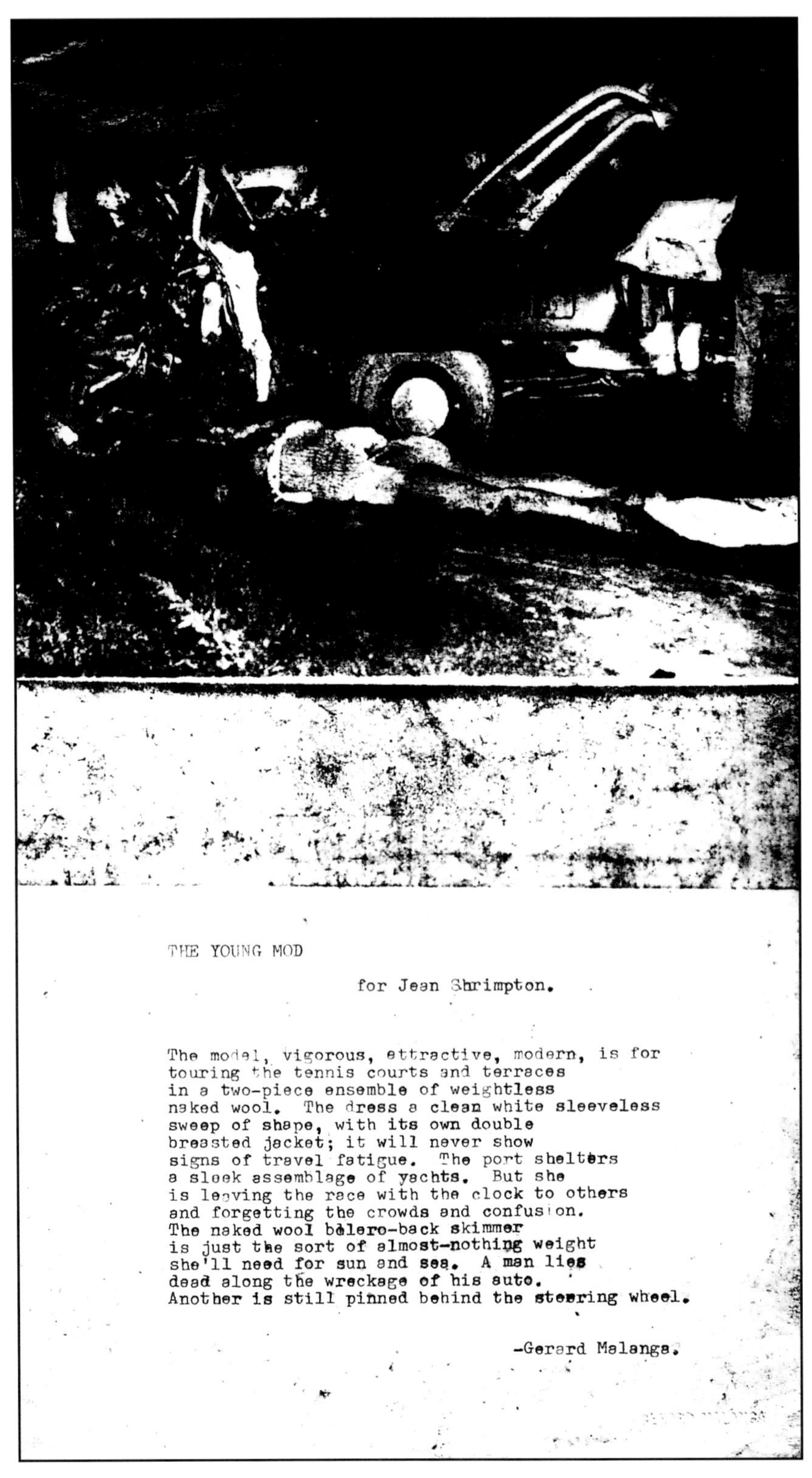



1. Gerard Malanga
   *The Young Mod* 1964
   Thermo-Fax and typed
   poem
   14 x 8 1/2

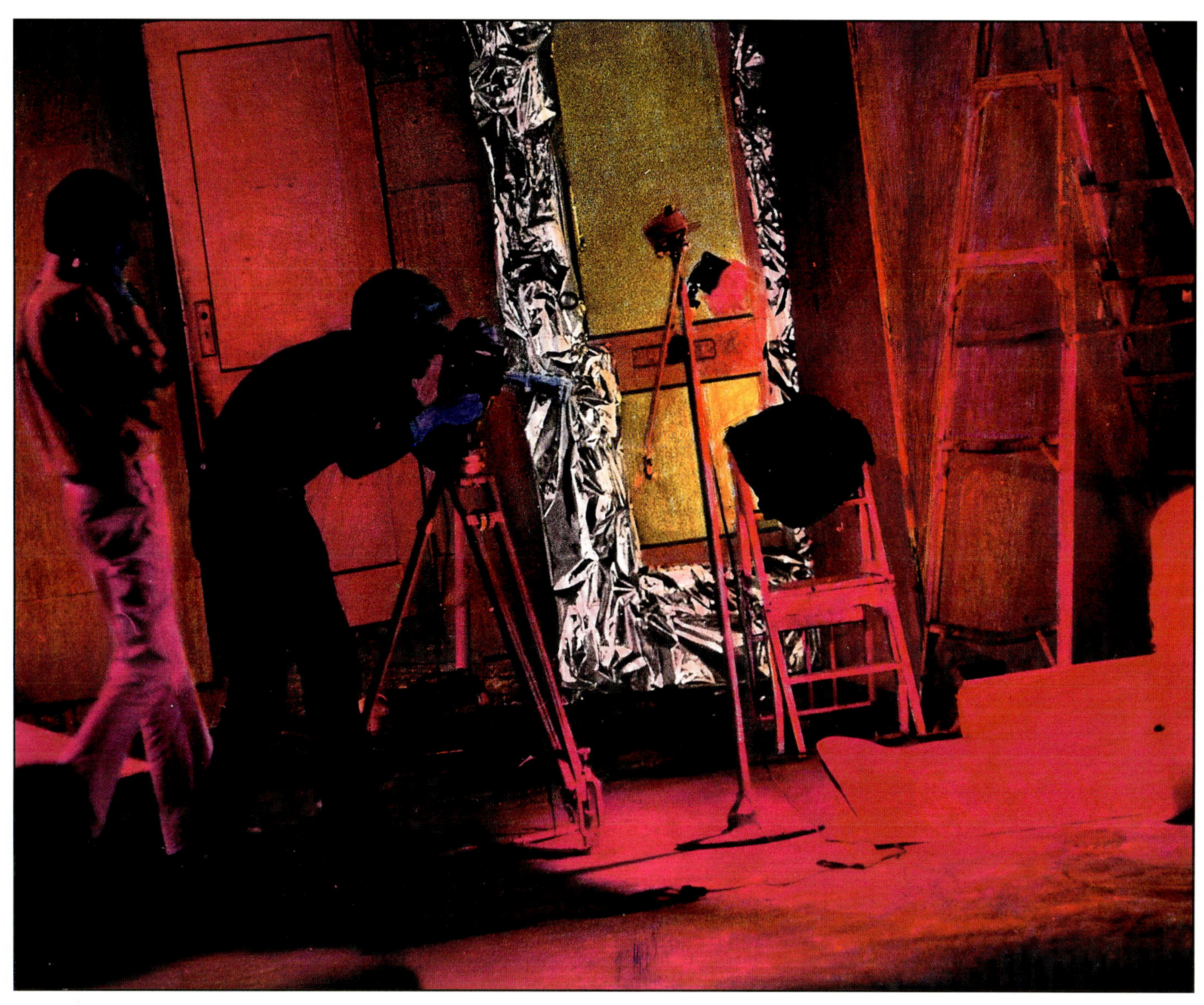

13. Billy Name
    *Andy Warhol Filming at the
    Factory*  c. 1965
    Hand-colored gelatin silver
    print
    7 1/4 x 9 1/2

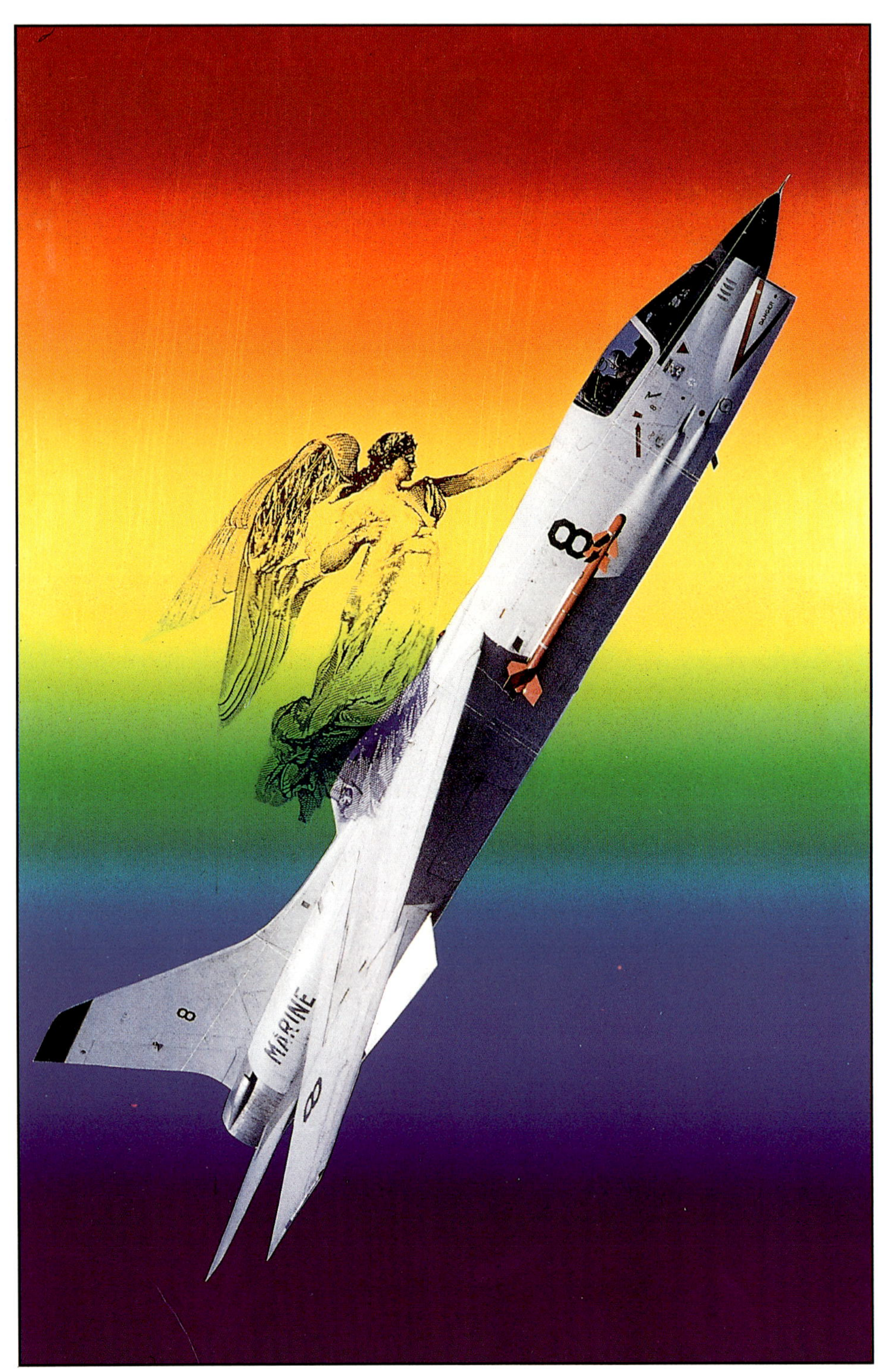

29. Ultra Violet
*Who but an Angel Can
Stop a Missile?* 1993
Computer-generated
print on paper
36 x 24

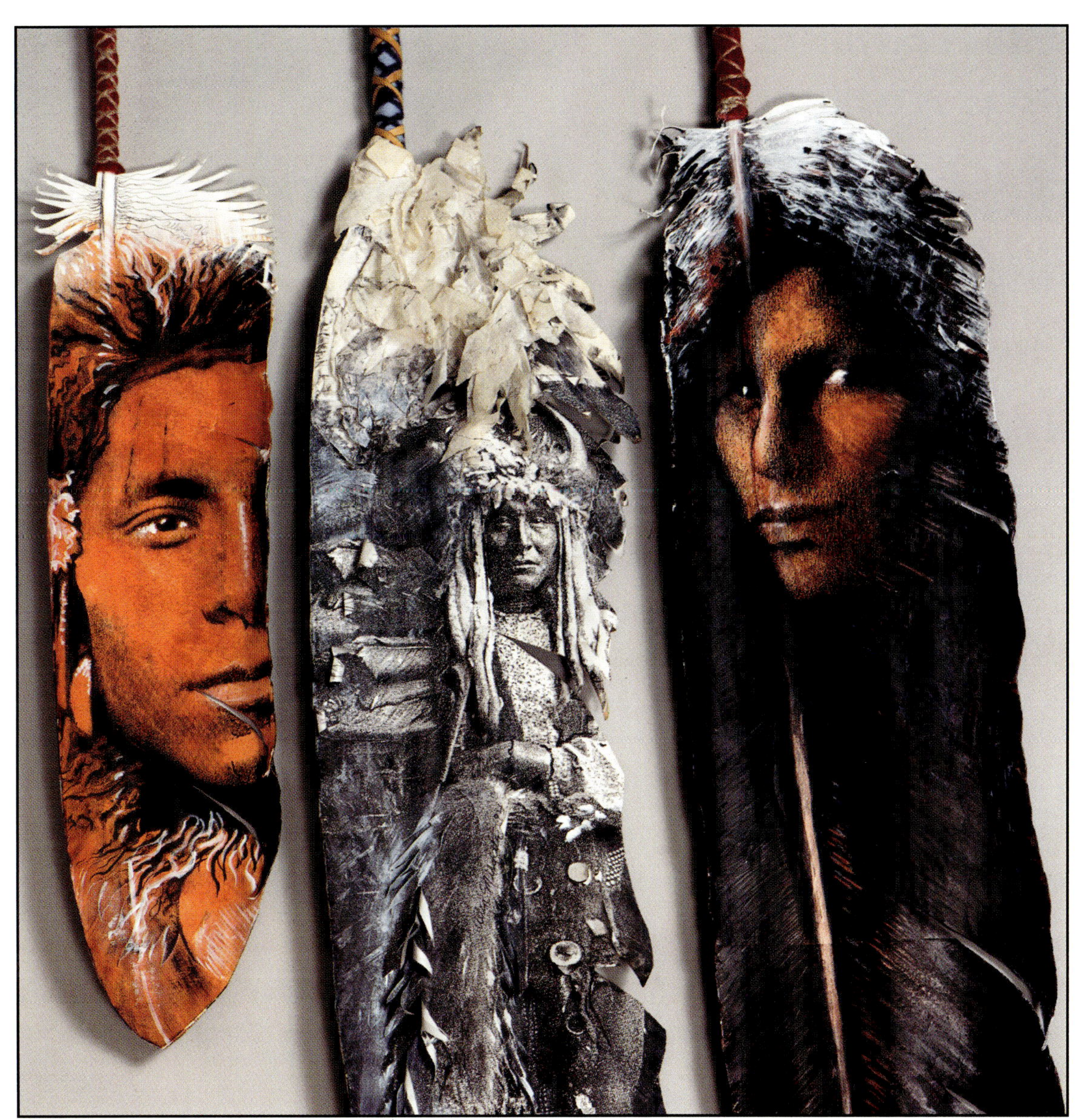

37. Allen Midgette
*Indian Portrait Feather
Tree* c. 1993-96
Mixed-media assemblage
(detail)

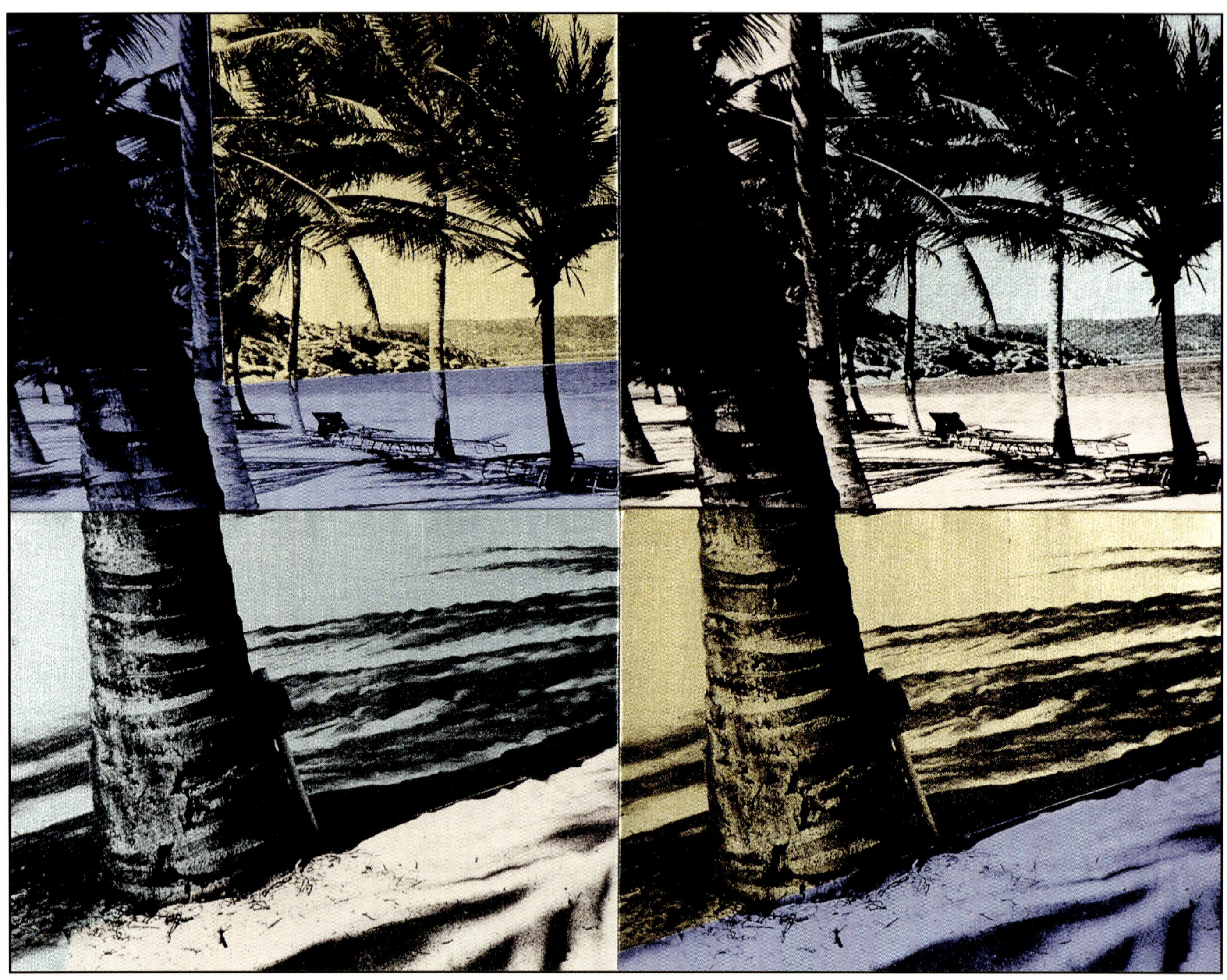

48. Christopher Makos
   *Paradise Painting*  1992
   Silkscreen on canvas
   23 x 29

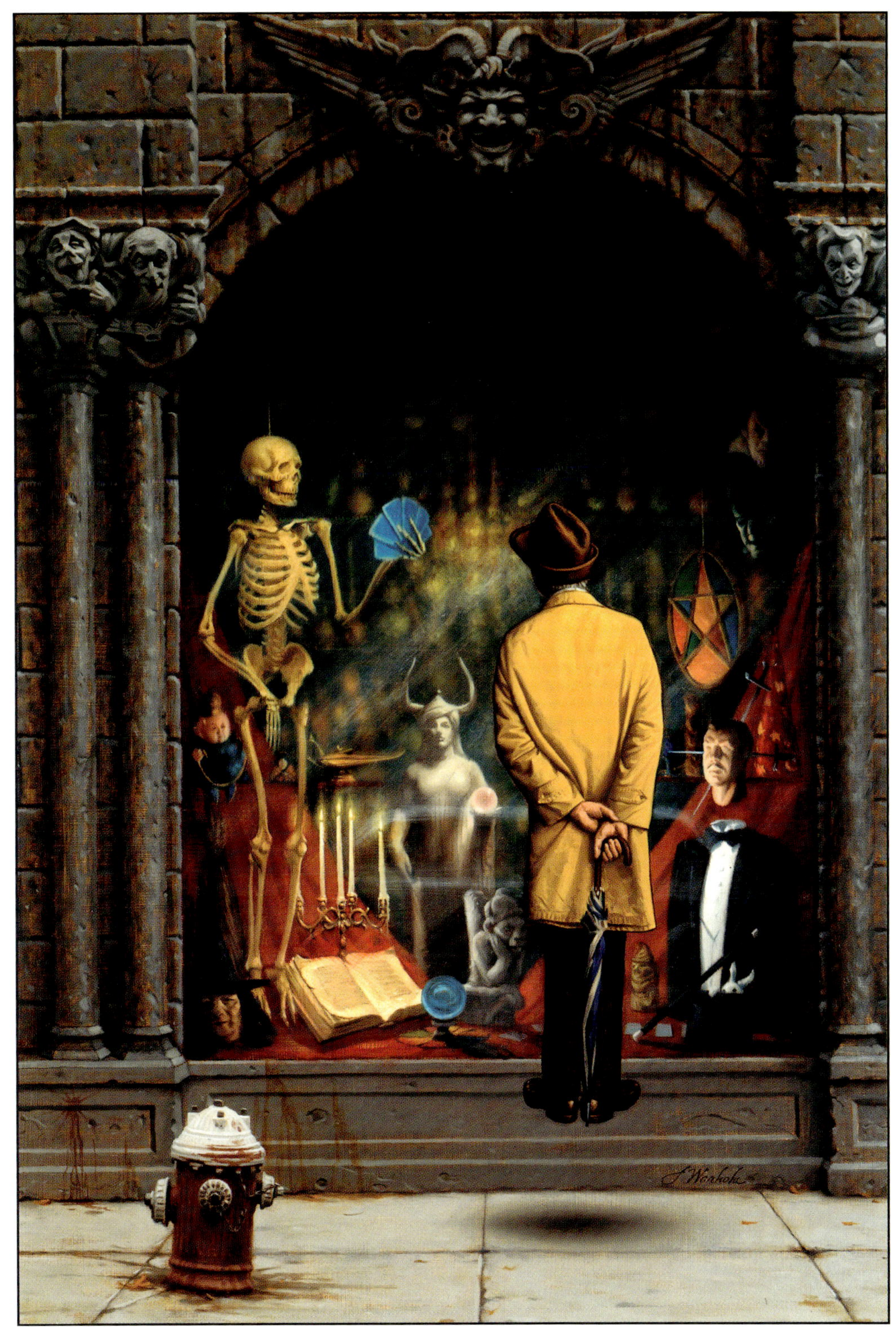

52. James Warhola
*The Magic Shop*  c. 1983
Oil on board
30 x 21

# NOTES

1. The sale was documented in a six-volume catalogue, *The Andy Warhol Collection* (New York: Sotheby's, 1988), distributed by Harry N. Abrams, Inc., New York.

2. See the inaugural publication, *The Andy Warhol Museum*, essays by Callie Angell, Avis Berman, Arthur C. Danto, Mark Francis, Richard Hellinger, Bennard B. Perlman, Helen Searing, and compact disc by Steve Rowland (Pittsburgh: The Andy Warhol Museum, 1994).

3. Q.v., Whitney Museum of American Art, *The Films of Andy Warhol: An Introduction* (New York: Whitney Museum of American Art, 1988); and Callie Angell, *The Films of Andy Warhol: Part II* (New York: Whitney Museum of American Art, 1994).

4. E.g., see Bruce D. Kurtz, *Keith Haring, Andy Warhol, and Walt Disney,* ex. cat. (Munich: Prestel Verlag, 1992): 14-17.

5. In the words of Christopher Makos, *Warhol: A Personal Photographic Memoir* (New York: New American Library, 1989): 17: "Andy was a very familial person, and he created his family as he went along."

6. Warhol's Superstars adopted names like International Velvet, Pope Ondine, Viva, Mario Montez, Mary Might, and Holly Woodlawn. Because of their outrageous public personas and improbable pseudonyms, Billy Name often now refers to himself as "a cartoon character."

7. E.g., Edie Sedgwick died of acute barbital intoxication in 1971; Andrea Feldman committed suicide by jumping out of a window in 1972; Candy Darling succumbed to cancer, probably induced by the female hormones she was taking as a pre-operative transsexual; Eric Emerson was found dead in 1975, the victim of either a hit and run accident or a drug overdose; Jackie Curtis overdosed on drugs in 1985; Ingrid Superstar disappeared from her home in Kingston, New York, in 1986, and was never heard from again; Ondine died of liver failure from years of drug and alcohol abuse in 1988; and Nico, a long-time heroin addict, fell off a bicycle in Ibiza in 1988 and died of a cerebral hemorrhage. Edie Sedgwick was the subject of a best-selling book by Jean Stein, *Edie: An American Biography*, ed. with George Plimpton (New York: Alfred A. Knopf, 1982); Candy Darling's writings were posthumously published in *Candy Darling by Candy Darling*, intro. by Jeremiah Newton (Madras and New York: Hanuman Books, 1992); and the last years of Nico's life were documented by James Young, *Nico: The End* (Woodstock, NY: The Overlook Press, 1993). Susanne Ofteringer's poignant film, *Nico Icon* (1995), chronicles the singer's tragic rise and fall; and the recent movie by Mary Harron, *I Shot Andy Warhol* (1996), recounts the bizarre story of would-be-Warhol-assassin Valerie Solanas, who died of bronchial pneumonia and emphysema in 1988.

8. Among the notable exceptions to this past trend are Patrick S. Smith's indispensable *Andy Warhol's Art and Films* (Ann Arbor: UMI Research Press, 1986) and *Warhol: Conversations about the Artist* (Ann Arbor: UMI Research Press, 1988); and David Bourdon's exemplary monograph, *Warhol* (New York: Harry N. Abrams, Inc., Publishers, 1989). Both authors, in their extensive research on Andy, located and interviewed as many of his collaborators as possible. Their focus, however, was on Warhol, and, thus, they did not consider at length the independent works and careers of those artists. More recently, books have appeared on the photography of Billy Name and Stephen Shore; q.v., Debra Miller, *Billy Name: Stills from the Warhol Films* (Munich and New York: Prestel Verlag, 1994); and Lynne Tillman, *The Velvet Years: Warhol's Factory 1965-67*, photographs by Stephen Shore (New York: Thunder's Mouth Press, 1995).

9. *The Shadow* was designed as one in a series of ten "Myths," which Warhol issued as both paintings and prints.

10. For a more detailed analysis of the Warhol films, see Callie Angell's insightful essay, "'Our Movies': Art-making, Personality, and Social Space in Warhol's Factory," in this catalogue.

11. For a succinct survey of Warhol's career, see Margery King, "Chronology," in *The Andy Warhol Museum, op. cit.*, pp. 167-91.

## GERARD MALANGA NOTES

1. Within the next few years, Malanga, along with several other of Warhol's friends and associates, helped to locate many of the macabre images Andy selected for silkscreening in his "Death and Disasters" series. The most extensive study of this subject to date is the exhibition catalogue compiled by the Menil Collection, *Andy Warhol Death and Disasters* (Houston: Houston Fine Art Press, 1988).

2. Malanga sold all but one of the Thermo-Fax poems to Jon Hendricks, who later resold many of them to various unknown parties.

3. According to Joel Lobenthal, *Radical Rags: Fashions of the Sixties* (New York: Abbeville Press, 1990): 18-19:

   The appellation "Mod" referred originally to a group of scooter-riding, clothes-obsessed young men, but the term was soon used generically to denote many pockets of youth whose appearance broadcast their independence.

The more fastidious "Mods" provided a contrast in fashion to the "Rockers," whose sartorial style revolved around motorcycle jackets, jeans, and leather boots (pp. 140-43).

4.  Significantly, "The Young Mod" is one of a series of fashion poems by Malanga, and the first ever written to incorporate the world of fashion into poetry (Gerard Malanga, conversation with author, 13 June 1995).

5.  The fatalities reached their zenith in the late 1960s and early 1970s at approximately 55,000 per year. See Barbara F. Reese, *Motor Vehicle Accident Deaths in the United States, 1950-67* (Rockville: United States Health Services and Mental Health Administration, 1970): 33. I would like to thank Suzy Hoffmann for providing this information.

6.  Gerard Malanga, *Chic Death* (Cambridge, MA: Pym-Randall, 1971): 131.

7.  Among them, the Irene Glascock Memorial Poetry Contest (1963), held annually at Mount Holyoke College; the New York City Writers Conference, organized each year at Wagner College, for which he was awarded the Avant-Garde Poetry Prize (1961) by Frances Steloff of the Gotham Book Mart in Manhattan; and the New School for Social Research in New York, where he and Jean Boudin shared the Dylan Thomas Memorial Poetry Prize (1962), which, that year, was judged by Arnold Weinstein and Kenneth Koch, and presented by Marianne Moore. His poems already were being published in such respected journals as the *Paris Review*, *Partisan Review*, *Poetry*, and the *New Yorker*. See Gerard Malanga, "Notes from a Non-Literary Life," *Contemporary Authors Autobiography Series* 17 (1994): 98-100.

8.  Malanga met Ford at one of the frequently held "salons" at Maas's penthouse in Brooklyn Heights. Ford, in turn, arranged the meeting of Andy and Gerard at a poetry reading at the New School for Social Research in Greenwich Village. Three years later, Warhol would cast Maas's wife, the experimental filmmaker Marie Menken, as Gerard's mother in *The Chelsea Girls* (1966). For Warhol's reminiscences of his first encounter with Malanga, see Andy Warhol and Pat Hackett, *POPism: The Warhol '60s* (New York: Harper & Row, 1980): 26-27.

9.  In the later production by director Stanley Kubrick (Warner Brothers, 1971), the role was played by Malcolm McDowell and the character's name was changed to Alex. For a more detailed discussion, see Debra Miller, *Billy Name: Stills from the Warhol Films* (Munich and New York: Prestel Verlag, 1994): 44-51.

10. Maurice Yacowar, *The Films of Paul Morrissey* (New York: Cambridge University Press, 1993): 17-18, gives a slightly different account of this event, in which the pivotal role of Malanga is not acknowledged. It is also described in Warhol and Hackett, *op. cit.,* pp. 144ff.; and Victor Bockris, *Transformer: The Lou Reed Story* (New York: Simon & Schuster, 1995): 101-03.

11. This was not an unusual role for Malanga to assume. In an interview of 13 December 1978, in Patrick S. Smith, *Andy Warhol's Art and Films* (Ann Arbor: UMI Research Press, 1986): 414, Gerard recalled:

> I guess I was a catalyst at the Factory…
> a lot of the people who passed through the
> Factory doors were people who came because
> I was there, and there was always an
> exchange of ideas between Andy and some
> of the people that I knew that he didn't
> know… I was responsible for bringing in
> people! Like Paul Morrissey, Ronnie Tavel,
> Rene Ricard, Allen Ginsberg…

Warhol himself commented, in Warhol and Hackett, *op. cit.,* p. 111:

> The way it was working out was that Gerard
> influenced everything we did away from the
> Factory… Gerard kept up with fashion
> and the arts and he was good at inviting
> all the celebrities we met to come by the
> Factory.

12. Malanga had met the statuesque German model, singer, and actress, who had a walk-on role in Federico Fellini's *La Dolce Vita* (1960), in London the preceding spring. When she arrived later that year in New York, she called Gerard at the Factory; he, in turn, invited her to the Cafe Bizarre to see the Velvet Underground perform. Upon meeting her, Warhol and Morrissey envisioned the icy beauty as the perfect lead singer for the band and insisted they include her in the group.

13. Although the multimedia show erroneously is assumed to have originated in San Francisco with the acid-rock generation, its true genesis can be traced to the East Coast and the "Happenings" of Allan Kaprow, an artist who studied at the New School for Social Research in New York in the 1950s with musician/composer John Cage; see John Gruen, *The New Bohemia* (Chicago: a cappella books, 1990): 144-45. Even before their association with Warhol, the Velvet Undergound, with their original percussionist Angus MacLise, had experimented with mixed-media stage presentations. In the spring of 1965, they presented the most significant of these, "Launching the Dream Weapon," which included underground movies, lights, slides, poetry, music, and dancers; see Victor Bockris and Gerard Malanga, *Up-Tight: The Velvet Underground Story* (New York: Omnibus Press, 1983): 20. See also Victor Bockris, *op. cit.*, pp. 125 and 133, for recognition of the Exploding Plastic Inevitable's impact in New York and Los Angeles.

14. Bockris and Malanga, *op. cit.*

15. Quoted in Victor Bockris, *The Life and Death of Andy Warhol* (New York: Bantam Books, 1989): 153.

16. Gerard Malanga and Andy Warhol, *Screen Tests/A Diary* (New York: Kulchur Press, 1967). For background on this important collaboration between artist and poet, see the subjective interpretation of Reva Wolf, "Collaboration as Social Exchange: *Screen Tests/A Diary* by Gerard Malanga and Andy Warhol," *Art Journal* 52, 4 (Winter 1993): 59-66, and the critical responses it engendered from Debra Miller and Elsa Schmidt, "Letters to the Editor," *Art Journal* 53, 2 (Summer 1994): 112.

17. See Malanga, "Notes from a Non-Literary Life," *op. cit.,* pp. 108-15, for a detailed account of their relationship. In a recent interview, Barzini inexplicably denied her well-documented involvement with Malanga; see Glenn O'Brien, "Benedetta: Supermodel at Twenty, Superperson at Fifty," *Mirabella* 65 (Oct. 1994): 150.

18. Gerard Malanga, *Three Poems for Benedetta Barzini* (New York: Angel Hair Books, 1967); idem, *The Last Benedetta Poems* (Santa Barbara: Black Sparrow Press, 1969); idem, *Ten Years After: The Selected Benedetta Poems* (Santa Barbara: Black Sparrow Press, 1977); and idem, *100 years have passed: prose poems* (Los Angeles: Little Caesar Press, 1978).

19. Barzini's troubled, early life is discussed in O'Brien, *op. cit.*, pp. 148-53, and Lobenthal, *op. cit.*, pp. 187-90.

20. Malanga, "Notes from a Non-Literary Life," p. 118.

21. Later, he would be appointed photo archivist for the New York City Department of Parks, a position he held from 1985-88. During his service there, he curated more than two dozen historical photography exhibitions, and single-handedly conserved and catalogued the Robert Moses historic negative collection.

22. The "Paris Review Interview" was published in its entirety in Charles Olson, *Muthologos: The Collected Lectures & Interviews*, ed. by George F. Butterick (Bolinas, Ca.: Four Seasons Foundation, 1977): II, 105-53. It had appeared in a slightly different form in *The Paris Review* 49 (1970).

23. For an introduction to Olson's life and works, see Eniko Bollobas, *Charles Olson* (New York: Twayne Publishers, 1992); and Paul Christensen, *Charles Olson: Call Him Ishmael*, with a foreword by George F. Butterick (Austin: University of Texas Press, 1975). A detail of Malanga's portrait of Olson was used for the cover of Christensen's book.

24. On the history, faculty, and alumni of Black Mountain College, see Mary Emma Harris, *The Arts at Black Mountain College* (Cambridge, MA: MIT Press, 1987); Martin Duberman, *Black Mountain: An Experiment in Community* (New York: Dutton, 1972); Sally Banes, *Terpsichore in Sneakers* (Boston: Houghton Mifflin, 1979); and Mervin Lane, ed., *Sprouted Seeds* (Knoxville: University of Tennessee Press, 1990).

25. Dennis Cooper, "POPISM: 15 Portraits by Gerard Malanga," *Little Caesar* 8 (Feb. 1979): 32.

26. Robert Creeley, "OverView," unpublished manuscript, 1990 (Malanga Archives), p. 4.

27. Charles Olson, note to Malanga, 1969 (Malanga Archives).

28. Warhol and Hackett, *op. cit.*, p. 223.

29. *Ibid.*, p. 151.

30. Warhol, as a frail and sickly child, had done much the same. For Andy, going to the movies, reading movie magazines, and collecting publicity stills of the stars became an early obsession. Malanga, too, was fascinated at a young age by "not just movies but movie posters, movie stars, and movie studios." He subscribed to the trade publication *Boxoffice*, and years later gave all his back issues to Andy; see Malanga, "Notes from a Non-Literary Life," p. 97.

31. Although Gerard had left the ranks of the Factory in 1970, he maintained both friendships and working relationships with many of his cohorts from the Warhol circle.

32. The movie was produced and filmed by Warhol, and written, directed, and edited by Morrissey. Jed Johnson assisted on camera work, sound, and production.

33. Candy Darling, *Candy Darling*, with an introduction by Jeremiah Newton (Madras and New York: Hanuman Books, 1992): 115, extracted from Candy's journals of 1970-72.

34. *Ibid.,* p. 74.

35. The song first appeared on Reed's album *Transformer* (RCA, 1972). For the complete lyrics, see Lou Reed, *Between Thought and Expression: Selected Lyrics of Lou Reed* (New York: Hyperion, 1991): 42.

36. Warhol and Hackett, *op. cit.*, p. 299.

37. Gerard Malanga, ed., *Scopophilia: The Love of Looking*, with an afterword by Gerard Malanga and a foreword by Robert Creeley (New York: Alfred van der Marck Editions, 1985): 127.

38. These works were used as the cover illustrations for Gerard Malanga, *Three Poems for Benedetta Barzini*; idem, *Ten Years After: The Selected Benedetta Poems*; and idem, *100 years have passed: prose poems*, respectively.

39. Gerard Malanga, *Three Diamonds* (Santa Barbara:
    Black Sparrow Press, 1991): 41-42.

40. *Ibid.,* p. 213.

41. Gerard Malanga, conversation with author, 13 June
    1995.

42. From the poem "Extended Sonnet," in Malanga,
    *Three Diamonds*, p. 42.

43. It is important to note here that Malanga does not
    portray his female models in any manner in which he
    himself had not been depicted at a comparable age
    (i.e., in full nudity and in sexual situations), both in
    Factory films and photographs, and in his own works.

44. More accurately, they tend to look much younger than
    they are, although each is at least eighteen years old
    and has attained the legal age of consent.

45. The title of an exhibition of Malanga's photography at
    303 Park South Gallery, New York, in 1985.

46. Gerard Malanga, *Good Girls* (Tokyo: Kawade-
    Shoboshinsha Co., Ltd., 1994): n.p.

47. Gerard Malanga, "Anatomy of the Gaze," in Malanga,
    ed., *Scopophilia: The Love of Looking, op. cit.,* p.
    120.

48. *Ibid.,* p. 122.

49. E.g., Song of Solomon (6:10-13):

    Who is she that looketh forth as the morning,
    fair as the moon, clear as the sun, and
    terrible as an army with banners?…
    Return, return, O Shulamite; return, return
    that we may look upon thee.

50. The most compelling survey of the art historical
    tradition of the nude remains Kenneth Clark, *The
    Nude: A Study in Ideal Form* (Princeton: Princeton
    University Press, 1956). For a more recent study of
    the female nude, see Christine Mitchell Havelock,
    *The Aphrodite of Knidos and her Successors* (Ann
    Arbor: University of Michigan Press, c. 1995).

51. In this respect, it differs markedly from most of the
    other plates included with it in *Good Girls*, Malanga's
    monograph of erotic photographs in which the tone is
    decidedly sexual.

52. On Praxiteles, see Oscar Arvid Antonsson, *The
    Praxiteles Marble Group in Olympia* (Stockholm: O.
    Antonsson, 1937); Carl Blumel, *Der Hermes eines
    Praxiteles* (Baden-Baden: W. Klein, c. 1948);
    Antonio Corso, *Prassitele: Fonti Epigrafiche e
    Letterarie: Vita e Opere* (Rome: De Luca, 1988-90);
    and Havelock, *op. cit.*

53. Gerard Malanga, conversation with author,
    13 June 1995.

54. A.A. Brill, *Lectures on Psychoanalytic Psychiatry*
    (New York: Vintage Books, 1946): 227.

## BILLY NAME NOTES

1.  For Billy Name's early background, see Debra Miller,
    *Billy Name: Stills from the Warhol Films* (Munich and
    New York: Prestel Verlag, 1994): 10 and 12.

2.  Billy Name, conversation with author, 18 March 1993.

3.  Jonas Mekas, "The Filmography of Andy Warhol," in
    John Coplans, *Andy Warhol* (Greenwich, CT: New
    York Graphic Society Ltd., 1970): 147, in which it is
    erroneously stated that "Billy Linich gets his hair
    cut." For the most recent discussions of Warhol's
    various versions of the subject, see Debra Miller, *loc.
    cit.*; and Callie Angell, *The Films of Andy Warhol:
    Part II* (New York: Whitney Museum of American
    Art, 1994): 12.

4.  Earlier, in 1960, James Waring had sent his own piece
    entitled "Haircut" to the avant-garde composer La
    Monte Young, a mutual friend of Waring and Billy
    Name:

    Use a stop watch. Watch and time three
    minutes. During that time say "haircut"
    as [sic] least, or as many times as you
    like.

    James Waring, correspondence to La Monte Young,
    December 1960 (La Monte Young Archives, New
    York).

5.  On the seventeenth-century Italian artist, see The
    Metropolitan Museum of Art, *The Age of Caravaggio*,
    ex. cat. (New York: The Metropolitan Museum of Art,
    1985).

6.  Andy Warhol and Pat Hackett, *POPism: The Warhol
    '60s* (New York: Harper & Row Publishers, 1980):
    63.

7.  Mike Wrenn, *Andy Warhol in his own words*
    (London: Omnibus Press, 1991): 12, 16, and 19,
    respectively.

8.  Warhol and Hackett, *op. cit.*, p. 74.

9.  The original Thermo-Fax machine from the Factory is
    still extant; presently it is stored at the Andy Warhol
    Museum in Pittsburgh.

10. My thanks to Suzy Hoffmann for this observation,
    and for providing the following statistical data on
    guns in America, cited in notes 15-16.

11. Around the same time, Pop artist Roy Lichtenstein
    executed a series of silkscreens on the theme of the
    gun, including *Trigger Finger* and *Fastest Gun* of
    1962.

12. Billy Name, quoted in Vassar College Art Gallery, "The Billy Name Collection: The Silver Era at Warhol's Factory," ex. cat., Warburg Print Room, Vassar College, Poughkeepsie, NY, 21 January-10 March 1989, n.p.

13. Neil Printz, "Painting Death in America," in The Menil Collection, *Andy Warhol Death and Disasters* (Houston: Houston Fine Art Press): 22, has noted:

> During the 1980s, Warhol… introduced new subjects relating to the theme [of Death and Disasters], including paintings of guns and knives…, an earthquake in Italy…

Although these subjects were new for Andy, they had been Thermo-Faxed nearly twenty years earlier by Billy Name, and left in Billy's silver trunk at the Factory after his departure in the winter of 1969-70. They, along with the rest of the trunk's contents, were returned to Billy by the Warhol Estate after Andy's death.

14. Billy Name, quoted in Vassar College Art Gallery, *op. cit.*, n.p.

15. Colin Wilson, *A Criminal History of Mankind* (New York: Carroll & Graf, 1990): 605.

16. "Big Shots," *Time Magazine* (2 August 1993): 20-27.

17. Warhol and Hackett, *op. cit.*, 74.

18. *Ibid.*

19. See Lynne Tillman and Stephen Shore, *The Velvet Years: Warhol's Factory, 1965-67* (New York: Thunder's Mouth Press, 1995). Shore currently serves as Chairperson of the Department of Photography at Bard College, Annandale-on-Hudson, New York.

20. The task of painting the Factory silver and draping it with expanses of aluminum foil and Mylar occupied Billy from January to April 1964, during which time he took up residence there. He continued to live in Warhol's studios until his departure from New York in the winter of 1969-70.

21. For a full study of this subject, see Debra Miller, *op. cit.*

22. *Ibid.,* pp. 38-39. During the course of the film, Montez is chided into admitting that 'she' is, in fact, a man. Preceding *Screen Test #2*, Montez was featured in Warhol's *Harlot* (filmed on 13 December 1964); later he appeared in *Camp* (1965), *Hedy* (1965), *More Milk Yvette* (1965), and *The Chelsea Girls* (1966).

23. For a survey of Montez's career, see F. Michael Moore, *Drag! Male and Female Impersonators on Stage, Screen and Television* (Jefferson, NC: McFarland & Co., Inc., 1994): 186-89. He appeared in the productions of such underground luminaries as Ron Rice, Piero Heliczer, Bill Vehr, and Charles Ludlam, in addition to those of Warhol and Smith. In 1968, Montez had a role in Terry Southern's *Candy* and in Frank Simon's documentary, *The Queen.*

24. This piece is just one of several vintage, hand-colored, and cut-out photographs by Billy Name that have never before been catalogued, illustrated, or exhibited.

25. Kornman's publicity still of Marilyn Monroe, marked with Warhol's 23, is in the archival collection of the Andy Warhol Museum, Pittsburgh.

26. The advertisement for the presentations at the Cinematheque appeared in the *Village Voice* XI, 17 (10 Feb. 1966): 22. In it, Billy Name is listed as Billy Linich.

27. One of the original posters from the event at Rutgers is preserved in the Billy Name Collection. Although Billy Linich [Name] is listed on the poster, he did not make that trip to New Brunswick.

28. Victor Bockris, *The Life and Death of Andy Warhol* (New York: Bantam Books, 1989): 184. According to Billy Name, conversation with author, 5 December 1990, he arrived at his new surname by simply copying the question on a form he was filling out. Fred Lawrence Guiles, *Loner at the Ball: The Life of Andy Warhol* (London and New York: Bantam Books, 1989): 50, gives a different explanation—that Andy named Billy after a friend's dog!

29. See Victor Bockris and Gerard Malanga, *Up-Tight: The Velvet Underground Story* (New York: Omnibus Press, 1983): 30-31; and Warhol and Hackett, *op. cit.*, pp. 155-57. The following year, the same site would become the Electric Circus.

30. *Village Voice* XI, 24 (31 March 1966): 30. The ad is cited in Warhol and Hackett, *op. cit.*, p. 162, with the explanation (p. 152) that "it wasn't 'Exploding' yet." According to Paul Morrissey (quoted in Bockris and Malanga, *op. cit.*, p. 31), the name, "Exploding Plastic Inevitable," was his invention, composed from random words off the liner notes of Bob Dylan's record album, *Bringing It All Back Home* (Columbia, 1965). His recollection is faulty, however, as the closest word to appear on that album cover is "explosion." But Dylan's notes on *Highway 61 Revisited* (Columbia, 1965) contain the words "erupting," "Inevitables," and "plasma" (not "plastic").

31. *Village Voice* XI, 25 (7 April 1966): 29.

32. These include: *White Light/White Heat* (Verve, 1967); *The Velvet Underground* (MGM, 1969); *Nico: Chelsea Girl* (PolyGram, 1967); and *Songs for Drella* (Sire, 1990).

33. Lou Reed, quoted in Bockris and Malanga, *op. cit.,* p. 104.

34. Susan Dunn Whittier Bottomly was the very tall, sixteen-year-old, brunette daughter of a Boston district attorney who had come to New York in 1966 to embark upon a career in modeling. Gerard

Malanga discovered her for the Factory and gave her the name International Velvet, after the 1940s movie *National Velvet* starring Elizabeth Taylor, whom he thought she resembled. She first appeared in Malanga's film portrait of 1966, *Prelude to International Velvet Debutante*, then was featured later that year in Warhol's *The Chelsea Girls*. Billy Name considered her "the most beautiful of all the women at the Factory. Her face, her hair, her body—everything was perfect." (Billy Name, conversation with author, 18 March 1993).

35. According to Billy Name, their photo session occurred at the Factory prior to the actual filming of Warhol's movie; see Debra Miller, *op. cit.*, pp. 86-88. But Allen Midgette, conversation with author, 27 April 1995, disputes the photographer's recollection and remembers Billy's still photography and Andy's motion picture being shot simultaneously.

36. Billy Name did not use a flash until after the Warhol atelier's move from East 47th Street to Union Square in 1968.

37. Cf. Richard Avedon, *Avedon, Photographs, 1947-1977*, ex. cat. (New York: Farrar, Straus, & Giroux, 1978); and George Hurrell, *Hurrell Hollywood: Photographs 1928-1990* (New York: St. Martin's Press, 1992).

38. Billy's sudden disappearance was immortalized with the publication of the note he left for Andy ("Andy—I am/not here/ anymore but/I am fine/Love, Billy") in Warhol and Hackett, *op. cit.*, p. 300.

39. A selection of this material was exhibited in the Warburg Print Room of the Vassar College Art Gallery, Poughkeepsie, New York, 21 January-10 March 1989.

40. With the new glossy RC stock, the artist is able to achieve his aesthetic goal of more brilliant whites and more intense blacks. Furthermore, its archival life far surpasses that of the organic fiber paper, resulting in longer-lived and more stable tonal contrasts, free from fading or patina.

41. The largest published collections of Billy Name's Factory Fotos to date appear in Andy Warhol, Kasper König, Pontus Hultén, Olle Granath, eds., *Andy Warhol*, ex. cat. (Stockholm: Moderna Museet, 1968) and Debra Miller, *op. cit.*

42. On the history and techniques of cameraless photography, see Patra Holter, *Photography Without a Camera* (New York: Van Nostrand Reinhold, 1980).

43. For example, Man Ray's famous Rayographs—comprising cameraless images of actual two- and three-dimensional objects placed on sensitive paper and exposed to various light sources—recreate in photography the collages popular in the artist's youth; see Man Ray, *Les Champs Délicieux: Album de Photographie* (Paris: 1922).

44. Gerard Malanga recalled the purpose of the blank canvas in Patrick S. Smith, *Warhol: Conversations about the Artist* (Ann Arbor: UMI Research Press, 1988): 165-66:

    …it was painted the same color as the background [of the pendant painting]… There is no image. The reason why he did that was because it doubled the value of the painting.

45. For a survey of the avant-garde artists active in New York during this period, see Barbara Haskell, *Blam! The Explosion of Pop, Minimalism, and Performance 1958-1964* (New York: Whitney Museum of American Art, 1984); Ronald Sukenick, *Down and In* (New York: Collier Books, 1987); John Gruen, *The New Bohemia* (Chicago: a cappella books, 1990); and Sally Banes, *Greenwich Village 1963* (Durham, N.C. and London: Duke University Press, 1993).

46. Cf. John Cage's piano piece "4'33"", in which the pianist silently sits at the keyboard for that duration of time.

47. In "Satori Interview: Billy Name," *Satori* 2, 2 (Summer 1989): 14-17, the artist discusses these lost years of his life.

48. Billy, speaking of what it was like to be a young artist in this circle, recalled: "Just being around John Cage at that time, you felt his edge, and you became cut by that." Quoted in *ibid.*, p. 15.

49. Among Cage's works are "Credo in Us," a percussion quartet scored for a radio and other instruments; "Imaginary Landscape No. 5," for any 42 recordings; "Speech for 5 Radios and Newspaper;" and "Radio Music," scored for as many as eight radios. Q.v., Paul Griffiths, *Cage* (New York: Oxford University Press, 1981).

50. See David Bourdon, "Cosmic Ray: An open letter to the founder of the New York Correspondence School," *Art in America* (Oct. 1995): 108-11.

51. Warhol and Hackett, *op. cit.*, p. 64.

52. *Ibid.*

53. *Ibid.*, p. 65.

54. *Ibid.*, p. 83.

55. The song was first recorded on the album *The Velvet Underground and Nico* (Verve, 1967); it begins with the verse, "I'll be your mirror, reflect what you are/In case you don't know;" see Lou Reed, *Between Thought and Expression: The Selected Lyrics of Lou Reed* (New York: Hyperion, 1991): 3.

56. Quoted in Penelope Mason, *History of Japanese Art* (New York: Harry N. Abrams, Inc., Publishers, 1993): 29.

57. Shunryo Suzuki, *Zen Mind, Beginner's Mind* (New York: Weatherill, 1991): 106.

58. Eugene Wildman, *Anthology of Concretism* (Chicago: Swallow Press, 1969): viii-ix.

59. Mary Ellen Solt, *A World Look at Concrete Poetry* (Bloomington: Indiana University Press, 1968): 7. Solt's *Forsythia,* for example, uses the word forsythia, spelled out horizontally, as a base from which new words, such as out, space, yellow, etc., vertically stem, then break up into individual letters that spiral out in all directions, rather like an untrimmed forsythia bush.

60. See Judi Freeman, *The Dada and Surrealist Word-Image* (Cambridge, MA: MIT Press, 1989); and Carol P. James, "An Original Revolutionary Messagerie Rrose, or What Became of the Readymade," in *The Definitely Unfinished Marcel Duchamp,* ed. by Thierry Du Duve (Cambridge, MA: MIT Press, 1991): 281.

61. Quoted in Marc Dachy, *Dada Movement* (Geneva: Skira, 1990): 24.

62. Freeman, *op. cit.,* p. 25, translates it as "She has the hots."

63. On this practice, see John D. Erickson, *Dada: Performance, Poetry and Art* (Boston: Twayne, 1984): 98.

64. Cited in Robert Motherwell, ed., *The Dada Painters and Poets: An Anthology* (Boston: G.K. Hall, 1981): xxviii.

65. On Fluxus, see Janet Jenkins, ed., *In the Spirit of Fluxus,* ex. cat. (Minneapolis: Walker Art Center, 1993); and the review "All is Flux," *Art News* (Sept. 1992): 16. The exhibition was mounted on the thirtieth anniversary of the Fluxus movement.

66. Quoted in Bourdon, *op. cit.,* p. 109.

67. See Carter Ratcliff, "Joseph Cornell, Mechanic of the Ineffable," in Kynaston McShine, ed., *Joseph Cornell,* ex. cat. (New York: Museum of Modern Art, 1980): 48. Cornell made numerous trips into Manhattan to collect the artifacts that became his boxes and collages; interestingly, he called his found objects "signs."

68. "Satori Interview: Billy Name," *op. cit.,* p. 17.

69. *Ibid.* Billy's sonic system is not unlike that of Kurt Schwitters, whose "Sonate" begins: "Grim Glin Gnim Bimbin."

**ULTRA VIOLET NOTES**

1. Quoted in Michael Smith, *Village Voice* XIII, 7 (30 Nov. 1967): 33.

2. Andy Warhol and Pat Hackett, *POPism: The Warhol '60s* (New York: Harper & Row, 1980): 250.

3. Smith, *loc. cit.*

4. Quoted from an interview with Ondine of 17 December 1978, in Patrick S. Smith, *Andy Warhol's Art and Films* (Ann Arbor: UMI Research Press, 1986): 453.

5. John J. O'Connor, *Wall Street Journal* CLXX, 101 (22 Nov. 1967): 16; cited also in Ultra Violet, *Famous for 15 Minutes: My Years with Andy Warhol* (New York: Harcourt Brace Jovanovich, Publishers, 1988): 125.

6. For recent discussions of the film, see Callie Angell, *The Films of Andy Warhol: Part II* (New York: Whitney Museum of American Art, 1994): 29-30; and Debra Miller, *Billy Name: Stills from the Warhol Films* (Munich and New York: Prestel Verlag, 1994): 118-23.

7. The movie was created for New York's Hudson Theater, on 44th Street near Times Square, in response to owner Maury Maura's request for something along the lines of the erotic Swedish hit *I, a Woman.*

8. Howard Thompson, *New York Times* CXVI, 40,025 (25 Aug. 1967): 23, cites the length as 100 minutes, but Gold's review of the film in *Variety* 248, 2 (30 Aug. 1967): 6, gives the total running time as 99 minutes.

9. See the review by Gene Youngblood, "New Warhol at Cinematheque," *Los Angeles Free Press* (16 Feb. 1968): 10, 12-13. This is consistent with Ultra Violet's recollection of flying to San Francisco with Warhol, Morrissey, and Nico to meet the Los Angeles-based Tom Baker for filming in California; see Ultra Violet, *op. cit.,* p. 115. Other segments of *I, a Man,* such as Valerie Solanas's appearance in a stairwell at the Factory, obviously were filmed in New York and comprised the earlier version shown there.

10. Warhol and Hackett, *op. cit.,* p. 211.

11. Ultra Violet, *op. cit.,* p. 138.

12. The original document is quoted in Angell, *op. cit.,* p. 35, n. 7.

13. Ultra Violet, *op. cit.,* p. 115. Ultra achieved the purple tint of her hair by rinsing it with cranberry juice or jelly (p. 82).

14. Warhol and Hackett, *op. cit.,* pp. 280-81.

15. Ultra Violet, *loc. cit.*

16. Morrissey filmed and released *Flesh* in 1968, following the shooting of the party scene in *Midnight Cowboy* (which was not completed for theatrical

release until 1969). He later featured actress Sylvia Miles, who had been nominated as Best Supporting Actress for her role in Schlesinger's movie, in *Heat*. For a sensitive analysis of the hustler trilogy, see Maurice Yacowar, *The Films of Paul Morrissey* (New York: Cambridge University Press, 1993).

17. For an insider's account of this period, see Françoise Gilot and Carlton Lake, *Life with Picasso* (New York: McGraw-Hill Book Company, 1964): especially pp. 210ff.

18. Ultra Violet, *op. cit.*, p. 61.

19. The present portrait originally was designed as a hand-made book in Ultra Violet's large-scale installation, *The Apocalyptic Library*, which combines milestones from the history of civilization with quotations from the Biblical Book of Revelation.

20. Cf. Picasso's *Still Life with Owl and Three Sea Urchins*, 1946, oil on plywood, 81.5 x 79 cm., Picasso Museum, Antibes, illustrated in Danièle Giraudy, *Antibes/Guide to the Picasso Museum* (Paris: Hazan, 1987): 39.

21. Ultra Violet, *op. cit.*, p. 51.

22. *Ibid.*, p. 216.

23. Among the surveys of this popular artform, see Allan Schwartzman, *Street Art* (Garden City: The Dial Press, 1985) and Francesca Alinovi, et al., *Arte di Frontiera: New York Graffiti*, ex. cat., Galleria communale d'arte moderna, Bologna, March-April 1984 (Milan: Mazzotta, 1984).

24. On Ruscha and the use of words as artistic subject, see Anne Livet, et al., *The Works of Edward Ruscha*, ex. cat., San Francisco Museum of Modern Art, March-May 1982 (New York: Hudson Hills Press, 1982) and *Edward Ruscha: Paintings*, ex. cat., Boymans-van Beuningen Museum, Rotterdam, March-April 1990.

25. Ultra Violet, *L'ULTRATIQUE* (Lodève: Karedys Editions, 1991).

26. Ultra Violet, quoted in the exhibition brochure by Debra Miller, "Apocalyptic Angels: The Works of Ultra Violet," Department of Art and Art History, Gettysburg College, PA, February-March 1995.

27. Ultra Violet, "An Interactive Presentation: Andy Warhol and Art History," Warhol's Worlds, The Andy Warhol Museum, Pittsburgh, PA, 22 April 1995.

28. *Ibid.*

29. *Ibid.* Among the numerous recent volumes dedicated to the subject of angels are Malcolm Godwin, *Angels: An Endangered Species* (New York: Simon and Schuster, 1990); Morris B. Margolies, *A Gathering of Angels: Angels in Jewish Life and Literature* (New York: Ballantine Books, 1994); and Sophy Burnham, *A Book of Angels* (New York: Ballantine Books, 1990), *Angel Letters* (New York: Ballantine Books, 1991), and *The President's Angel* (New York: Ballantine Books, 1993). The play *Angels in America*, written by Tony Kushner, debuted at the Walter Kerr Theatre in New York on 4 May 1993 (*Part I: The Millennium Approaches*). On television, *Touched by an Angel*, began its run on the CBS network in 1994. I am indebted to Maria J. Keane and Joseph Moskal for providing me with bibliographic and background information on angels.

30. Scholars have dated the writings of the Pseudo-Dionysius to c. 500 A.D.; Thomas's *Summa* was composed 1266-73.

31. E.g., in the Book of Daniel (8:15ff. and 9:21ff.), Gabriel interpreted a vision and explained a decree; in the Gospel of Luke (1:11-20), he announced the coming birth of a son to Elizabeth and Zacharias, and declared his name to be John [the Baptist].

32. Ultra Violet, "Apocalyptic Angels: A Message of Light from Ultra Violet," unpublished ms., 1994, p. 6.

33. Dr. William Haseltine, Dana Farber Cancer Institute, Harvard University, quoted in Gina Kolata, "AIDS Research Finds 13 Vulnerable Spots in Life Cycle," 1993.

34. The inconsistencies in this paradigm for AIDS have led some researchers to doubt the causative effect of HIV; see the controversial article by B. Elswood, Dr. R. Stricker, and W. Neves, "AIDS: Why Is Science Failing," translated and reprinted in *Critical Path AIDS Project* 3, 2-3 (Feb.-Mar. 1992): 4-7.

35. Statistics provided by the AIDS Information Network of Philadelphia, based on data compiled by the World Health Organization and the Global AIDS Policy Coalition to 1994. See *AIDS and Families* (Washington, DC: American Association for World Health, 1994): 15-16; and Steven J. Goodwin, exec. ed., *AIDS Reference Guide* (Washington, DC: Atlantic Information Services, Inc., 1995): 1-8.

36. They are eulogized in Ultra Violet, *Famous for 15 Minutes, op. cit.,* pp. 248-51.

37. This is a paraphrase from Joseph Smith, trans., *The Book of Mormon*, 1st ed. 1830 (Salt Lake City: The Church of Jesus Christ of Latter-Day Saints, 1986):

> …for it is by faith that miracles are wrought; and it is by faith that angels appear and minister unto men (Moro. 7:37).

38. Ultra Violet donated the use of this image to the AIDS Information Network, Philadelphia, for its educational and fundraising efforts.

39. The Friedmann-Lemaître models describe an expanding universe, based on Albert Einstein's gravitational field equations. They were independently confirmed by American astronomer

Edwin Hubble in 1929. For a comprehensible
explanation of the Big Bang, see James S. Trefil, *The
Moment of Creation* (New York: Charles Scribner's
Sons, 1983) and Joseph Silk, *The Big Bang: The
Creation and Evolution of the Universe* (San
Francisco: W.H. Freeman and Company, 1980). It has
been refuted in Eric J. Lerner, *The Big Bang Never
Happened* (New York: Vintage Books, 1992).

40. Ultra Violet, "Apocalyptic Angels: A Message of
Light from Ultra Violet," *op. cit.,* p. 3.

41. This was confirmed by British astronomers observing
the solar eclipse of 29 May 1919, on the west coast of
Africa and northern Brazil. The equation and its
explanation were provided to Ultra Violet by D.B.
Ostrowsky.

42. *Ultra Violet's World*, videography and editing by
Dana Sardet, Nice and Oggio La Gaude, 1995.
Distributed the The Currituck Company, Kennett
Square, PA.

43. I am indebted to Suzy Hoffmann for providing me
with the historic and technical information on
computers cited in this entry.

44. In her use of existing sources as the basis for her own
original artwork, Ultra Violet follows in the tradition
of Andy Warhol's photo-silkscreening process. One
consequence of Warhol's unauthorized appropriation
of existing images was the successful lawsuit filed
against him by photographer Patricia Caulfield.
Nevertheless, the art of appropriation continues, most
notably in the work of Jeff Koons (who has also faced
legal action, initiated and won by California
photographer Art Rogers); q.v., Martha Buskirk,
"Appropriation under the Gun," *Art in America* 80
(June 1992): 37-41; *Jeff Koons*, ex. cat., San
Francisco Museum of Modern Art, 1992; and
Christopher R. Young, *The Purloined Image*, ex. cat.,
Flint Institute of Arts, Flint, MI, March-May 1993. It
is important to note that, historically, in Renaissance
and Baroque art theory (based on Pliny),
appropriation was termed *aemulatio* and considered
the highest form of praise for the work so emulated.

45. Ultra Violet, "Apocalyptic Angels: A Message of
Light from Ultra Violet," *loc. cit.* Similar concerns
had been expressed earlier in the scholarly, scientific
community; e.g., F.C.D. III, "Rockets and Guided
Missiles," *The Encyclopaedia Britannica* 19
(Chicago: William Benton, Publisher, 1966): 424:

> Whenever a new scientific frontier has
> been penetrated the eventual results have
> been of economic benefit to mankind. It
> could only be hoped that in moving into
> this new dimension man would also learn
> better the art of living with his neighbors,
> and that the rocket, developed as a machine
> of war, would become a tool for peaceful
> research and understanding.

46. For a succinct chronology and survey of Renoir's life
and career, see Denis Rouart, *Renoir,* trans. by James
Emmons (Geneva: Editions d'Art Albert Skira, 1954).

47. Ultra Violet, "Apocalyptic Angels…," *loc. cit.*

48. "Chocolate!," curated by Carin Kuoni and Ingrid
Schaffner, Swiss Institute, New York, 6 April-20 May
1995.

49. Ruscha's painting (c. 1973-74, chocolate on canvas)
was inspired by a phrase frequently uttered by Ultra
Violet during the period of their involvement. It was
one of the canvases he presented to her as a gift; the
other, *Oro Puro*, was stenciled in gold paint mixed
with Ruscha's own blood. The most notorious of
Ruscha's chocolate pieces was the *Chocolate Room*
he created for the Venice Biennale of 1970. In it, he
used 28 tubes of Nestlé's chocolate paste, which he
silkscreened onto 360 sheets of paper, installed like
shingles on a wall. The installation came to an abrupt
end when ants invaded the gallery, after which the
insects themselves became a recurrent motif in
Ruscha's art; see Henry T. Hopkins, "Director's
Foreword: Ed Ruscha: Three Contact Prints," in
*Edward Ruscha: Paintings, op. cit.,* p. 11.

50. Ultra Violet, conversation with author, 25 March
1995.

51. Ultra Violet, conversation with author, 31 August
1995.

## ALLEN MIDGETTE NOTES

1. Allen Midgette, conversation with author, 21 March
1996.

2. Recalled by Allen Midgette, lecture, University of
Delaware, Newark, 27 April 1995. This comment is
particularly perplexing in light of the fact that
Midgette has American Indian blood.

3. Q.v., Robert Phillip Kolker, *Bernardo Bertolucci*
(New York: Oxford University Press, 1985).

4. Allen Midgette, lecture, University of Delaware,
Newark, 27 April 1995.

5. David Bleiler, ed., *TLA Film & Video Guide 1996-
1997* (Philadelphia: TLA Publications, 1996): 42.

6. Noted in the review of the film, "In Cannes Critics
Section," *Variety* (6 May 1964): 16.

7. The "best party of the sixties" is described at length
in Andy Warhol and Pat Hackett, *POPism: The
Warhol '60s* (New York: Harper & Row, Publishers,
1980): 101-05.

8. Allen Midgette, lecture, University of Delaware,
Newark, 27 April 1995.

9. According to Billy Name, conversation with author, 14 August 1993.

10. See Debra Miller, *Billy Name: Stills from the Warhol Films* (Munich and New York: Prestel Verlag, 1994): 124, especially n. 2; and *Andy Warhol, Cinéma* (Paris: Centre Georges Pompidou/Editions Carré, 1990): 262.

11. Allen Midgette, lecture, University of Delaware, Newark, 27 April 1995.

12. Based on the account by Allen Midgette, lecture, University of Delaware, Newark, 27 April 1995; see also, David Bourdon, *Warhol* (New York: Harry N. Abrams, Inc., Publishers, 1989): 266-69. Midgette's version of the story is significantly different from Warhol's, who attributed the idea of the impersonation to Allen; see Warhol and Hackett, *op. cit.,* pp. 247-48.

13. Warhol and Hackett, *op. cit.,* p. 248.

14. Quoted in a press clipping, "POPPED ART," in Allen Midgette's scrapbook.

15. The auction was held from 23 April-3 May 1988, at Sotheby's New York.

16. As a result of his renewed impersonation, in 1992, Midgette was cast in the role of Warhol for playwright Richard Lay's off-Broadway comedy, *Andy Warhol's Secret Girlfriend*, at the Intar Theater on 42nd Street. But creative differences with the play's director, John Wall, led both Midgette and his leading lady, Helene Beth Abrams, to quit the show prior to its opening. See Frank DiGiacomo and Joanna Molloy with Florence Anthony, "PAGE SIX: Casting Off," *New York Post* (2 September 1992): 6; and Jerry Talmer, "ON THE TOWN: Art imitates artist," *New York Post* (30 September 1992).

17. Mitchell first released "Woodstock" on her album *Ladies of the Canyon* (Reprise Records, 1969). The lyrics are printed on the album cover.

18. Allen Midgette, conversation with author, 18 April 1996.

19. Andy Warhol, *Andy Warhol's Index (Book)* (New York: Random House, 1967). The pop-up book of life at the Factory was Warhol's answer to the "Catholic Index"—the church's list of forbidden movies and books.

20. E.g., see H. Perry Chapman, *Rembrandt's Self-Portraits: A Study in Seventeenth-Century Identity* (Princeton: Princeton University Press, 1990).

21. For a visual survey of selected examples of Warhol's self-portraiture, see Museum of Modern Art, *Andy Warhol: A Retrospective*, ed. by Kynaston McShine, ex. cat. (New York: Museum of Modern Art, 1989): 82-99.

22. Ivan Karp, quoted in Warhol and Hackett, *op. cit.*, p. 17. Of course Warhol had executed self-portraits well before his conversation with Karp, including a pencil drawing of 1942 (Private Collection) and the controversial tempera painting *The Broad Gave Me My Face, But I Can Pick My Own Nose* of c. 1948-49 (Collection Paul Warhola Family).

23. Allen Midgette, conversation with author, 18 April 1996.

24. Warhol first silkscreened *Marilyn* in 1962, shortly after the star's shocking suicide on 5 August.

25. *Flowers* was first issued in 1964. The composition was appropriated from a color photograph of hibiscus blossoms that was printed as a two-page fold-out in *Modern Photography* (June 1964), by the magazine's executive editor, Patricia Caulfield. Caulfield sued Warhol for the unauthorized use of her photograph and eventually received a cash settlement and twelve portfolios from Warhol's original edition of 250. See David Bourdon, *op. cit.,* pp. 191 and 311, n. 42.

26. The design was used for the cover of *The Velvet Underground and Nico* album of 1967 (Verve). According to Allen Midgette, conversation with author, 14 March 1995: "I never really got into the Velvet Underground; I just came to the Factory to work."

27. Andy's first series of *Campbell's Soup Cans* was silkscreened in 1961-62. *Life Savers* and *Van Heusen (Ronald Reagan)* were a part of Warhol's portfolio of ten *Ads,* created in 1985.

28. The series of *Dollar Signs* was begun in 1981. Warhol produced them as photo-silkscreens, based on his own hand drawings.

29. Allen Midgette, conversation with author, 14 March 1995.

30. *Ibid.*

31. Wounded Knee, South Dakota, was the site of the massacre of hundreds of captive Indians by the United States Cavalry in 1890; q.v., Dee Alexander Brown, *Bury My Heart at Wounded Knee: An Indian History of the American West* (New York: Holt, Rinehart & Winston, 1971). The charges filed against Means for his participation in the takeover of 1973 were dismissed by U.S. District Court Judge Fred Nichol, who disputed the truthfulness of government allegations and was shocked by reports of the use of paid FBI informers against the defendant; see *New York Times* (14 March 1975): 77.

32. On 5 May 1976, Means and another AIM member, John Thomas, were shot and wounded in the housing area of the Indian reservation at Yankton, South Dakota, where they were planning the schedule for an AIM treaty conference to be held later that summer. On 10 June 1975, reports confirmed that Means had been shot in the abdomen by a policeman from the

Bureau of Indian Affairs at Fort Yates, North Dakota, during a scuffle at Standing Rock Indian reservation. Later that year (30 July 1975), Means was reported to have suffered a minor head wound in an apparent assassination attempt while driving on South Dakota's Rosebud Indian reservation.

33. See "2 Held in Shooting," *New York Times* (4 March 1975): 27.

34. This respect for Indian culture became evident, too, in Warhol's personal effects. By the time of his death, he had accumulated an extensive collection of Native American art, which was catalogued and auctioned in the sale of his movable estate; see *The Andy Warhol Collection. Vol. IV. American Indian Art* (New York: Sotheby's, 1988), distributed by Harry N. Abrams, Inc., New York.

35. Allen Midgette, conversation with author, 14 March 1995. He recounts:

> One time, in 1954, when we were visiting relatives in Cape Hatteras, I had this annoying wart on my knee. It was always rubbed raw from my jeans. Uncle Gus told me that he had a cure. He took a potato and rubbed the wart and said some chants to evoke the favor of the spirits. Then he told me not to think about the wart for one week. I actually really forgot about it. Several months later, my dad asked me, "Whatever happened to that wart?" "Oh," I said, "it must be gone, because I have not been miserable with it since Uncle Gus told me not to think about it!"

36. The "Mighty Midgettes" (alternately Midget, Midyett, or Midgett) were among the first European families to settle on the island of Cape Hatteras; see Jo Anna Heath Bates, *The Heritage of Currituck County, North Carolina, 1985* (Winston-Salem: The Albemarle Genealogical Society, Inc., 1985). Allen's father, Jarvis Midgette, served in the Coast Guard's Corps of Engineers there. The Midgettes were, in fact, the first Coast Guards of the Cape, and were thus featured in a television commercial. After being promoted to Captain, Jarvis was transferred to New Jersey, where he met his first wife Dorothy (Allen's mother), who was of Welsh heritage (Allen Midgette, conversation with author, 16 April 1996).

37. Allen Midgette, conversation with author, 14 March 1995.

38. Allen Midgette, conversation with author, 21 March 1996. Among Allen's recognizable portraits is the elderly Sitting Eagle, an unidentified Sioux warrior, whose face is seen in extreme close-up, and a Piegan named Iron Breast, whose image, derived from a photograph by Edward Sheriff Curtis of c. 1890, occupies one of the largest feathers on the tree; see Christopher Cardozo and George P. Horse Capture, *Native Nations: First Americans as Seen by Edward S. Curtis* (Toronto: Little, Brown and Company, Bulfinch Press, 1993): 41.

39. Allen Midgette, conversation with author, 21 March 1996.

40. *Ibid.*

41. For an understanding of the social climate of the 1960s, see Martin A. Lee and Bruce Shlain, *Acid Dreams: The CIA, LSD and the Sixties Rebellion* (New York: Grove Press, 1985).

42. Allen Midgette, conversation with author, 18 April 1996.

43. Allen Midgette, conversation with author, 14 March 1995.

44. The use of the shield became ritualized in ceremony and dance as these activities lessened, "partly due to [US] government programs of relocation and termination, and partly to an inevitable process of acculturation;" see Norman Feder, *American Indian Art* (New York: Harry N. Abrams, Inc., Publishers, 1965): 11.

45. Allen Midgette, conversation with author, 18 April 1996. According to Alvin M. Josephy, Jr., *America in 1492* (New York: Vintage Books, 1991): 85-117, Indians used to corral antelopes and deer, killing as many of them as seemed necessary for tribal survival. The deer provided not just sustenance, but also ornaments, clothing, tools, shoes, threads, and toys. Norman Feder, *op. cit.,* p. 12, also notes that:

> As a rule, the Indian artist generally used whatever material was most readily available: wood and wood products were the dominant materials in the Northwest Coast and Woodland areas, buffalo hides on the Plains, and clay in the Southwest. However, almost everywhere the rare material was eagerly sought because of the prestige its ownership brought.

46. In particular, the eagle feather was highly esteemed. The eagle was the Indians' brother, and elaborate ceremonies took place over the slain body of an eagle. A hunter would conceal the carcass in a brush-covered pit and perform rituals to placate the eagle's spirit; see Cardozo and Horse Capture, *op. cit.,* p. 154.

47. Josephy, Jr., *op. cit.,* p. 116.

48. Allen Midgette, conversation with author, 14 March 1995.

49. Allen Midgette, conversation with author, 18 April 1996.

50. *New Larousse Encyclopedia of Mythology*, intro. by Robert Graves (London, New York, Sydney, and Toronto: The Hamlyn Publishing Group Limited, 1959): 427.

51. Allen Midgette, conversation with author, 14 March 1995.

52. On Klimt, see Susanna Partsch, *Klimt: Life and Work* (Munich: I.P. Gesellschaft GmbH, 1993).

53. The impact of Byzantine mosaics on Klimt was enhanced by his trip to Ravenna in 1903; their lasting impression was reflected in the artist's "Golden Style."

54. On the Stoclet frieze, see Partsch, *op. cit.,* pp. 218-28; and Werner M. Schweiger, *Wiener Werkstätte: Design in Vienna 1903-1932*, intro. by W.G. Fischer (New York: Abbeville Press, 1984): 155-62.

55. Partsch, *op.cit.,* p. 142.

56. The Flöge Sisters (Emilie, Pauline, and Helene—who had married Klimt's brother Ernst in 1891) opened their fashionable shop on the Mariahilfstrasse in the summer of 1904.

57. Allen Midgette, conversation with author, 18 April 1996.

## CHRISTOPHER MAKOS NOTES

1. On Man Ray, see Merry A. Foresta, et al., *Perpetual Motif: The Art of Man Ray*, ex. cat. (New York: Abbeville Press, 1988).

2. Makos stated in an interview that it was Man Ray, not Andy Warhol,

   > who was really my mentor, because I'm much more into surrealism and Dadaism and all of that from the '20s and '30s… [but Andy] was more accessible than Man Ray.

   See Chip Butterman, "15 minutes with Makos," *Spunk* 2.7 (1994): 50.

3. Quoted in Glenn Albin's Introduction in Christopher Makos, *Warhol: A Personal Photographic Memoir* (New York: New American Library, 1989): 11.

4. Christopher Makos, *White Trash* (New York: Stonehill Publishing Company, 1977): jacket notes.

5. In the 1970s, Makos's photographs appeared in such noteworthy publications as *Daily News, Esquire, Interview,* and *Rolling Stone.*

6. Makos in Butterman, *op. cit.*, p. 45.

7. By his own admission, Makos "never made a good assistant." After locking Williams's bulldog in a closet and leaving his typewriter on an airport minibus, he was relieved of his position, although the two men remained friends; see Chip Butterman, *op. cit.*, p. 48.

8. *Ibid.*, p. 50.

9. Christopher Makos, *White Trash, loc. cit.*

10. Andrew J. Crispo, in his introduction to *ibid.,* n.p.

11. E.g., Ivana Trump chose Makos to photograph her for the back cover of her autobiography, *For Love Alone* (New York: Pocket Books, c. 1992).

12. A group of the self-portraits was exhibited at Pace/MacGill Gallery in New York from 7 May-26 June 1992, and published in the catalogue *Andy Warhol Polaroids 1971-1986* (New York: Pace/MacGill Gallery and Andy Warhol Foundation for the Visual Arts, Inc., 1992): 100-11. The show traveled to the Anthony d'Offay Gallery, London, and the Galerie Liliane & Michel Durrand-Dessert, Paris.

13. Bob Colacello, *Holy Terror: Andy Warhol Close Up* (New York: HarperCollins Publishers, 1990): 443.

14. Noted by Christopher Makos, *Warhol: A Personal Photographic Memoir*, p. 75. See also Marjorie Garber, *Vested Interests: Cross-Dressing and Cultural Anxiety* (New York and London: Routledge, 1992): 161. For further associations between Warhol and Duchamp, see Anne d'Harnoncourt and Kynaston McShine, *Marcel Duchamp* (New York: The Museum of Modern Art, 1973): 227. I am indebted to Barbara Macklem for providing me with useful information for this catalogue entry.

15. *Ibid.,* p. 112.

16. Christopher Makos, *Warhol: A Personal Photographic Memoir*, p. 122. Makos selected a related portrait of Warhol wearing glasses, from the same photo session, for the cover of his book.

17. The date of Warhol's signing with Zoli is incorrectly given as 1983 in *ibid.,* p. 14. In 1985, Andy switched his representation to the Ford modeling agency.

18. Andy Warhol, *The Andy Warhol Diaries*, edited by Pat Hackett (New York: Warner Books, Inc., 1989): 370.

19. Colacello, *op. cit.,* p. 442. The caustic author goes on to opine: "it was obvious that he was being used for his joke value."

20. Makos, *Warhol: A Personal Photographic Memoir, loc. cit.* This is in contrast to other authors, who make much of Andy's earlier insecurities about his nose, his complexion, his body, and his baldness; e.g., cf. Victor Bockris, *The Life and Death of Andy Warhol* (New York: Bantam Books, 1989): 30-32.

21. Makos, *ibid.,* pp. 13-14.

22. My thanks to Barbara Macklem for this sensitive observation.

23. See Stephen Koch, *Andy Warhol Photographs* (New York: Robert Miller Gallery, c. 1987).

24. Makos, *Warhol: A Personal Photographic Memoir*, p. 104.

25. *Ibid.*, pp. 104, 112. Makos also noted (p. 34) that:

> Andy was fond of stealing ideas, and
> the way he did this was by surrounding
> himself with interesting and different
> kinds of people…

26. Makos's venues in 1995 included King (January) and Tiffany & Co. (March) in New York; Chicago Art Expo, Mars Gallery (May) and Gallery Wabi Sabi (September) in Chicago; and Site Santa Fe/ Throckmorton (July) in New Mexico.

27. Three additional photographs of Harry appeared in the book; see Christopher Makos, *White Trash*, pp. 30, 31, and 40-41.

28. Vincent Fremont, "Andy Warhol's Portraits: A Recollection by Vincent Fremont," in Henry Geldzahler and Robert Rosenblum, *Andy Warhol Portraits of the Seventies and Eighties*, ex. cat. (London: Thames and Hudson in association with Anthony d'Offay Gallery, 1993): 31-32.

29. Makos, *White Trash,* pp. 17, 35, and 69.

30. This exhibition was followed by another show of "Eyes" in February 1990 at Hokin, and in November 1990 at Jan de Bourvrie Gallery in Bussum, The Netherlands; and "Eye and Mouth Paintings" in April 1990 at Pucci Gallery, New York.

31. Among the impressive list of Makos's commercial clients are: Armani A/X; Listerine/Warner Lambert; Optical Affairs, International; SONY Corporation, America; Polaroid, Europe; Compaque Computer; and Forbes, International.

32. Warhol used the image for a series of silkscreens in 1962, then for the lithograph *Marilyn Monroe I Love Your Kiss Forever Forever*, in the unbound book by Walasse Ting, *1¢ Life*, edited by Sam Francis (Bern: E.W. Kornfeld, 1964).

33. A selection of the photographs that document his journeys has been published in Christopher Makos, *Warhol: A Personal Photographic Memoir*. His photographs of Venice were exhibited in a one-man show at the Ken Taranto Gallery, New York, in August 1993.

34. In the artist's own words (Christopher Makos, conversation with author, 15 April 1996): "I was just blown away by the natural beauty of the place."

35. Quoted in Butterman, *op. cit.*, p. 50.

36. *Ibid.*

37. Q.v., David Bourdon, *Warhol* (New York: Harry N. Abrams, Inc., Publishers, 1989): 361.

38. Christopher Makos, press release for *Makostyle*, 1993.

39. Makos, quoted in Butterman, *op. cit.*, p. 45.

40. *Ibid.*

41. *Ibid.*

## JAMES WARHOLA NOTES

1. For the most complete biography and study of James Warhola's career, see Susanne Mahoney Pepperman, "'Look to See to Remember:' The Life and Art of James Warhola," M.A. thesis, University of Delaware, Newark, 1995.

2. According to the artist, "You had to paint realistic figures with good brushwork." James Warhola, conversation with author, 11 April 1994.

3. John Stanley, *Creature Feature Movie Guide* (New York: Warner Books, 1982).

4. Carnegie-Mellon University was called the Carnegie Institute of Technology when Andy studied pictorial design there, from 1945-49. See David Bourdon, *Warhol* (New York: Harry N. Abrams, Inc., 1989): 20.

5. An example of Andy Warhol's light-hearted spirit is his last hand-colored picture book, *Wild Raspberries*, of 1959—a 40-page novelty cookbook containing eighteen illustrations. The title itself is a playful take-off on Ingmar Bergman's film, *Wild Strawberries*. Q.v., *ibid.*, pp. 66-67.

6. Avram Davidson, *Magic for Sale* (New York: Ace Science Fiction Books, 1983).

7. James Warhola, conversation with author, 2 December 1994.

8. Ron Goulart, *Suicide, Inc.* (New York: Berkley, 1985).

9. James Warhola, conversation with author, 4 January 1995.

10. The set of Fantasy Art Trading Cards was published by FPG of Pittsburgh in 1995. Each package consists of ten randomly inserted cards from a 90-card series, which could include the artist's biography, an autograph, and/or a checklist of his works, along with reproductions of Warhola's paintings (primarily a sampling of his favorite works executed in oil, but with a few examples of his watercolors). On the back of each of the art cards is the title of the painting, a brief quotation about it by the artist, and a preliminary sketch or conceptual drawing of the work reproduced on the front.

11. See Spider Robinson, *Callahan's Crosstime Saloon* (Short Hills, NJ: R. Enslow, 1978). Jamie's cover design was for a later edition of the book.

12. Directed by George Lucas and released in 1977, *Star Wars* was the first in a phenomenally successful trilogy of science-fiction films, completed by *The*

*Empire Strikes Back* (1980) and *Return of the Jedi* (1983).

13. James Warhola, conversation with author, 4 January 1995.

14. James Warhola, conversation with author, 14 May 1995, acknowledges that the art and working methods of these renowned illustrators had the most profound influence on his own career. Q.v., Douglas Allen and Douglas Allen, Jr., *N.C. Wyeth* (New York: Bonanza Books, 1984); Thomas S. Buechner, *Norman Rockwell, A Sixty Year Retrospective* (New York: Harry N. Abrams, Inc., 1972); and Terry Booth, *Brandywine Spirit Art* (Chicago: The Brandywine Fantasy Gallery, 1988).

15. James Warhola, conversation with author, 2 December 1995.

16. James Warhola, conversation with author, 4 January 1995.

17. The current popularity of fantasy and science-fiction art can be traced back to the counter-culture of the 1960s, when young people embraced values and ideas different from those of past generations; see Robert E. Weinberg, *A Biographical Dictionary of Science Fiction and Fantasy Artists* (New York: Greenwood Press, 1988): 27. Heinlein's controversial novel, first published in 1961 (New York: G.P. Putnam's Sons), became a best-seller among college students and members of the hippie movement.

18. James Warhola, conversation with author, 4 January 1995.

19. Robert A. Heinlein, *Stranger in a Strange Land* (New York: G.P. Putnam's Sons, 1961): 21.

20. This episode is told in *ibid.,* pp. 143-49.

21. Heinlein's story concludes with a reference to the Archangel Michael pushing back his halo to get to work *(ibid.,* p. 408).

22. James Warhola, conversation with author, 25 August 1994.

23. Bruce B. Cole, *The Pumpkinville Mystery*, illustrated by James Warhola (New York: Prentice-Hall Books for Young Readers, a Division of Simon and Schuster, 1987).

24. James Warhola, conversation with author, 25 August 1994.

25. See Iona and Peter Opie, *The Classic Fairy Tales* (Oxford: Oxford University Press, 1974): 163.

26. *Jack and the Beanstalk*, retold by Susan Pearson and illustrated by James Warhola (New York: Simon & Schuster Books for Young Readers, 1989). The book measures 10 1/4 x 8 1/4" and contains 40 pages. Warhola designed twelve double-page illustrations, five full-page illustrations, six small-scale or floating illustrations, a title-page illustration, and a wrapped cover.

27. Opie, *op. cit.,* p. 206.

28. *The Tinderbox* by Hans Christian Andersen, retold by Peggy Thomson and illustrated by James Warhola (New York: Simon & Schuster Books for Young Readers, 1991). The book measures 11 1/4 x 8 1/4" and has 38 pages, containing nine double-page, six full-page, thirteen small-scale or floating, and two title-page illustrations, and an illustrated wrapped cover.

29. The Brothers Grimm were the first substantial collectors and students of folktales, and the first to write them down exactly as ordinary people had told them. Although they realized that the folktales in their collection shared a common European tradition of storytelling, they were very interested in rediscovering their own ethnic past and wanted to emphasize the Germanic qualities in their versions of the stories. They stated that their fairy tales were based on "the wealth of German poetic literature in early times" and oral versions of folktales, of which there were wide variations. See James M. McGlathery, *Grimms' Fairy Tales, A History of Criticism on a Popular Classic* (Columbia, S.C.: Camden House, Inc., 1993): 6, 29-30.

30. *The Brave Little Tailor* by the Brothers Grimm, retold by Peggy Thomson and illustrated by James Warhola (New York: Simon & Schuster Books for Young Readers, 1992). The book measures 11 1/4 x 8 1/4" and contains 40 pages, with nine double-page illustrations, eight full-page illustrations, eighteen small-scale or floating illustrations, both a title-page and endpaper illustration, and a wrapped cover.

31. James Warhola, conversation with author, 25 August 1994.

32. Traveling with his mother, Ann Warhola, Jamie visited Prague (in the Czech Republic) to meet his father's cousins, and then went on to Bratislava, the capital of Slovakia, for additional family reunions. Leaving Bratislava, the Warholas traveled ten hours to Michova, the little village in Eastern Slovakia that was the ancestral home to Jamie's paternal grandparents (Andy Warhol's parents). Five miles from Michova is the city of Medzilaborce, where a modern concrete Warhol Museum stands in homage to the Warhola family's contributions to the history of art. Jamie was honored to donate two of his favorite fantasy oil paintings, *The Enforcer* of c. 1980 and *The Wizard's Workshop* of c. 1987, to this museum; they hang in a side gallery, along with the work of Paul Warhola, Jamie's father (Andy's brother). The main gallery is devoted to limited edition prints by Andy Warhol, donated by the Andy Warhol Foundation for the Visual Arts (created and funded by the Warhol Estate, as stipulated in the artist's will). "It's rewarding to see how many Eastern Europeans know and respect Andy Warhol for the important artist he

was," Jamie notes with pride. James Warhola,
conversation with author, 22 February 1995.

33. Sarah Weeks, *Hurricane City*, illustrated by James
Warhola (New York: Harper Collins, Inc., 1993). The
book measures 9 1/4 x 11 1/4" and contains 32 pages
with three double-page illustrations, twenty-four full-
page illustrations, and two title-page illustrations. The
cover is wrapped.

34. See James R. Mellow, "Art: American Illustration,
Paintings that Capture the Sentiments of an Era,"
*Architectural Digest* (Oct. 1990): 250.

35. This practice has a centuries-long tradition in art
history; Albrecht Dürer, the great master of the High
Renaissance in Germany, numbers among the many
artists who kept verbal and visual diaries of their
travels; q.v., Fedja Anzelewsky, *Dürer: His Art and
Life*, trans. by Heide Grieve (New York: Alpine Fine
Arts Collection, Ltd., 1980).

## CALLIE ANGELL NOTES

1. Quoted in Jean Stein, *Edie: An American Biography*
(New York: Alfred A. Knopf, 1982): 228.

2. Conversations with author, August 1994.

3. Andy Warhol, *The Philosophy of Andy Warhol* (*From
A to B and Back Again*) (New York: Harcourt Brace
Jovanovich, 1975): 99.

Campbell's, Day-Glo, Gillette, Life Savers, Mylar,
Polaroid, Thermo-fax, Van Heusen, Verifax,
Wonderbread, and Xerox are all registered trademarks.